T0339009

Crisis!

CRISIS!

*When Political Parties Lose
the Consent to Rule*

Cedric de Leon

STANFORD UNIVERSITY PRESS
Stanford, California

STANFORD UNIVERSITY PRESS
Stanford, California

Printed in the United States of America on acid-free, archival-quality paper

LIBRARY OF CONGRESS CATALOGING-IN-PUBLICATION DATA
Names: Leon, Cedric de, author.
Title: Crisis! : when political parties lose the consent to rule / Cedric de Leon.
Description: Stanford, California : Stanford University Press, 2019. | Includes
      bibliographical references and index.
Identifiers: LCCN 2019004977 (print) | LCCN 2019006598 (ebook) |
      ISBN 9781503610651 (ebook) | ISBN 9781503603554 (cloth; alk. paper)
Subjects: LCSH: Political parties—United States—History. | Crises—Political
      aspects—United States—History. | Legitimacy of governments—United
      States—History. | United States—Politics and government.
Classification: LCC JK2261 (ebook) | LCC JK2261 .L455 2019 (print) | DDC 324.273—dc23
LC record available at https://lccn.loc.gov/2019004977

Cover design: Rob Ehle

Cover images: Nineteenth-century political cartoons via Wikimedia Commons

Text design: Kevin Barrett Kane

Typeset at Stanford University Press in 11/15 Brill

CONTENTS

Crisis!

1

THE CRISIS SEQUENCE

To hear **Martin Van Buren** tell it, losing the 1840 presidential election was the best thing that ever happened to him. The former president returned to his farm in upstate New York and watched his potatoes grow after directing a troubled economy for four years. Three of his sons lived nearby and his first grandson was born later that summer.

But Van Buren was either fooling himself or putting on a show, for his actions suggested that he was carefully planning a political comeback. He went on a national tour in early 1842, not even a year after his removal from office, to lay the groundwork for the next presidential campaign. This was no mean feat: Americans did not then have the modern conveniences of air or even train travel. On the first leg of his trip, the former president traveled overland down the Eastern Seaboard and then turned west across the Deep South. On the last leg, he traveled north through the Midwest and became the first former president to visit the boomtown of Chicago.[1]

Van Buren returned to his farm on July 28, 1842, having traveled some seven thousand miles. He had reestablished his relationships with the heads of all the major local and state Democratic Party machines and in the process burnished his credentials as a leader with nationwide appeal. No other Democrat came close to his stature midway through the opposition's administration, and it was clear to any casual observer that he was the party's presumptive nominee in 1844. Soon after the national tour, the *Democratic Review* published a sonnet to him. It began, "Fallen? No thou art not!"[2]

Martin Van Buren therefore had good reason to believe that he would prevail at the 1844 Democratic National Convention. A majority of the party's delegates had pledged themselves to him by 1843. The opposition only helped to strengthen his self-assurance. President William Henry Harrison, leader of the Whig Party, had died in the first weeks of his administration, leaving the White House to his vice president, John Tyler, whose accidental tenure was marked above all by gross ineptitude. Democrats in Congress shared their leader's confidence, so much so in fact that they counted their chickens before they were hatched, electing a staunch Van Burenite, John W. Jones of Virginia, Speaker of the House to push through their presumptive leader's legislative agenda.

Since the 1840s, American voters have become well acquainted with the phenomenon of the frontrunner. The perennial frontrunner in our own time has been Hillary Clinton. Like Van Buren before her, Senator Clinton headed into the 2008 Democratic primary elections with the swagger of an odds-on favorite, while Barack Obama bore the mantle of the quixotic challenger. In January 2007, Mrs. Clinton announced her candidacy for the highest office in the land from the living room of her home in Washington. Seated comfortably on her couch in her trademark pantsuit, the senator from New York said, "I'm in, and I'm in it to win." One reporter for the influential online magazine *Politico* expressed what was on everyone's minds when he called her "Hillary the inevitable."[3]

This was not just a theme imposed upon the race by a cynical mass media, for the Clinton campaign itself deliberately cultivated the air of inevitability. Indeed, this seemed to be the core of the campaign's strategy: to shock and awe the American public into a Clinton coronation. The Obama campaign countered by painting Senator Clinton as just another candidate. In one instance of this back-and-forth, Obama strategist David Plouffe released a memo saying that Senator Clinton's advantages were similar to those of an incumbent, whose support was broad but thin. Clinton strategist Mark Penn responded with his own memo, citing over forty polls in which his candidate was not only winning but widening her lead over the Democratic field. Penn wrote, "Hillary's electoral strength has grown in the last quarter and she is better positioned today than ever before to become the next President of the United States."[4]

The Clinton campaign had plenty of reason to crow. Their candidate was a U.S. senator, heir-apparent to the throne of the Democrats' leading faction, the centrist Democratic Leadership Council, and First Lady to the hugely popular president Bill Clinton, the party's newest patriarch. George W. Bush had by that point led the country into the quagmire that was the Iraq War and bungled the rescue and resettlement of Americans in Hurricane Katrina. In 2006, the voters issued a signal rebuke to the Bush administration by turning both houses of Congress over to the Democrats for the first time since the early 1990s. It was clear to most observers that whoever became the Democratic nominee would almost certainly become the next president, and no one stood a better chance of winning the nomination than Hillary Clinton.

Of course, we now know that neither frontrunner did what they set out to do. James K. Polk, who was by all accounts a washed-up politician in 1844, was drafted in the last minute to break a deadlocked Democratic convention. The original "dark horse" candidate, he defeated Van Buren and went on to beat Henry Clay by the thinnest of margins to become president. Barack Obama, though certainly the star of his party's convention in 2004, was a first-term senator and a long shot for the nomination, yet he defeated the most powerful Democrat in America to become the nation's first black president.

This book is about the events that followed the unanticipated victories of presidents Polk and Obama and that led in each case to a "crisis of hegemony," a moment in which the party system disintegrates into factions and the people withdraw their consent to be governed by the establishment. The major parties of the nineteenth century were coalitions of northern and southern states that united on either side of economic issues, in large part to avoid the politicization of slavery. Keeping the electorate's eyes on the tyranny of banks and tariffs meant that voters and legislators paid less attention to the scourge of bonded servitude. Mr. Polk's election was a mandate for "Manifest Destiny," a program of aggressive territorial expansion that promised cheap land to less affluent white men and a life of economic independence out West. Far from delivering on that promise, however, the further colonization of indigenous lands and what was then still northern Mexico led instead to a toxic debate over whether slavery would be permitted in the new territories. That dispute led to the factionalization of the two-party system, the secession of eleven southern states from the Union, and eventually to the Civil War in 1861.

I use the case of the Civil War to help us make sense of our own time. The nineteenth and twenty-first centuries are by no means historical twins, but there is a shared logic or pattern at work in which the politics of race and economics backfires on the political establishment. Until recently, the contemporary party system studiously avoided the politicization of racial inequality and neoliberal economic policies like free trade and deregulation. That globalization was good, that government was bad, and that the struggle for civil rights was settled became received wisdom. To run afoul of those conventions was to commit political suicide. The Great Recession of 2008, the worst economic downturn since the 1930s, created the conditions for a break with the status quo, and Barack Obama came to symbolize that break. Though he steered clear of civil rights policy, Mr. Obama promised an ambitious regulatory overhaul of Wall Street and an unprecedented expansion of government spending to update the country's ailing infrastructure and thereby put the unemployed back to work. Far from welcoming this challenge to politics-as-usual, the establishment moved in to suppress "the New New Deal." The failed promise of the Obama agenda, in turn, factionalized the major parties, rendering them incapable of stopping Donald Trump's epic rise in 2016. The Trump phenomenon, in other words, is not the beginning of the story but the end result of party polarization and fracture since the Great Recession.

The sequence of partisan reactions and counter-reactions to insurgent political programs—Manifest Destiny in the nineteenth century and the

New New Deal in the twenty-first century—eventuated in a crisis of public confidence. Though party politics were at the center of these watershed moments, commentators tend to downplay the importance of parties and politicians in causing such crises, instead attributing them to changing social and economic dynamics on the ground. With few exceptions, students of electoral "realignments," for example, explain shifts in power from one political party to another by pointing to shocks like depressions or wars.[5] Similarly, prominent historians argue that the U.S. Secession Crisis reflected the social conflict over slavery, especially the threat that abolitionism posed to the largest slave owners' economic interests.[6] Today debates on populism and the rise of the Far Right focus on the social disruption caused by economic downturns, changing moral values, and mounting class inequality.[7] In few instances do political parties play a role.

One key problem with these theories is that they cannot explain the *timing* of political crises. Changes like globalization have been playing out for at least two generations: so why is the Far Right coming to power only now? The conflict over slavery was at least a century old by the time of the Civil War, going back to the American Revolution and the colonial period before that. If the threat to the largest slave owners' economic interests was the root cause of the Civil War, then why did the South secede in 1861 and not before?

The Puzzle of Time

To solve the puzzle of timing I focus on the back-and-forth dynamic that follows an unexpected challenge to the party system. Such a challenge has the potential to touch off a "crisis sequence," a chain of partisan reactions and counter-reactions that destabilizes the relationship between political parties and their constituents and ends in a crisis of hegemony.

The basic idea is this. Party systems typically want to debate some things but not others and in doing so tend to reinforce a particular kind of social order.[8] Since its founding as a white settler colonial state, the United States government has maintained certain racial, class, and gender compromises that form the basis of American society. Thus, the political elites of the slaveholding republic promised universal white manhood suffrage at the expense of the rights of people of color and women. Similarly, the postracial neoliberal order of 1968–2008 conceded civil rights but resisted the desegregation of schools, neighborhoods, and workplaces; at the same time, establishment politicians conceded the right of workers to organize and bargain collectively, even as they dismantled the social safety net and either outsourced union jobs overseas or destroyed jobs through automation.

Every once in a while, however, politicians and social movement activists insist on debating issues that the major parties want to avoid. This unanticipated challenge to the status quo convinces politicians and voters alike to defect from the mainstream parties. But the establishment does not take a challenge to its power lightly, and rather than yield to the insurgency it tries to reabsorb the defectors—that is, to lead them back to politics-as-usual. If the establishment succeeds, then the story ends there and the political crisis is contained; but in a crisis sequence the process of reabsorption backfires and leads to a full-blown crisis of hegemony. In brief, the four episodes of the crisis sequence are (1) unexpected challenge, (2) defection, (3) failed reabsorption, and (4) crisis.

The timing of the U.S. Secession Crisis makes sense if we think about it as the endpoint of a political back-and-forth that went awry. The crisis sequence in this case began with the unexpected challenge to the status quo posed by James K. Polk, whose candidacy shifted public debate from economic issues, which Van Buren employed deliberately to depoliticize slavery, to territorial expansion, which was the pet project of Mr. Polk, southern Democrats, and a new generation of party leaders called "Young America" Democrats. The resulting colonization of northern Mexico, from Texas to Northern California, led to a bitter debate over whether or not slavery would be permitted there. To cool the ensuing strife between the North and South, the political establishment passed the Compromise of 1850, thereby settling the debate over slavery for good, or so they thought. But the dynamics of compromise unintentionally led to a second defection that emboldened the secessionist "Southern Rights" faction of the Democratic Party, gave rise to the Republican Party in the North, and permanently destroyed the Whig Party. The destruction of the existing two-party system in turn led to the exodus of eleven southern states from the Union in 1861.

The election of Donald Trump also makes sense if we think of how it might also represent the endpoint of a crisis sequence. That sequence began with the campaign and election of Barack Obama and his advocacy of the New New Deal, which challenged the free market fundamentalism of the post–Civil Rights era. That vision inspired voters and politicians alike to defect to Mr. Obama's insurgent campaign and vault him past Hillary Clinton and John McCain to the presidency. The neoliberal establishment refused to roll over. Clinton Democrats infiltrated the Obama transition team and administration from the inside, while congressional Republicans, with the initial support of the Tea Party, stonewalled the president's legislative agenda and defeated him in the 2010 midterm elections. Not even halfway through his administration, then, Mr. Obama had bowed to the establishment and traded the New New Deal in for a tax-cutting neoliberal agenda. But the reabsorption of the president's self-styled insurgency did not ultimately save the establishment, for the reabsorption strategy backfired badly, fueling infighting across the political spectrum. On the left, Barack Obama's neoliberal turn meant that economic and racial inequality festered, touching off successive insurgencies from Occupy Wall Street to Black Lives Matter and the Bernie Sanders campaign. On the right, the Tea Party shut down the government in 2013 and inspired a rebellion of disgruntled factions within the Republican Party from "birthers," evangelicals, and libertarians, ensuring that no two candidates could unite with sufficient strength to defeat Donald Trump in the 2016 Republican primaries. With the party system in crisis, Mr. Trump was able to capture the Republican nomination and defeat a weakened Democratic Party. In the Rust Belt in particular, those who had voted for Barack Obama's New New Deal in 2008 defected in the thousands: white union members voted for Donald Trump's economic nationalist agenda, while black voters in city centers stayed home on Election Day.

In both instances, we see a pattern of unexpected challenge, defection, failed reabsorption, and crisis. Each step in the sequence is a necessary condition for the next. An unanticipated challenge to the status quo is necessary to prompt a defection. Otherwise politics-as-usual would be sufficient to maintain party loyalty. Defection is necessary to prompt reabsorption— absent a defection, the political establishment would not need to reabsorb anyone. Finally, the failure to reabsorb is a necessary condition for the last event in the sequence, which is a crisis of hegemony, because a party that reabsorbs the power that was slipping from its grasp by definition regains the people's consent to govern.[9]

The Setting

Of course, making the U.S. Secession Crisis the reference point for understanding our present crisis is tricky, and comparisons between the Civil War and contemporary politics extend only so far. The two crises take hold at different moments in the development of American politics, race relations, and capitalism, a fact that limits just how much we can say in the comparison. We can, however, suggest that political crises in general evince shared features, namely, the fracturing of the political system and a corresponding shift in the allegiances of regular people who were once loyal to the system. We can also safely say that this has something to do with the ability of the establishment to hold on to its power. Finally, as recent controversies involving police violence and immigration make clear, both crises share a racial logic owing to the fact that America was founded as, and remains, a white settler colonial state.

But to the degree that we can outline the dynamics of political crisis, we run into another problem, which is that these changes happen not just at the national level but at local, state, and regional levels. This is especially true of pre–Civil War or antebellum politics, when the national parties were coalitions of local and state party machines. To balance these various concerns, I ground the story of southern secession, which takes up the first half of the book, in the state of Alabama, with special attention to Tuscaloosa County.

There are several reasons for this choice. The first set of reasons has to do with the symbolic importance of the town and state in the development of the secessionist agenda. The town of Tuscaloosa was the capital of Alabama for much of the antebellum period. Tuscaloosa connected, via plank road and the Black Warrior River, the poorer hill counties of northern Alabama and the affluent plantation counties of the southern half of the state. Indeed, the county itself was very much a cross-section of Alabama, for its hilly eastern half was home to small farmers and herdsmen, whereas its western half, particularly the southwest, housed sprawling plantations (and now houses the University of Alabama). With respect to states, it was important for me to choose a case other than South Carolina, which has received so much attention to the exclusion of other states that supposedly seceded in a herd once South Carolina took the first fateful step. In this, one could do no better than Alabama. Alabama was in the vanguard of the South as the national crisis over slavery deepened. It was an early seceder and a member state of the so-called Deep South. Alabama was distinguished even in this group, for the country's leading secessionist, William L. Yancey, was an Alabaman and Alabama hosted the first capital of the Confederacy, Montgomery. If Illinois was the "Land of Lincoln," then Alabama was the "Heart of Dixie."

The second set of reasons has to do with addressing the dominant explanation for secession within the social sciences, which is that the largest slaveholders led the South out of the Union in order to protect their "property." As we shall soon see, the Whig Party and its base among the largest planters actually *resisted* secession until the mid-1850s. In their view, slavery was safer within the Union than it was outside of it. It was only because of a series of strategic missteps that southern Whigs and their wealthy constituents were at last maneuvered into supporting secession, and then only grudgingly. This will run counter to what many social scientists and laypeople think they know about the Old South (historians will know better). Accordingly, I will have to first show *that* southern planters and Whigs resisted secession and second explain *why* they resisted secession only to give in. Doing so requires local voting data because of the secret ballot and the absence of individual-level survey or polling data (pollsters started doing voter surveys in the 1930s). The best we can do is look at voting by precinct or "beat" and watch as planter-dominated neighborhoods give their ballots to one party and then another. Whenever possible, I will provide electoral returns for every county in Alabama and try to point out patterns in how planter counties voted in contrast to less affluent hill counties. However, because a county is much bigger and more diverse than a precinct, it is harder, at least on the basis of secret ballot returns, to say definitively how planters were responding to party politics if at all. This is why the precinct-level vote from Tuscaloosa County is so important.

All data on Alabama and the U.S. Secession Crisis were collected from the Hoole Special Collections Library at the University of Alabama in Tuscaloosa and the Alabama Department of Archives and History in Montgomery. For the leadership's public statements, I use speeches, letters to the editor, and where party elders were also the editors of local party newspapers, their editorials. For insight into party leaders' behind-the-scenes maneuvers, I rely upon their correspondence, memoirs, and diaries when available. The behavior of Tuscaloosa County planters tracked closely with the actions of four prominent Whig politicians: U.S. Congressman George W. Crabb, Congressman William R. Smith (Crabb's protégé and successor to Crabb's congressional seat), State Senator Robert Jemison Jr. (also the second-largest planter in the county), and Congressman Henry Hilliard (former professor at the University of Alabama and the most prominent Whig in the state).

To show that these statements and maneuvers connected with voters on the ground, I rely mainly on county electoral returns by precinct from 1840 to 1860. The returns have been cross-checked against manuscript census reports and other data that describe differences in class, ethnic, and religious residential patterns. Newspaper articles, letters to the editor, and the minutes of local rank-and-file party meetings in turn offer insight into the reasons that voters maintained or changed their political allegiances in this period.

Remembering the Civil War and Secession

But why go through all the trouble of collecting precinct-level voting data and poring over dusty old letters? Don't we already know what we need to know about the Civil War? Apparently not. A Pew Research Center poll conducted in 2011, the 150th anniversary of the war, asked a random sample of Americans to identify the main cause of the conflict. A plurality of respondents sidestepped the importance of slavery. Forty-eight percent said that the war was fought over "states' rights," the doctrine that southerners were free to conduct their affairs without federal interference. Thirty-eight percent said the primary cause was slavery. Nor was the states' rights answer confined to senior citizens who might have participated in the resistance to racial integration in the 1960s. Fully 60 percent of people under the age of thirty invoked states' rights as the leading cause of the war, the highest percentage of any demographic group.[10]

There is a greater consensus among scholars, many of whom suggest that the crisis originated with the threatened economic interests of the largest southern slave owners or planters.[11] One problem with this account is that the largest slave owners were doing quite well in this period. By one estimate, Mississippi and Alabama planters owned 94 percent of agricultural wealth in 1860 compared to 92 percent in 1840. Not content to dominate, the rich were actually increasing their share of the pie. This leaves a crucial question unanswered: if planters were doing so well under the existing system, why would they ever support leaving the Union? If it ain't broke, why fix it?

A similar school of thought grew out of sociologist Barrington Moore's classic work *Social Origins of Dictatorship and Democracy* (1966). Moore argued that economic conditions made the Civil War possible. Despite a long history of commercial interdependence in which South Carolina supplied raw materials to Rhode Island mills, for example, southern planters were able to break with their business associates to the north because of their increasing reliance on trade with Britain (northeastern industrialists meanwhile were more and more dependent on midwestern consumers). To southern planters, secession made economic sense as a means of defending slavery, because they no longer needed New England to make money.[12]

Scholars of secession continue to stress the importance of slave owners' interests, but they do so in different ways. Political scientist Barry Weingast has argued that in the 1850s politicians violated the "balance rule," in which slave states were inducted to the Union at the same time as free states so that neither section would have more representation than the other in the U.S. Senate.[13] Daniel Carpenter held that secessionism represented a counter-movement to abolitionism in the North.[14] Still others suggest that secession reflected a southern ethos of male honor, modeled by affluent planters, such that the exodus from the Union was motivated in part by the wounded pride of southern men.[15]

One problem with all such accounts is that they emphasize features of the social, economic, and political landscape that were not unique to 1861 and therefore cannot explain the timing of the South's dramatic turn away from the Union. The gendered appeal to "manly independence" was a consistent refrain in antebellum proslavery rhetoric, while abolitionism and southern hostility to it are as old as American slavery itself, preceding even the founding of the republic.[16] The Senate's balance rule was tested repeatedly by the logistics of territorial expansion in the 1840s, from the annexation of Oregon and Texas to the status of slavery in the newly colonized northern half of Mexico known as the Mexican Cession.

Moreover, the clash of northern industrial and southern slave-owning interests predicts the wrong outcome. The dispute between the North and South turned on whether slavery should be permitted in the western territories. If northerners had let the South secede, they could have claimed title to the West and prohibited slavery unilaterally. One might plausibly argue that it was in the interest of northerners to let the South go without a fight. Conversely, in seceding, southern slave owners forfeited their right to the western territories. One could say that it was in their interest to remain in the Union, reach a compromise, and thereby ensure slavery's expansion into the West albeit on a limited basis. Instead the exact opposite occurred: northerners moved to crush the southern rebellion; the white South seceded and in defeat witnessed the end of slavery; and the toll of war climbed to upwards of 750,000, the largest number of deaths of any war in American history.[17]

In sum, the timing of secession does not follow from economic interests, even if we assume that northerners and southerners had competing interests. Slavery was of course the all-important context of the crisis. A dispute over the prohibition of slavery in the western territories makes no sense outside a social order in which white supremacists treated black people as chattel. However, slavery does not, by itself, explain the sequence of events that made the crisis come to a head in 1861 and not before.[18]

Thinking through Our Present Crisis

Social and economic interests are also poor predictors of the timing of Far Right success today. Here it is helpful to do a rough comparison of the United States and other countries where right-wing ethnic nationalists have gained significant traction in recent years. We can do this by examining data collected by the World Bank on inequality, immigration, unemployment, and crime—all hot-button issues in Far Right rhetoric that speak to voters' changing interests and policy preferences. In the United States, the Gini coefficient, which is a widely used measure of inequality, has increased modestly since the mid-1980s but leveled off and even decreased slightly between 2007 and 2013, just in time for Donald Trump's rise. One can observe the same moderate up-and-down trend in the Gini coefficient where the Far Right experienced some success but ultimately failed, for example, in Canada. Immigration, another centerpiece of Donald Trump's campaign, is equally problematic as a predictor of the Far Right's recent popularity. Since its peak in 1997, immigration to the United States has been in free fall and now matches levels of immigration from 1992, when Americans elected the Democrat Bill Clinton to office and rejected the populist candidacy of Ross Perot. By contrast, in Canada immigration has actually risen steadily in the same period, yet the Far Right there was isolated and absorbed into the mainstream party system.[19] Much the same can be said of crime and unemployment, which have also been in decline in the United States, though Mr. Trump himself has suggested that the country is gripped by these social problems. In France, where Marine Le Pen's nativist and Eurosceptic Front National posted its largest-ever vote share in the 2017 presidential election, unemployment rose steadily from 7.5 percent in 2008 to 10.4 percent in 2013 but has since leveled off and in 2016 dipped below 10 percent to roughly 2012 levels, when the French elected the socialist François Hollande president. France's homicide rate, like that of the United States, has been in steady decline since 1995. Even terrorism is an inconsistent indicator: the Far Right has substantial support in countries not only where terrorist activity is relatively high, like India, the United Kingdom, and France, but also where terrorism is relatively low, like Hungary and Belgium.[20]

There are of course more sophisticated studies that focus on the economic side of the story. One account traces the twin triumph of Donald Trump and Brexit to wage stagnation and corporate irresponsibility, especially since the 2008 recession.[21] But as many of us know, real wage growth for the typical American worker stalled out in the 1970s and has been a consistent feature of the economic landscape ever since.[22] This is to say nothing of the countless examples of corporate malfeasance in the same period. The question is why an ethnic nationalist like Donald Trump has not upended the party system until now.[23]

Other observers suggest that the rise of the Far Right in the United States has more to do with culture than with economics. One influential account traces the culture war over issues like gay marriage and abortion to an "empathy wall" that divides the white conservatives of the Louisiana bayou from the white liberals of Berkeley, California. The former are Tea Party activists, while the latter are true-blue Democrats, and neither group shows any inclination to scale the empathy wall to undercut their own interests.[24] Putting aside the controversial claim that voters are more to blame for polarizing American society than politicians are, the problem with this point of view is once again timing. Political polarization in the modern era began as early as the 1960s and intensified in the early 1990s.[25] The fact that the empathy wall has been in place now for quite some time begs the same vexing question that economic explanations do: why Trump and why now?

Parties and Political Crisis

This book is inspired by a growing skepticism with the idea that everything has to do with how voters confront a changing world in defense of their interests. "The people" provide a necessary but insufficient explanation for political crises. Historians of the so-called modern revisionist school, for example, stress the importance of unanticipated or "contingent" events, including the sometimes surprising decisions of politicians, in sparking the American Civil War.[26] Likewise, there is mounting recognition that political parties themselves are responsible for the rise of the Far Right in Europe. For instance, political scientist Herbert Kitschelt has argued that as conservative parties move to the political center in order to compete for moderate voters, they alienate parts of their base and make them available for recruitment by the radical right.[27] Lastly, a new generation of political sociologists argues that parties can, under certain conditions, remake the social order by politicizing social differences like race and religion.[28]

Though these alternatives to existing theories help us better understand political crises, few if any scholars suggest, as I do here, that they originate in "reactive" or "nonlinear" sequences of political maneuvers to contain or capitalize upon challenges to the status quo. This kind of sequence—the crisis sequence—adds a missing chapter to the stories we tell ourselves about the Civil War and our current political climate.[29]

Rather than look to voters' interests and policy preferences for the sources of crisis, I look to parties and politicians. Social and economic change matters in the sense that a recession, for example, has the potential to undermine the popularity of the party in power. However, "change" has no natural affinity for the left or right. Whether change leads to socialism or ethnic nationalism depends a great deal on what competing parties do to exploit or dampen the political effects of a disruption to people's lives.

The secession crisis and the election of Donald Trump suggest that politicians and voters blow up the party system not only because people are suffering but also and at the same time because the system itself is unable to absorb an existential challenge to its power. This is not a value judgment that it is better for the political establishment to contain a crisis than it is for the establishment to be overthrown. For example, both slavery and neoliberalism were called into question because politicians broke their promise to safeguard white men's privileged access to land and labor: I do not and cannot endorse either the social orders themselves or the mechanism of their demise. Nor do I look back fondly on the counterexample to the U.S. Secession Crisis and our present crisis: the Democratic Party's co-optation of the American labor movement during the Great Depression. The relationship between the Democratic Party and organized labor has been disempowering to workers in many respects, from the decline in direct action to the loss of jobs due to trade deals negotiated by both parties.[30] My observations about the politics of reabsorption are motivated by empirical evidence and historical analysis.

The book does have political implications, though, and those I do not shy away from. The fact that our crisis is so similar to the U.S. Secession Crisis makes a strong historical analysis a matter of utmost urgency. It is perhaps no accident that President Trump compared the present moment to the American Civil War.[31] Though his insinuation that he or Andrew Jackson could have prevented the war is beside the point, the comparison hits closer to home than perhaps he realizes. Like the triumph of ethnic nationalism today, secession was partly the result of broken promises and partisan maneuvers, the outcome of which many people underestimated. The United States and the world now teeter on the brink of a right-wing ethnic nationalist wave, from Donald Trump in the United States and nativists in the United Kingdom, France, and Hungary to the AKP in Turkey and the BJP in India. What political elites and civil society organizations do now can mean the difference between fascism and democracy, just as the American Civil War meant the difference between the survival of a slaveholding republic and the birth of liberal democracy.

2
THE APPEAL OF
MANIFEST DESTINY

Each year, or so the story goes, President Andrew Jackson would direct his staff to place a big block of cheese in the main foyer of the White House. In a spirit of openness to the people, for which his presidency was so well known, Jackson invited the surrounding community to partake of the cheese and take some home with them for good measure. Though the block weighed over a ton, it would disappear in the span of two hours.

The story is, as some might suspect, apocryphal. There was only one block of cheese (not one every year) and it smelled to high heaven, so much so that the president, inspired more by desperation than egalitarianism, came up with the scheme to get rid of it as quickly as possible. That the legend persists as a symbol of the seventh president's populism is nevertheless anchored in something quite real, and it defined an era.

Jackson's unlettered and modest background was important to the Democratic Party's popularity with less affluent white men. He hailed from the

Tennessee frontier, not from the gentry of the original thirteen colonies, and he was infamous for a boorish tendency to lash out in public and talk out of turn. Presaging Karl Rove's packaging of George W. Bush many years later, the Democrats put Jackson's coarseness to use by appealing to farmers and workers as an aggrieved class of common men, whose economic situation had grown worse with the advent of factories, banks, and the market economy.[1]

Jacksonian rhetoric was anchored in more than just a cult of personality. It had its roots in a worldview, a "discourse of dependency."[2] Dependency was a state of noncitizenship reserved for landless white men, slaves, and women. These groups were barred from voting because it was thought that they were too desperate to make good decisions about the country as a whole. White wageworkers in particular, who labored for other people rather than for themselves, were stigmatized very much as slaves were for being subservient to a master class. In contrast, white male farmers and artisans were the icons of independence: they could vote because it was imagined that they lived comfortably enough off their own labor that their votes could not be bought.

This idea of dependency fueled Democratic rhetoric in the 1830s and early 1840s. Democrats said that they alone could be trusted to make a life of economic independence accessible to the common man, whereas their opponents, the Whig Party, were the party of the rich and powerful, the "aristocracy." Thus, the Jacksonian Democratic Party worked to curb the power of economic institutions like the Second Bank of the United States. Banks, Democrats said, intensified economic dependency, because they ensnared unsuspecting farmers and workers in a cycle of debt; when they failed to repay the bank, debtors often went to prison.[3]

Preserving the Slaveholding Republic

In keeping the public's eyes fixed on economic issues, the Jacksonian party system (1828–44) served another and perhaps more vital purpose to the Union, namely, to prevent the politicization of slavery. The design of the party system originated with the tumultuous period immediately prior, which is ironically referred to as the "Era of Good Feelings" (1816–28). James Monroe, fifth president of the United States and the last president of the revolutionary generation, sought to push his legislative agenda through Congress without resorting to the old parties, the Federalist Party of George Washington, Alexander Hamilton, and John Adams and the Republican Party of Thomas Jefferson and James Madison. In his first inaugural address, President Monroe said, "Discord does not belong to our system. . . . The American people have encountered together great dangers and sustained severe trials with success. They constitute one great family with a common interest. . . . To promote this harmony . . . will be the object of my constant and zealous exertions."[4]

Far from promoting harmony, however, Monroe's antiparty approach, known as his "consolidation policy," created space for other divisions to emerge, including sectional divisions pitting northern free states against southern slave states.

The sectional conflict became most acute when Congress considered the admission of Missouri to the Union in 1819. Those sympathetic to the North held that the central government had the right to "restrict" slavery in the unsettled western territories, whereas those siding with the South insisted that the government had no such right. This had the effect of fracturing once powerful interregional alliances like that of Pennsylvania and Virginia. Talk of "disunion" was hot in the nation's capital. Legendary statesman Henry Clay, for instance, wrote in private correspondence about the mood in the U.S. Senate. "The words, civil war, and disunion," he said, "are uttered almost without emotion."[5] Future president John Quincy Adams of Massachusetts mused privately whether the dissolution of the Union would be so bad from the North's perspective. In a diary entry dated February 24, 1820, he wrote, "A dissolution, at least temporary, of the Union as now constituted, would be certainly necessary. . . . The Union might then be reorganized on the fundamental principle of emancipation."[6]

Though Congress arrived at the Missouri Compromise of 1820, which prohibited slavery north of the Mason-Dixon line, the experience scarred all those who went through it, and none more so than Martin Van Buren, the architect of the Jacksonian party system. Unlike Monroe, Van Buren believed that political parties—especially those that knit regional economic interests together—were the only effective check to sectionalism. In a letter dated

January 13, 1827, to Thomas Ritchie, a likeminded newspaper editor in Virginia, Van Buren wrote, "We must always have party distinctions, and the old ones are the best. . . . If the old ones are suppressed, geographical differences founded on local instincts or what is worse, prejudices between free and slave holding states will inevitably take their place."[7] Together with Ritchie, Van Buren inaugurated a party system of Whigs and Democrats based on competing interregional economic partnerships and in doing so contained sectional tensions over slavery for a generation.

Texas and Manifest Destiny

The shadow of a threat to this system began to grow in the 1840s. Van Buren, who eventually became president in the party system he himself created, lost reelection in 1840 to the war general and Whig, William Henry Harrison. The defeat was no danger to the party system in and of itself, but the ground began to shift when Harrison died one month into his administration. Harrison's vice president, John Tyler, became president and proceeded to throw the government into disarray. Tyler betrayed the probusiness principles of his own party and was a pariah among his colleagues. The Democrats, though gleeful, never accepted Tyler as one of their own. He was in effect a president without a party to accomplish his legislative agenda. In a last-ditch move to salvage his presidency, Tyler moved to annex Texas to the Union.

White settlers had been moving to that region for many years and in 1836 declared their independence from Mexico. In August 1837, just a few months into the first year of the Van Buren administration, the Texans requested annexation to the United States. Mindful of the intent of the Jacksonian party system, President Van Buren denied the request, "fearing an antislavery backlash and domestic turmoil." The Whigs were similarly disinclined toward Texas. Indeed, when Tyler asked his own Whig secretary of state, Daniel Webster, to consider a treaty of annexation, Webster rejected him outright.[8]

It was only toward the end of his administration, when Webster resigned his post in 1843, that Tyler was at last free to select a secretary of state who would push the Texas plan, but even this process was fraught with surprises and pitfalls. His second secretary of state, Abel Upshur, died before he could get on a head of steam, and his third secretary of state, the South Carolinian John C. Calhoun, was a polarizing figure, whose sectional sympathies were as likely to scuttle a Texas deal as to seal one. What Tyler needed came from an unlikely quarter that, while in favor of Texas annexation, was wholly unconcerned with the president's political fate. This group, more than any other, had the potential to disrupt a party system built on the depoliticization of slavery.

The 1840s witnessed the rise of a new generation of Democrats, whose pet project was nothing less than the expansion of American empire. "Young America" or "New" Democratic Party politics had three core themes: a vision of limitless empire preordained by God, known as Manifest Destiny; the old Jacksonian rhetoric of economic dependency; and a practical plan for achieving expansion that consisted in rapid economic development and settler colonialism, the practice of occupying land and removing or eliminating the nations and people who lived there.

It was Thomas Jefferson, the country's third president (1801–9), who first articulated the link between westward expansion and the economic fate of white men, but expansion took on new meaning as poor whites became increasingly trapped in a cycle of wage and debt dependency. Indeed, by 1860 employees would outnumber the self-employed for the first time in U.S. history.[9] This reality became an important resource to young Democrats, who sought new issues to eclipse their party elders while still allowing them to remain true to the egalitarian thrust of Jacksonian rhetoric. Accordingly, they talked up territorial expansion as a way to arrest wage dependency. As one New Democrat put it, the effect of cheap land in the West "would be to invite a large number of individuals who had settled in eastern cities, who were half-starved and dependent on those who employed them, to go to the West, where with little funds, they could secure a small farm on which to subsist and . . . get rid of that feeling of dependence which made them slaves."[10]

The solution to economic dependency, then, was a sprawling frontier to which a factory worker could escape and farm his own land, but crucially New Democrats also insisted that their plan was God's plan. In February 1844, Illinois congressman John Wentworth invoked divine providence in the U.S. House of Representatives to urge the seizure of Oregon from the

British. Responding to Congressman Thomasson of Kentucky, who cautioned against any premature occupation of that territory lest it bring war with Britain, Wentworth blustered, "In my opinion God never made this country for a colony of Great Britain or any other foreign power. . . . I say it, sir, with religious zeal, that the Almighty God bids us onward to take Oregon."[11] A week later, U.S. senator Sidney Breese laid out the larger vision, of which Oregon was merely a part. That territory, he said, was "fraught with the destiny of freedom," for beyond,

> in the dim distance I see it stretching far and wide upon the coast of the Pacific sea, rich in all the gifts of a most beneficent Providence, its beauty and its grandeur now shrouded in barbaric darkness, yet soon to be lighted up by the sun of freedom. . . . From that favored spot, the contagion of liberty and free principles may be caught, and the infection spread to the remotest lands, until all mankind shall be free. It is the destiny of man; it will be accomplished.[12]

Although the dependency of multitudes on the Eastern Seaboard was a key justification for westward expansion, the New Democrats also rationalized their legislative agenda as a matter of divine providence and destiny. For Breese, empire was nothing less than a restless and worldwide crusade that would not end until it spread like a contagion to the "remotest lands" and made "all mankind" free.

As a matter of practical logistics, however, the New Democrats looked not to the divine but to the legislative mechanism of land grants, first to encourage settler colonialism and, in doing so, stimulate local investments in infrastructure such as railroads, harbors, and canals that could connect the distant reaches of the American empire. "The general policy of the democracy," the *Democratic Review* (the national party newspaper) would later explain, "is to favor the settlement of the land, spread the bounds of the future empire, and to favor, by freedom of intercourse and external commerce, the welfare of the settlers."[13]

New Democrats thus employed a host of rhetorical and practical devices to press the agenda of American empire. There was, however, one enormous obstacle that New Democrats had to overcome if they were to turn their faction's political project into policy. They first had to defeat the leader of their own party: the architect of the Jacksonian party system, former president Martin Van Buren.

The 1844 Democratic National Convention

As we have already seen, Van Buren was intent on running for president in 1844. He was the consummate strategist, less given to ideological rigidity than he was to hardnosed pragmatism. It was therefore halfway surprising that Van Buren took a principled stand against Texas annexation just one month before the Democratic National Convention. It was *not* surprising in the sense that he had spent the better part of the preceding twenty years cultivating a party system whose attention to economic policy precluded issues that could ignite a sectional crisis of Missouri-like proportions. On the other hand, Van Buren could just as easily have made one of his famously noncommittal statements so his allies could say he was for Texas annexation in Alabama and against it in New York.[14] Instead, in a widely publicized letter dated April 20, 1844, to William Hammett, a Mississippi delegate to the approaching convention, he objected to annexation on not one but two grounds: that the United States must honor its treaty obligations with Mexico (of which Texas was still a part) and that the constitution did not permit the acquisition of Texas in the manner proposed.[15]

The Hammett letter earned Van Buren a host of powerful enemies. His friends in Virginia—anchor of the South in the famous North-South alliance that he himself had resuscitated after the Missouri debacle—withdrew their support. Other southerners were sneakier. U.S. senator Robert J. Walker of Mississippi, a diminutive and shrewd pol, persuaded Van Buren to hold the convention in the spring of 1844 instead of the fall of 1843; had it been held earlier with Texas not so much on the front burner, the New Yorker might well have prevailed. Young America Democrats in the North sharpened their knives, too. James Buchanan, the new boss of the Pennsylvania machine, privately pronounced Van Buren "a dead cock in the pit."[16]

Despite the political chaos that followed publication of the Hammett letter, Van Buren remained confident of his prospects at the 1844 DNC. Indeed, when asked later whether he would retract his statement on Texas, Van Buren famously responded that he would not "trim his sails to catch the passing breeze."[17] Such stubbornness suggests a candidate who was self-assured and unwilling to bend to the controversy of the moment. Recalling the prelude to the convention, Van Buren wrote in his autobiography that he held the majority of pledged delegates to that assembly. "Defeated in 1840 . . . the great majority of the democratic masses rallied for the restoration of their overthrown principles, by the instrumentality of my re-elevation to the Presidency," he wrote, adding, "More than three fourths of the States instructed their delegates either in express terms, or thro' unmistakable avowals of their preferences, to vote for my nomination."[18]

As Van Buren ruefully noted, however, he was "defeated at the Baltimore Convention by the intrigues of politicians."[19] The 1844 DNC was the conjuncture of competing political forces, each seeking either to resurrect fallen stars like lame duck president John Tyler, former House Speaker James K. Polk, and Martin Van Buren or to further elevate the rising stars of the party's Young America faction, men like Lewis Cass of Michigan and James Buchanan of Pennsylvania.

Tyler was after legacy, and that legacy was Texas. His original plan had been to persuade Congress that Britain had designs on Texas. The only way to counter the plot of their ancient enemy, Tyler insinuated, was the immediate annexation of Texas as a slave state.[20] But by 1844 Tyler had still not been able to annex Texas. Unwilling to give up, he now threatened a third-party challenge from the South in concert with his secretary of state, John C. Calhoun, should the Democratic Party fail to nominate a proannexation candidate. Tyler held an anemic convention in Baltimore near the site of the DNC as a reminder of what might happen if things did not go his way. Years later, Tyler would confide that the third-party ploy was meant to make the Democrats realize that "a Texas man or defeat was the choice left."[21]

James K. Polk was eager for a comeback. His political career had begun promisingly enough. After serving as Speaker of the U.S. House of Representatives, he was elected governor of Tennessee in 1839. But by 1844, he had been defeated for that state's executive office not once but twice, by a country yokel named Lean Jimmy Jones. In a last-ditch bid to hold off permanent irrelevance, Polk deployed two Tennessee DNC delegates to Baltimore, General Gideon J. Pillow and Cave Johnson, to orchestrate what he privately admitted would at best culminate in the vice presidential nomination. On May 15, just one week before the convention, he wrote, "I think it probable that my chief hope will be for the second office, and if so, I wish my name to go before the Convention at all events." Of course, he desired the presidency above all, but for his name to appear at the top of the ticket it was critical that the suggestion come not from the Tennessee delegation but from Van Buren's own strongholds in the North. Because of Polk's long-standing relationship with the former president, any appearance of collusion to deny Van Buren the nomination would automatically turn the formidable northern delegations against him.[22]

Van Buren and the Democratic establishment sought to avenge their humiliating loss to the Whig ticket in 1840. Van Buren entrusted his floor operation to George Bancroft of Massachusetts, head of the New England delegations, and to his fellow New Yorker, Benjamin Butler. Their main objective was to defeat a vote in favor of the infamous "two thirds rule," which required that the presidential nominee win a supermajority of convention delegates. Word on the street was that the motion would come from one of two quarters: either the Young America bloc aligned with Cass and Buchanan or southern Democrats aligned with John C. Calhoun and the Mississippi annexationist Robert J. Walker. If Van Buren's floor generals could avert or defeat a vote on the two-thirds rule, Van Buren would almost certainly win the nomination on the first ballot.[23]

The Young America or New Democratic wing sought nothing less than to seize the party from the Jacksonian old guard. Their sole means of achieving that result was the two-thirds rule. In the event that Van Buren could not secure a supermajority, Buchanan hoped that the party would turn its anxious eyes to him. Accordingly, he played both ends against his middle: he told the Van Buren managers that he was with them but secretly persuaded the Pennsylvania delegation to support the two-thirds rule.[24] Meanwhile, Lewis Cass had built a strong organization among the delegations of the Southwest and West. The latter announced in Baltimore that they were prepared to bolt the convention if Cass were not nominated.[25]

The stage was set then for what one historian has called "one of the slea-
ziest conventions in history."[26] The players convened at the Egyptian Saloon,
the upper-level ballroom of the Odd Fellows Hall on Gay Street in Baltimore.
As the name implies, the saloon was decorated with faux scenes of ancient
Egyptian "culture," complete with the Nile River, pharaohs, and inscrutable
hieroglyphs. Equally inscrutable at this moment was the ultimate outcome
of the assembly, which erupted in pandemonium at 10:00 A.M. on Monday,
May 27.

The first major episode of the convention was the fight over the two-thirds
rule, which, to repeat, was opposed by the Van Buren establishment and supported by his challengers. Action on that question began when Walker quietly
sent Calhounite Romulus Saunders of North Carolina to nominate Hendrick
Wright of Pennsylvania to chair the convention. Wright was an unknown to
Van Buren's New York delegation and relatively obscure within the Pennsylvania delegation, so he seemed on the surface to be an innocuous choice.
No sooner had Wright assumed the chair than Romulus Saunders moved
the two-thirds rule, arguing that the DNC had done so in 1836 and 1840 and
should do so again to ensure a unanimous choice. Cave Johnson, Polk's man
masking as a Van Burenite, then rose ostentatiously to challenge the motion. Van Buren's floor general, Benjamin Butler of New York, followed with
another procedural hurdle. The DNC by this point had devolved into what
might charitably be called a loosely disciplined mass meeting.[27]

After months of backdoor intrigue, Mississippi senator Robert J. Walker
at last rose to make his strategy plain. He argued that the simple majority
rule was a misnomer—that it should be renamed the minority rule, since so
few states in the North actually voted for Van Buren in 1840. The only way to
ensure a Democratic victory in 1844, he said, was to nominate a candidate
with near-unanimous support. Romulus Saunders then rose to remind his
colleagues that the party's motto was "principles not men" and that sticking
with Van Buren out of mere personal loyalty was a betrayal of the party's
mission.[28] In response, Van Buren's floor general, Benjamin Butler, made a
long and impassioned speech insisting that no one could carry a two-thirds
majority under the circumstances and that if the DNC adopted the rule, it
would lead inevitably to a minority candidate. The crowd reportedly loved

Butler's speech and had he called the question at that point, he might well have defeated the two-thirds rule, but the Walker-Calhoun managers called for adjournment and Butler was too tired to oppose it.[29]

At 9:00 the next morning, Tuesday, May 28, Saunders moved to reinstitute the rules of the 1836 and 1840 conventions, which included the two-thirds rule. The roll call began with John W. Tibbatt of Kentucky voting in favor. This was significant, as the Kentuckian Richard M. Johnson had been Van Buren's running mate in 1836. In the end, Saunders's motion carried. The South voted in a bloc in support of two-thirds; Maine, New Hampshire, and New York voted against; while Pennsylvania and the remaining New England states split their votes.[30]

With the rules now out of the way, the balloting could begin. Not surprisingly, Van Buren put in a strong showing on the first ballot. He garnered 146 votes—a commanding lead but shy of two-thirds. The Young America Democrat Lewis Cass placed second with 83 votes; Van Buren's old running mate Richard M. Johnson came in third with 24 votes; and Calhoun and Buchanan brought up the rear with 6 and 4 votes respectively. As the balloting continued, the transfer of votes to Cass accelerated. By the seventh ballot, Cass led with 123 votes and Van Buren had fallen to 99. The fear at this point was that the party would stay hopelessly divided, with no one able to carry two-thirds of the convention. The southern and Young America factions remained decidedly against Van Buren, while the establishment refused to hand their ballots to the "damned rotten corrupt venal Cass cliques."[31]

As the drama of the first seven ballots unfolded, Polk's floor manager Gideon Pillow carefully worked to secure the vice presidential nomination, only ever hinting at his patron's availability for the top of the ticket. Pennsylvania and Massachusetts were the first northern delegations to bite: they approached Pillow to discuss his man as a compromise presidential candidate. Recall that Polk's strategy from the outset was to avoid the appearance of orchestrating Van Buren's demise. That strategy, disguised as a campaign for the vice presidency, was beginning to bear fruit. Pillow, now with Van Buren's surrogate, George Bancroft of Massachusetts, would go to work on the northern delegations late into the evening. Their argument was that only Polk could stop Cass.

The eighth round of balloting began on Wednesday morning, May 29. New Hampshire, the second delegation to be called in the roll, gave its votes to Polk, and the Egyptian Saloon erupted in cheers. Massachusetts, Tennessee, and Alabama would follow suit, giving Polk 44 votes. With Polk on the move, Reah Frazier of the powerful Pennsylvania delegation then moved a ninth ballot, reminding those assembled that Polk was "the bosom friend of Old Hickory," the affectionate nickname of Andrew Jackson, the party's patriarch. Then the influential Samuel Medary of Ohio announced that his delegation was willing to sacrifice their first-choice candidate and vote for Polk in the interest of "brotherly affection."

By this point, New York and Virginia—anchors of the once unstoppable North-South Jacksonian coalition—had left the saloon to caucus. All held their breaths to see what these powerhouses would do. In the middle of the balloting, William Roane of Virginia returned to the convention and threw his delegation's votes from Cass to Polk to what the *Washington Globe*, an organ of the national Democratic Party, described as "thunders of applause." At that point all that remained was Van Buren's home state, and soon Butler entered the saloon to announce that Van Buren had approved his withdrawal from the race to save the party. With Butler's announcement, the rush was on to Polk and by 2 P.M. on Wednesday, James K. Polk was declared the unanimous choice of the Democratic convention.[32]

In the denouement, the convention offered New York a consolation prize: the nomination of Van Buren ally Silas Wright for the vice presidency. Butler grasped at the chance to save face. He reached out to Wright by the fastest means available—a new technological marvel called the telegraph—to see whether he would accept the nomination. In a sign of the sectional tensions to come, Wright ominously rejected the offer, the first person ever to do so. Henry David Thoreau was to write of the incident, "Simply because the South and North could now speak more quickly to each other did not mean that they had anything to say."[33]

Wright's undisguised contempt for the Polk ticket suggests that the Democratic Party had at last done what Jacksonian Democrats once worked so hard to avoid, namely, introduce to mainstream politics an issue of territorial policy that could irreparably divide the Union. This unanticipated break with the past was hardly lost on the political establishment. Whig presidential nominee and "Great Compromiser" Henry Clay predicted that a war for Texas would "sow the seeds of a dissolution of the Union."[34] Van Buren Democrats were equally suspicious. One month after the Baltimore convention, on the floor of the U.S. Senate, Thomas Hart Benton of Missouri said, "Disunion is at the bottom of this long-concealed Texas machination. Intrigue and speculation cooperate; but disunion is at the bottom; and I denounce it to the American people. Under the pretext of getting Texas into the Union, the scheme is to get the South out of it."[35]

The Whigs React

Polk's nomination upended the national Whig message just as it was gaining traction. The hyperpartisan Van Buren had been president during the economic downturn of 1837, and the Whigs relished the prospect of advancing an alternative vision of principled partisanship and responsible economic stewardship. One Whig likened Van Buren to a steer "so poor and weak it had to be *held up* to be shot" (emphasis in original). Another declared, "If we cannot beat Van Buren, we can beat no one." By the spring of 1844, the Whigs had invested considerable time and money circulating anti–Van Buren speeches, song-sheets, and pamphlets.[36]

The Whigs were nevertheless able to regroup and advance a gamely response to the Democrats' expansionist agenda. Alabama Whigs, in particular, struck a posture of amused contempt. Targeting the Democrats' wanton disregard for treaties, the *Independent Monitor*, Tuscaloosa's Whig Party newspaper, reported that a Democratic spokesman at a local campaign rally for James K. Polk simply "declared that the treaty between the United States and Spain, in 1819, by which Texas was ceded to the latter, is void."[37] Similarly, the Whigs mocked the needless expansion of American empire and the preposterous claims of the republic's manifest "destiny." Joking that Democrats had imperial designs on the entire globe, including China and Australia, they quipped, "The names of these [last] two countries end with 'a,' just like America. How conclusive that they are destined to form part of our Union, and that all the intermediate countries, north of the Cape of Good Hope, shall be as one great political brotherhood, nursed by the old American Eagle?"[38]

But this was not the core of the Whig message, nor could it be. Partisan debate in this period turned on a racialized discourse of dependency, within which each party stigmatized the policies of the other as ones that would enslave free white men. Southern Democrats warned that the Whigs' pro-business agenda would eventually turn landless whites and small slaveholders into the wage dependents of wealthy planters, making them no better in the status hierarchy of the time than African slaves. As the social superiors of farmers and herdsmen, the planter base of the Alabama Whig Party recoiled from the subversive implications of Democratic rhetoric. In contrast to the latter's economic populism, Whigs offered a corporatist vision of progress known as "the American System," which through moral improvement and commercial measures was intended to enrich the collective life of the nation over time and allow all white men to share in the prosperity of a wealthy nation.[39]

Whig corporatism found a friendly audience among economic elites who were enthusiasts of benevolent societies. Antebellum Tuscaloosa County saw the proliferation of Bible, tract, Sunday school, and temperance societies. Like Whig politicians, Tuscaloosa planters believed that moral improvement was the solution to what the Reverend Randolph Reddins referred to as the "lamentable destitution" of the piney hills in the county's eastern backcountry. Accordingly, much of the planter elite's benevolent work centered on evangelizing the poor.[40]

To turn back the Democratic charge of elitism—a charge that was only reinforced by the condescension of evangelicals toward less affluent whites—the Whigs worked to tilt the focus of political debate toward the virulent partisanship of the opposition. If there were any scheme to undermine the economic independence of white men, they argued, it consisted in the Democrats' demagogical opposition to commercial progress.[41] It was the Democrats, the Whigs countered, who inculcated slavish loyalty among their constituents and were dependents themselves on the spoils of party patronage.[42]

In the heat of the 1844 presidential campaign, for example, the Whig *Independent Monitor* spoofed a fictional conversation between an anti-Bank Democratic voter and a new "Texas" Democrat. The voter shows the Democratic operative what a great follower of Andrew Jackson he is by displaying "all his measures engraved on this collar round my neck." Later in the conversation, the operative says, "Let us examine that collar you wear. . . . File off these inscriptions, and engrave 'immediate annexation' in their place."[43] The collar is of course an allusion to the bonds of slavery. The author implies that Democratic promises of ending economic dependency are all an illusion, for "immediate annexation" is merely another device to subordinate the people to the dictates of party.

In contrast to the Democrats' system of political dependency, the American System was a modern and mixed economy, both industrial and agricultural, in which each class of people depended on the others for prosperity. Instead of offering the common man a farm out West as the Democrats did, the Whigs preached self-improvement and promised a fluid hierarchy, in which factory operatives could save enough to start their own shop—a "competency"—and eventually become capitalists and manufacturers who might then furnish employment for a new generation of ambitious operatives. Likewise, nearby farmers would not pick up stakes and move to Texas but instead benefit from local industrialists, whose needs would provide the necessary capital to buy land, increase crops, and make improvements.

Whig rhetoric in the age of expansion therefore worked to refute the Democratic claim that American empire would necessarily increase the "area of freedom" for all present and future citizens. The editor of the Whig *Monitor* addressed the trouble with empire head on:

> If the people of Alabama would feel themselves settled for life, instead of looking to new and delusive prospects in Texas, California and other distant regions, and would apply all their energies to building up a system of internal improvement, and manufactures, for which the materials are so ample and convenient, we should soon behold prosperity and content in every plain, valley and mountain. . . . Let each man cultivate his own acres, or pursue his proper business, without being led off by tales of fiction, or a morbid desire for new countries. Then, and not before, will there be general and abiding prosperity.[44]

Rather than expand across "space" and attempt to reproduce the utopia of a producers' republic, the Whigs offered improvement over "time."[45] In this passage the Whigs characterize Democratic promises of cheap land in Texas and California as "delusive prospects" and "tales of fiction," in comparison with the concrete and improvable reality of the here and now. They urge Alabamans to build up "a system of internal improvement, and manufactures," the only sure way to generate a "general and abiding prosperity."

The Whigs applied the same principle to the republic's political institutions, preferring to develop them gradually over time instead of spreading them precipitously at the point of the bayonet. Congressman Henry Hilliard, a former professor at the University of Alabama at Tuscaloosa and the most prominent Whig in the state, was not as averse to territorial expansion as other Whigs were, but he was cautious in ways that were typical of his party's approach to public policy.[46] In a speech on the war with Mexico in the U.S. House of Representatives on January 5, 1847, he warned:

> Our government is one of consent. . . . If we should become engaged in wars for the extension of our sway, overrunning neighboring states, and bringing into our confederacy a reluctant people, the whole character of our political system will be changed; it will be converted into a political despotism. . . . Our national character and the purity of our political system are of far more consequence to us than any amount of territory which we can acquire.[47]

Hilliard states in no uncertain terms that the preservation of republican institutions is more important than their proliferation across the continent. The speech underlines an important difference in the parties' competing approaches to territorial expansion. Whereas the Democrats sought to preserve the republic by expanding across space and allowing ever more people the chance to become independent farmers, the Whigs thought it a fool's errand, for it was precisely the abrupt acquisition of land and peoples that would radically change the republic at its core, transforming it into a "political despotism."

The 1844 Presidential Election

After the initial surprise of Polk's nomination, the Whigs thus circled back to first principles and offered the American System as a more responsible alternative to Manifest Destiny. The question remains, though, how a generational struggle for the leadership of the Democratic Party could cause defection among Whig leaders and voters. After all, shouldn't the Whigs have benefited from Democratic strife?

On the contrary, leadership succession in the Democratic Party introduced a new crosscutting cleavage of pro- and anti-expansionist interests into American politics. After Whig presidential candidate Henry Clay announced his opposition to Texas annexation, mirroring Van Buren's stance on the issue, southern Democrats framed slavery's expansion into the Southwest as a way to preserve slavery within the Union. Because the northern white population was then outstripping that of the South, southern Democrats became acutely aware that their representation in the U.S. House of Representatives was also slipping, making the South vulnerable to legislation that might undermine slavery. They observed that whereas southerners had six fewer congressmen in 1810, by 1840 that deficit had grown to fourteen. Thus, on July 11, 1844, the editor of Tuscaloosa's *Democratic Gazette* referred to annexation as "a measure of safety and deliverance to the South." Congressman William L. Yancey referred to Texas as a "bond" that would protect slavery: "We ask 'no preponderance in the Government,' but we demand safety. . . . Losing relative strength in the representative branch of the Government; having compromised away all possibility of retaining an equality even in the Senate . . . with the world arrayed against, and its most subtle and efficient nation using every means to subvert, our favorite institution, can we be true to ourselves if we do not demand 'the bond'[?]"[48]

With slavery apparently at risk, Tuscaloosa Whigs suffered the defection of two of their most prominent leaders. Just two months before the presidential election, the *Monitor* reported that U.S. congressman General George W. Crabb performed a "somerset . . . from the Whigs to the Democracy" at a "Polk and Dallas dinner" by "condemning Clay's views on the annexation of Texas."[49] William R. Smith, whom Crabb put through school and hired to work in his law office, became the mouthpiece of the local Whig Party in 1838 when he became editor of the *Monitor*, but he too left the party prior to the 1844 election over similar disagreements with Henry Clay.[50] Two factions thus emerged: "Texas Whigs," advocates of territorial expansion led by Crabb and Smith, and "old line Whigs," Clay loyalists led by State senator Robert Jemison Jr., owner of the county's second-largest plantation.[51]

The split resulted in an unprecedented erosion of Whig electoral support, and the Democrats carried Tuscaloosa County for the first time ever.[52] Most planters, especially in the southwest quadrant of the county, followed the lead of their fellow planter, Robert Jemison Jr., but Texas Whigs peeled off enough of the old base to deliver a majority to Polk with the Democrats' more rural base to the east. Although the Democrats also carried one other planter beat, by far the biggest coup was Northport, the second-largest town in the county next to Tuscaloosa. The Democrats' presidential vote share in Tuscaloosa County increased nine percentage points from 42.4 percent in 1840 to 51.7 percent in 1844.[53]

Nor was this defection an isolated incident. The Democrats did better in planter counties across Alabama in 1844 than they had done in previous elections. The Democratic presidential vote share across so-called Black Belt counties, a band of counties across the southern third of the state where planters owned on average fifty slaves or more, increased overall from 44 percent in the 1840 presidential election to 46.1 percent in 1844. Though the Whigs still carried much of the Black Belt, the Democrats succeeded in flipping two counties. Polk posted unprecedented victories in planter-heavy Sumter and Wilcox counties, a dramatic improvement on their performance in 1840. In Wilcox, for instance, the Democrats went from a paltry 36 percent of the vote in 1840 to 51.8 percent in 1844, an almost sixteen percentage-point swing.

The promise of new farmland out West and the "safety" of southern slavery thus touched off a defection in the Alabama Whig Party, both in Tuscaloosa County and across the Black Belt. The Whigs worked hard to keep the public's eye on economic policy, but James K. Polk's entrance into the race distracted from the old issues, so much so in fact that the preservation of slavery emerged as a key theme in the debate over Texas annexation.

Slavery was not a troublesome issue for the political establishment yet, but it would be soon enough. The dynamics of the 1844 presidential election nationally foreshadowed this threat. Indeed, if proslavery advocates like William L. Yancey enabled Polk to carry the South, then in a parallel process, the abolitionists paradoxically delivered the North. With the abolitionists now organized as an independent third party, the open question above the Mason-Dixon line was just how many votes Liberty Party presidential nominee James G. Birney would take from the two-party system. The Whigs were especially vulnerable to Birney, for the northern wing of the party consisted of proud antislavery reformers.

With the Electoral College count at 134 for Polk and 105 for Clay, New York's 36 electoral votes decided the election. In the Empire State, Birney received 15,812 votes, a full quarter of his nationwide total, while Polk won a plurality of 5,106 votes in the statewide tally. Had Birney not run and had a mere third of his votes gone to Clay, Polk would have lost New York and the presidency by a count of 141 to 134 Electoral College votes. As it happened, Polk carried New York and the nation.

Already the issue of territorial expansion was beginning to reorganize the party system and politicize slavery. If the major parties did not do something, and fast, the political system might descend into factional chaos. As we will see next, the party system did precisely that, but the Whigs then struck upon a strategy that would allow them to reabsorb their renegade factions and take back power: the message of unionism.

3

THE TUG OF UNIONISM

The Whigs' defeat in 1844 turned out to be a blessing in disguise. The incoming Democratic administration, convinced that the election was a mandate for its imperialist agenda, predictably set about acquiring new territory, beginning with the topmost priorities of Texas and Oregon. Skirmishes on the so-called border between Mexico and the self-proclaimed Republic of Texas, in turn, eventuated in the Mexican-American War (1846–48) and the colonization of northern Mexico, encompassing what is today the southwestern United States and all of California.

Though it appeared as though the Democrats were going from strength to strength, in fact they were setting the stage for a bitter debate over the status of slavery in the newly acquired territories. Technically speaking, the dispute began in 1846 when Congress took up debate on President Polk's proposal to compensate Mexico for the lands that would later be known as the "Mexican Cession." Democratic congressman David Wilmot of Pennsylvania attached a condition to the appropriations bill, the Wilmot Proviso, that slavery be prohibited from any such territory.

Wilmot was an unlikely champion for such an amendment as he was no abolitionist. Prior to this moment, Wilmot had been the most reliable of establishment Democrats. But then President Polk vetoed federal funding for northern canals, harbors, and other infrastructure projects. Just as curiously, the president negotiated half of Oregon away to the British after insisting on annexing *all* of Texas. Northern Democrats seemed to be drawing the short end of the stick. Accordingly, Wilmot and other party stalwarts began to connect the dots from the betrayal of Van Buren at the 1844 DNC to a "slave power conspiracy," in which a southern minority schemed to thwart the will of the northern majority.

If the slave power could impose Texas annexation as a litmus test for the 1844 presidential nomination, then Wilmot and his colleagues wanted to show that two could play at that game. Calling themselves "Free Soil Democrats," Wilmot's supporters sought to bar slavery from the western territories on the grounds that a monopoly of the land by wealthy planters would prevent free white men from escaping wage dependency in the nation's cities. Southern Rights Democrats in turn pressed their right to settle in the West. The so-called Alabama Platform, which was that state's position on territorial organization, declared "indefensible in principle" the notion that an act of Congress could "prevent any citizen from removing to, or settling in such territory, with his property, be it slave property or otherwise." Stuck in between these two warring factions was the new Democratic leadership. Polk and Young America Democrats like Lewis Cass and Stephen A. Douglas advocated a middle-of-the-road position called "popular sovereignty," according to which white settlers could decide by referendum whether their territory should be incorporated into the Union as a free or slave state.[1]

Within this toxic soup of Democratic factionalism, the Whigs found the ingredients for a political comeback. Boiled down to its essence, the Whig message was "I told you so." They blamed the political turmoil on the Democrats' reckless territorial policy, which alone was responsible for the rise of disunionism in the North and South. The solution, the Whigs insisted, was to elect a president (from their own party), whose love of the Union would put the slavery issue back in the proverbial bottle where it belonged and reunify the party system behind the founders' vision of a slaveholding republic. The Whigs packaged their candidate, General Zachary Taylor, as the second coming of George Washington himself, and in doing so reabsorbed the defection caused by Manifest Destiny in 1844. Shortly thereafter, a bipartisan coalition of establishment politicians led by Henry Clay and Stephen A. Douglas pushed a series of small compromises through Congress until at last the entire Compromise of 1850 was passed. Together the Taylor presidency and the Compromise defeated the Free Soil and Southern Rights factions of both parties. What those in the establishment did not know—what they did not expect—was that they were merely extending the life of the slaveholding republic by a few short years.

Texas, Oregon, and War

Van Buren Democrats were not just relitigating the 1844 DNC out of spite, for both the annexation of Texas and the division of the Oregon territory with the British were dirty double crosses. Recall that a treaty of annexation was blocked repeatedly in the early 1840s both by elements within the Tyler administration itself, like Daniel Webster, and by the Senate, which rejected the treaty proposed by Tyler's third secretary of state, John C. Calhoun. For obvious reasons, the outcome of the 1844 presidential election softened the ground in Congress for annexation.

Some Whigs felt that their position on Texas had cost Henry Clay the White House. It was in fact a Tennessee Whig, Milton Brown, who proposed the winning Texas plan in the U.S. House of Representatives. On January 25, 1845, by a vote of 120 to 98, the House agreed to admit Texas as a single slave state (not a territory as the Democrats had originally proposed), but stipulated that Texas could be divided into as many as four additional slave states below the Missouri Compromise line, while the territory above it would be free. The Senate Foreign Relations Committee rejected the Brown plan, but in a gesture of comity the Van Buren Democrat Thomas Hart Benton of Missouri proposed an alternate plan in which the more populous eastern frontier would be admitted as a slave state, while the rest would remain unorganized territory. Robert J. Walker of Mississippi then offered a critical amendment that would have empowered the incoming president to offer Texas the choice of a renegotiated treaty of annexation or a joint resolution of Congress. In a private meeting President-elect Polk gave his word to Benton that he would support the Senate plan when he assumed office, and this prompted all northern Democrats and three Whigs to vote in favor of annexation, thereby breaking the deadlock in the Senate. The House then supported the Senate version of the bill. But in his last days in office, President Tyler, feeling his oats, dispatched his chargé Andrew J. Donelson to Texas to present the *House* resolution with no mention of the Benton plan or the Walker amendment. Texas happily accepted the terms of the offer in July 1845, and the settler colony was formally admitted to the Union in December. Though he was arguably within his rights to revoke the deal, President Polk refused to do so and reneged on his promise to Benton.[2]

All might have been forgiven had the president agreed to end the joint occupation of Oregon with Britain and take over the entire territory, but this too he refused to do. Northern Democrats, above all Senator William Allen of Ohio, held that the United States should inform the British of its unwillingness to tolerate the ambiguity of split sovereignty. Allen, who coined the slogan "Fifty-Four Forty or Fight," pressed for a full occupation of the territory up to 54 degrees 40 minutes on the map, which would have swallowed up most of present-day British Columbia including Vancouver. Meanwhile, though the British certainly desired Oregon as a foothold to markets in China and the Sandwich Islands (later Hawai'i), the British foreign minister Lord Ashburton sent signals that he was unenthused about deploying troops to defend their claim. Rumors began to swirl about a compromise to divide the territory once and for all at the forty-ninth parallel. To preempt such a proposal, Allen and his compatriots howled at the betrayal. Polk, being from a slave state himself, could not be counted on to defend Oregon, they said, while conversely the ultra-southern John C. Calhoun of South Carolina argued against a war with Britain for Oregon after calling for the annexation of Texas. In the end, the president agreed to the compromise that remains in place today, with the Americans taking Seattle and the mouth of the Columbia River and the British, later the Canadians, holding Vancouver.

The war with Mexico and the subsequent colonization of the territory from Texas through Northern California known as the Mexican Cession only served to inflame sectional tensions. The war originated with Texas and spread from there into a full-blown continental conflict. Whereas the British had formally recognized the United States' claim to Oregon, Mexico had never recognized Texas independence and still considered Texas a state. Additionally, the western boundary of that state as it existed in Mexico was the Nueces River, not the Rio Grande, which lay farther to the west and which implied a much larger American territory. The independence and western boundary of Texas comprised the initial sticking points between Mexico and the United States, but these disputes in and of themselves did not necessitate war.

But then Polk sent General Zachary Taylor to the disputed territory and eventually to the banks of the Rio Grande itself in 1845. Meanwhile Mexico's new president, General Mariano Paredes, vowed to restore Texas to its rightful owner, touting the country's military prowess. Paredes ordered the Mexican army to push back the American invasion from the Rio Grande, and the ensuing skirmishes between April and May of 1846 inaugurated the war. Congress issued its official declaration of war on May 13.[3]

Paredes's bluster proved to be just that, for the U.S. armed forces had routed their Mexican counterparts by the beginning of 1848. The American advantage became especially apparent between the spring and fall of 1847 with a series of victories at Buenavista, Veracruz, Cerro Gordo, Contreras, Churubusco, Molino del Rey, and Chapultepec. On September 14, General Winfield Scott occupied Mexico City itself and as the winter set in, the United States effectively controlled New Mexico and Upper California. The balance of forces put the president in a strong bargaining position in treaty negotiations, but for all these victories Polk failed to achieve the peace, as Mexico simply refused to surrender. In the end, Polk's envoy Nicholas Trist was able to prevail on the Mexican government to negotiate. On February 2, 1848, Trist signed the treaty ending the Mexican-American War. Under those terms, the United States acquired New Mexico and Upper California, compensated Mexico for its lost lands to the tune of $15 million, and assumed the claims of American citizens against the Mexican government up to $3.25 million.[4]

The treaty met with the goals of Polk and his secretary of state, James Buchanan, but it did more than that. First, it established the United States as a world power. Up to that point, the United States had successfully defended its sovereignty, most famously against Great Britain in the War of 1812. The Mexican-American War proved that the United States—equipped as it was with a citizen army as opposed to a professional one—could not only defend itself but also expand its territory against a well-resourced foreign sovereign in Mexico.[5] Second, the favorable terms of the treaty made Young America Democrats hungry for more territory, most of all Cuba and the so-called Orient, suggesting that the politics of expansion were here to stay for the foreseeable future. Third and most important for our purposes, the treaty begged the question of how to organize that territory. Congress had just endured bruising sectional battles over Texas and Oregon, but even then disunion was deployed mainly as a threat rather than a promise. Would the debate over the Mexican Cession produce more of the same routine grandstanding, or would it permanently damage the reigning vision of the slaveholding republic? The political stakes were high. The Democrats were effectively doubling down on territorial expansion as their signature political issue, but if the Whigs were to prevail in the 1848 presidential election before the new territories were organized, the Democrats might well lose the entire Mexican Cession owing to the Whigs' critical stance toward Manifest Destiny. Indeed, as Congress debated the Wilmot Proviso, some Whigs rallied around a "No Territory" doctrine, according to which the United States should not acquire a single inch of land from Mexico.[6]

The Slaveholding Republic under Attack

The debate over the organization of the territories was an unprecedented attack on the idea of a slaveholding republic. In this it was distinct from previous sectional debacles. In the debate over the admission of Missouri in 1819, for example, the restriction of slavery was a secondary issue and was in fact the very means of compromise, advanced to the great relief of the contending parties. The debate over the Mexican Cession, by contrast, was a struggle over whether the North or South would control the government. This is due to the fact that it centered on the authority of Congress over the common territory. It was not, contrary to popular notions of "states' rights," about the authority of the individual states over their own domestic institutions. What put the republic to the test was that congressional authority itself was being questioned, and the staggering size of the Mexican Cession made the evasion of that test impossible.[7] The debate over territorial organization was also different from the debates over Texas and Oregon. Whereas Manifest Destiny had the effect at least for a time of uniting the parties in nationwide pro- and anti-expansionist coalitions, the debate over the Mexican Cession, which was shaped by Wilmot's opening salvo at the start of the war, exposed the salience of the single institution that divided North and South: slavery.[8]

There were, broadly speaking, four positions on the status of slavery in the territories. The first, the Free Soil position, must not be confused with the call for the abolition of slavery. Free Soilism sought to protect the ability of landless whites to escape wage and debt dependency in the East and migrate westward, where they could own their own land and become economically independent. As one Free Soil Democrat clarified, "The question is not whether black men are to be made free, but whether white men are to remain free."[9] Combined with the Jacksonian critique of dependency was what we might call a "strict constructionist" approach to the U.S. Constitution. Free Soil Democrats opposed both the addition of any new powers to Congress and the reinterpretation of the Constitution itself. This much strict constructionists of northern and southern pedigree could agree on, but constitutional orthodoxy led Free Soil Democrats to insist that slavery was fundamentally a local institution that could not be extended to the territories already free without positive legislation by Congress.[10] The position of Ohio Free Soil statesman Salmon P. Chase was typical of this point of view. Chase held that the Constitution never recognized slavery "as a national institution, to be upheld by national law"; as such, he continued, "Slavery is Constitutionally impossible." David Wilmot likewise insisted that the debate over territorial organization was about whether slavery "shall be carried to new and distant regions, now free, where the footprint of a slave cannot be found." Exhorting his fellow Free Soilers, Wilmot added that if they failed to defend the Constitution against the heretical attacks of proslavery southerners, then "We are cowards, slaves, and deserve to have the manacles fastened upon our own limbs."[11]

Southern Rights Democrats were also strict constructionists, but they denied that Congress had the right to prevent citizens from taking their slaves into the territories. As Senator James H. Hammond of South Carolina declared, "The South venerates the Constitution and is prepared to stand over it forever, such as it came from the hands of our fathers." For Southern Rights Democrats, the territories belonged to the several states of the Union and thus were the states' joint and common property. The restriction of slavery would thus make second-class citizens of southerners. An editor from Montgomery, Alabama, wrote that restriction was an admission "that a free citizen of Massachusetts was a better man and entitled to more privileges than a free citizen of Alabama."[12] Similarly, James Seddon of Virginia accused his Free Soil counterparts of an "arrogant assumption of superiority." "Are they better men, wiser, purer, or greater?" he asked. "Have they accomplished more, or paid more proportionally for the Union than we of the South?"[13] Finally, Southern Rights advocates offered a racist rejoinder to Free Soil's own racially problematic advocacy of landless white men. On their account, slavery was the first line of defense against the exploitation of nonslaveholding whites.[14] So long as slavery persisted, planters would use black—not white—workers to do demeaning manual labor. Given that the debate over territorial organization threatened to subordinate free white men, Southern Rights forces held that submission to the logic of restriction would mean "we are far worse slaves than our vassals."[15]

In contrast, the political establishment of the major parties was oriented toward compromise, though each party advanced competing approaches. The Whig center advanced its long-cherished activist view of government, insisting that the power over the territories did in fact lie with Congress and that Congress should of course use its prerogative to preserve the republic.[16] The Democratic center offered two other approaches to compromise. A relatively small group wanted to divide the Mexican Cession along the existing 36 degrees 30 minutes compromise line between free and slave states.[17] But the majority of moderate Democrats championed the doctrine of popular sovereignty. By this logic, northerners and southerners would have equal access to the new territories by means of the ballot box: the people, not Congress, would vote on whether to enter the Union as a free or slave state.[18] Armed with this apparently elegant solution to the problem of territorial organization, moderate Democrats made popular sovereignty the campaign platform of 1848 Democratic presidential nominee Lewis Cass of Michigan.[19] They assaulted extremists in both sections as elites who doubted the intelligence and rights of territorial residents. Both restriction and slavery extension were premised on a strong national government, which, they reminded their supporters, had also been responsible for past examples of federal overreach like the national bank.[20]

Bringing up the rear in terms of numbers, but nevertheless a mounting concern to their more powerful antagonists, were the abolitionists, whose political vehicle, the Liberty Party, opposed the existence of slavery anywhere in the Union including the South. The abolitionists were not the least bit swayed by the South's threats of disunion, for if the Union was the sacrifice needed to atone for the original sin of slavery, they made it clear they were willing to pay the price. In the debate over territorial organization, the abolitionists harped on one point and one point only: that all of the above solutions to organizing the Mexican Cession involved the persistence or expansion of slavery. The abolitionist firebrand and newspaper editor William Lloyd Garrison saw more clearly than most the underlying politics of the slaveholding republic, which depoliticized and thereby enabled the continued existence of slavery. According to the proposed plans, "Slave states are to be created indefinitely," he warned in his organ *The Liberator*, adding, "On this condition alone is the Union to be maintained. Mark that, ye idolators of the Union!"[21]

With political discourse rife with factionalism and recriminations, it was unclear whether or how Congress would resolve the status of slavery in the Mexican Cession. As we have seen, the debate was made particularly intractable because each faction charged the other with despotism and exhorted its own forces to join in revolutionary battle.[22] Anyone who could break this monumental logjam stood to benefit politically.

For Taylor and Union

Seeking to exploit this moment of uncertainty, the Whig National Convention met at the Chinese Museum in Philadelphia on June 7, 1848. The city was reportedly a hive of activity with ten thousand Whigs descending on Philly from New York alone. General Taylor, a hero of the late war with Mexico, was expected to enter the convention with a small lead over his nearest rival, the 1844 Whig nominee Henry Clay, but not enough to clinch the nomination outright. To win, a candidate had to carry a simple majority—140 of the total 279 delegates assembled.[23]

The first ballot took place in the early evening of Thursday, June 8. Taylor claimed the plurality of delegates as expected with 111, but the big story was Clay's second-place showing of 97 votes, which was lower than political handicappers had predicted. Whereas Taylor, a Louisiana slaveholder with no established political views, took over 80 percent of the South's votes, Clay, the old-line Whig, split the northern vote with General Winfield Scott, another Mexican-American War hero. The other candidates, including Daniel Webster, were by that point clearly out of the running.[24]

The second ballot saw modest movement toward the frontrunner, but the convention remained deadlocked with the South holding firm with Taylor and the northern delegations shifting their support from Clay (who by then had lost the votes of his home delegation of Kentucky) toward General Scott. The Clay camp then maneuvered to adjourn the convention until the following morning. Though this was of course a ploy to stop the bleeding and guilt Clay's erstwhile supporters into returning to the fold, the Great Compromiser's chances actually worsened overnight.[25]

More consequential were the machinations of Truman Smith, head of the Connecticut delegation and chief strategist of the party's previous national campaigns. Though Smith had been a vocal Taylorite as early as December 1847, voting publicly for Taylor at the national convention might have jeopardized his political career in Connecticut, which was dominated by Free Soilers and abolitionists. The wily Taylor camp, led by the Southern Unionist John J. Crittenden and none other than Abraham Lincoln himself, would have none of this equivocation and trapped Smith in a corner. With nowhere else to run, Smith at last threw in with Taylor. Because of his national influence and because of Connecticut's early position in the roll call voting, Smith's vote caused a stampede toward Taylor, who won on the fourth and final ballot.[26]

The dynamics of the Whig convention evince two important patterns. The first is sectional division. The last-minute rush to Taylor from northern delegates obscures the rift over slavery, for although two-fifths of Taylor's total delegate count was from the North, the absolute number was just one third of all northern delegates. Further, over 80 percent of Taylor's vote on the first ballot came from southern delegates; by the end they comprised almost two-thirds of the Taylor coalition. This was a result of electoral math. To win, Taylor had to carry 140 votes, and the South only had 111 votes to give. Taylor badly needed northern delegates to defect from Clay and Scott. Finally, it bears pointing out that the convention nominated Millard Fillmore of New York as the party's vice presidential candidate. This was meant to appease northern delegates, who threatened to campaign against the party if it nominated the textile industrialist Abbott Lawrence of Massachusetts, a known collaborator of the Taylor faction and, by virtue of his business, a direct beneficiary of slave labor.[27]

The second pattern has to do with the biography of the leading candidates themselves, or what convention delegates referred to obliquely as the need for "gunpowder." Together the two Mexican-American War heroes, Taylor and Scott, carried a majority of the convention. At the end of the second ballot, for example, Taylor had 118 delegates and Scott 49, for a total of 167 votes or about 60 percent of all delegates. Most Whig delegates sought a nominee who would be identified with the entire country instead of either Southern Rights or the Proviso. We might therefore surmise that Taylor's nomination stemmed from the fractious debate over the Mexican Cession.[28]

The framing of General Taylor as a second George Washington, with no political bona fides except his sacrifice for the Union, paid dividends in an uncomfortably polarized political climate. The Whigs handed the 1848 Democratic candidate Lewis Cass a crushing defeat and one that signified the electorate's rejection of all existing solutions to territorial organization, including popular sovereignty and the Proviso. Old "Rough and Ready," as Taylor was repeatedly called during the campaign, won a majority of both the North and South and carried four states that Clay had lost in 1844. Contrary to fears that northern Whigs would refuse to turn out, Taylor received 98 percent of Henry Clay's votes in free states and swept four out of seven states in the Deep South.[29]

The Compromise of 1850 and the
Failed Southern Congress

Though Taylor's victory in 1848 seemed to suggest a national tilt toward compromise, in practice his administration was both enabling and constraining of compromise in Congress. In the months prior to the beginning of Taylor's term, Congress made two feeble attempts to organize the Mexican Cession. Democratic senator Stephen A. Douglas of Illinois sent up a bill to admit the entire cession as a single state. Whig congressman William B. Preston of Virginia introduced a bill in the House for California statehood. Both bills had just failed when Taylor was inaugurated on March 5, 1849. Few lawmakers expected anything brilliant from the old general as he had precious little political experience, but Taylor moved decisively. His first act in office was to dispatch the Georgia Whig Butler King to help California residents write a constitution prohibiting slavery. He attempted to do the same in New Mexico, but that plan was hampered by the stalemate in Congress and an ongoing boundary dispute with Texas, a dispute that Taylor himself urged the New Mexican territorial governor to handle militarily if necessary.[30]

His abrupt entrance into the fray kick-started the conversation that would eventually lead to the Compromise of 1850, albeit as an alternative to the president's plan. Henry Clay's compromise, presented in the Senate on January 29, 1850, consisted of five separate proposals: admit California as a free state; admit the rest of the cession (New Mexico and Utah) without restriction to slavery; assume Texas's debt in return for yielding in the boundary dispute with New Mexico; abolish the slave trade, but not slavery, in the District of Columbia; and establish a stronger fugitive slave law.[31] In February Senator Henry Foote of Mississippi worked to put Clay's separate proposals in a single bill with the added provision that the U.S. Supreme Court assume jurisdiction over all future constitutional disputes over the territories.

That so-called omnibus bill was defeated, in part because Taylor clung stubbornly to his own plans. Indeed, as the historian Elizabeth Varon writes, Taylor was "the most significant barrier to compromise."[32] Luckily, for the forces of moderation, the president died on July 9, 1850. Vice President Millard Fillmore, who had been snubbed by the president while in office and was appalled by his conduct in the New Mexico boundary dispute, assumed the presidency and quickly went to work. He collaborated closely with Stephen A. Douglas to pass each of the measures of the omnibus bill one by one. As individual bills, Clay's compromise passed, and Douglas, the new savior of the Union, became thought of as a potential Democratic presidential nominee.[33]

The effect of the Compromise in the North was to heal the internal divisions between the Free Soil and establishment wings of both parties. In Illinois, for example, the leading lights of the Free Soil Democracy, most importantly John Wentworth, who was the boss of the Chicago Democratic machine, reconciled with the popular sovereigntists.[34]

In the South, the establishment had to crush one last uprising before putting the concept of secession back in the bottle. Denouncing Clay's compromise plan as submission to the North, Southern Rights Democrats organized a Southern Congress to be held in Nashville in the summer of 1850. Historians call the run-up to that convention the "first secession crisis."

The lead organizers of the Southern Congress were General E. C. Wilkinson of Mississippi, James Hammond of South Carolina, and Beverly Tucker of Virginia—all Democrats. These were joined by zealous new converts, chief among them William Lowndes Yancey of Alabama, who had consistently championed southern rights within the Union through the 1840s but who, as a result of the debate over the Mexican Cession, grew disillusioned with unionism.[35]

The middle ground prevailed, however. When Clay proposed his compromise on the Senate floor his fellow southern Whigs rallied to his side. Their operatives in the press then took up the call. Regarding the Nashville convention, the *American Whig Review* wrote straightforwardly, "secession and dissolution are the very worst of all evils."[36] Sensing their advantage, the Whigs cloaked themselves once again, as they had in the 1848 presidential election, in the mantle of the Union. Their position, which reflected the enduring vision of the slaveholding republic, was "southern rights with peace," and they used it relentlessly to tarnish the Democratic opposition as radical disunionists and demagogues.[37]

The most prominent southern politicos fell into line, even in the Deep South. In Georgia, Whigs Robert Toombs and Alexander Stephens, who would later become the Confederacy's secretary of state and vice president, respectively, worked with the Democrat Howell Cobb to position themselves as a powerful procompromise bloc. Even Jefferson Davis of Mississippi, future president of the Confederacy, while open to the concept of the right of secession, nevertheless framed the abolitionists as the true disunionists in their midst, while his own southern compatriots were the ones who defended "the Union that our fathers bled to establish."[38] And even in South Carolina, the supposed vanguard of southern disunion, a coalition of Whigs and Calhoun Democrats handily defeated the secessionist opposition. Voters in the South Carolina Upcountry gave over 60 percent of their ballots to the "wait and see" side of the question. Outside the Upcountry, the coalition did less well, as the secessionists tended to hail from there, but even then the antisecessionist bloc carried the lower cotton belt and won the city of Charleston with over 70 percent of the vote. Under such immense pressure, the champions of the Southern Congress were forced to backpedal and say that the meeting was "not secessionist but merely consultative."[39]

Here it bears outlining the various arguments for and against secession. In support of secession, Southern Rights Democrats advanced what can only be described as a lurid white supremacist argument that conjured the specter of wage slavery and economic dependency for the nonslaveholding white majority. The South Carolina secessionist B. H. Rice told yeoman farmers, "We have as yet no privileged class. He who has no slaves today may soon— or his children . . . [but] if slaves are freed, whites will become menials."[40] Other secessionist warnings were even more lurid. One letter to the editor of the *Carolina Spartan* predicted a future of racial mixing:

> We will be compelled to endure equality with them—we will be forced to allow them the same privileges we enjoy. . . . They would insist on a right to

vote and send their negro brethren to our State Legislature and to the United States Congress—their children would go to school with your children—they would eat at your *tables*, sleep in your beds and drink out of the same *gourd* that you do; yea, they would do more than this, they would marry your daughters, in despite of everything you could do, and you will be deeply humiliated at the thought that your grand-children, those who shall inherit your name and your property, are of *mixed blood*.[41]

As was typical of the Whig style, the response to these racist diatribes was notably more measured and pragmatic. Richard Yeadon, a Charleston lawyer and journalist, wrote the following of the debate in Congress: "If no reasonable compromise can be obtained from our Northern brethren, I am ready for disunion as a dire and hateful alternative and refuge from intolerable insult [and] wrong—but I unhesitatingly prefer Clay's compromise to disunion and will resolutely stand up to that mark."[42]

Animating this point of view was a cautiousness and economic pragmatism that were characteristic of the Whig Party and their planter base. Armistead Burt, another South Carolinian, held that the secession of his state would not strengthen slavery in any way and would make it more difficult to retrieve fugitive slaves. The protection of slavery afforded by the Constitution would be lost; the value of slave property after secession, he predicted, would fall; and the people would lose access forever to the lands of the Mexican Cession.[43]

Note that Burt, like so many others who were skeptical of secession, sought to preserve slavery, but in their estimation slavery was safer inside the Union than outside of it. Here we see that the caricature of the Deep South as the consummate vanguard of disunionism does not stand up to scrutiny. The vision of the slaveholding republic remained extraordinarily difficult to dislodge even in the region where one would expect it to be most imperiled. Indeed, when Southern Rights Democrats went public in 1850 with their intention to leave the Union, they opened themselves up to attacks as radicals and extremists. As a result, the political establishment was able to contain the secessionist insurgency.

The View from Alabama

The trajectory of Alabama politics followed the sequence of division and reabsorption across the country. The state's Southern Rights Democratic position on the organization of the territories, for instance, was not unique. It viewed any prohibition of slavery in the Mexican Cession—whether by popular sovereignty or the Wilmot Proviso—to be a violation not only of southerners' constitutional right to transport their "property" wherever they wished, but also of their natural right to a life of economic independence as prospective landowners out West.

David Hubbard typified this position. Hubbard was a Democratic congressman from Alabama during the debate on territorial organization. He was later an elector to the Southern Rights presidential ticket of Breckinridge and Lane in 1860 and was appointed Indian Commissioner during the years of the Southern Confederacy.[44] In a speech before the U.S. House of Representatives opposing the restriction of slavery, he said of his constituents: "They have paid their part in money, and done their share of fighting for this Mexican country and expect me to get for them as partners, part of the land upon which they may go, carry their property with them, own and enjoy it, and remain part of this Union, undisturbed in their rights." In contrast, he continued, the "learned speeches" of his moderate Democratic colleagues on "non-intervention," or "non-action" actually "takes *all of the land*" from them. This, said Hubbard, had the effect of unjustly robbing southern whites of their freedom, observing that "instead of destroying the slavery of the black man," the various proposals for compromise "destroy . . . the liberty of the white man" (emphasis in original).[45] Hubbard concluded his speech with the threat of disunion:

> A Union formed of bad men, to break up the rights secured to the South, to put black and white races upon a footing of equality, and to degrade the southern States from their position in the Confederacy, to forge the white man's chains, and fasten him to "*a government of unlimited powers*," under pretense of setting the black man free—I am for no such Union.[46] (emphasis in original)

Here Hubbard breaks with the established orthodoxy of his party in two respects. First, in dismissing his colleagues' "learned" speeches on "nonintervention," he rejects the doctrine of popular sovereignty, which was the Democratic Party platform in the 1848 presidential election. That platform, he says, threatens to deprive southern whites of their birthright and make them second-class citizens relative to other Americans who paid their part in "money and fighting" for the Mexican Cession. Perhaps more important, Hubbard destabilizes the orienting assumption of antebellum American politics in general, namely, that slavery and the South were safer in the Union than they were outside of it. His continued support for the Union as the compromise debate now came to a close was conditioned upon whether southerners could go wherever they wished, "undisturbed in their rights."

Like his fellow Whigs, Alabama congressman Henry Hilliard's support of slavery and of the slaveholding republic was much more genteel. There was no race baiting, whether by speculating on the prospects of racial equality or warning of miscegenation. His white supremacy was contained—silently—in his love of the Union. This love he leveraged to paint, again only by implication and the plain presentation of contrast, the extremism of his Southern Rights colleagues. "I am a Southern man by birth, by rearing, by allegiance, by all the mighty sympathies which can bind the heart of a man to his people," Hilliard said in a speech advocating compromise on the new territories on February 10, 1849. "But," he clarified, "I claim the wider and still more glorious privilege of being a citizen of the American Union; and while I love the South, I should love the South less if it did not form a part of this Union."[47]

Hilliard's party pressed the very same message, from the debate over the Mexican Cession through the Compromise of 1850 and beyond. Taking their cues from their national and statewide leaders, Tuscaloosa Whigs rallied in 1848 around the presidential candidacy of General Taylor, whom they packaged as a new George Washington. What was needed in the now two-year-long congressional stalemate over the Wilmot Proviso, local Whigs argued, was not a disunionist Southern Rights Democrat but a man who privileged the Union above all other interests. The June 29, 1848, issue of the Whig

Independent Monitor quotes the establishment Whig planter Robert Jemison Jr. saying of Taylor, "Though like the father of his country he inclines to the leading tenets of one of the great political parties, he is not strictly and fully identified with either. He is above all party. . . . Such a man was Washington, and on such a man the patriots of all parties may unite." Instead of the competing sectional interests on display in the congressional debate over the Mexican Cession, the Whigs contrasted the interests of all those who loved the Union against the selfish few who sought its destruction.

As in the rest of the country, unionism was the right message at the right time: Jemison's establishment or old-line Whigs reabsorbed the renegade Texas Whigs of 1844. The average Democratic vote share in planter beats dropped precipitously from 38.1 percent in 1844 to 29.4 percent in 1848. In the Texas Whig beats, Springer's and Northport, the Democrats' share of the popular vote fell from the mid-to-high 50 percent range to a third.

Statewide archival data corroborate the more fine-grained precinct-level returns. Average Democratic vote shares across Alabama's planter or Black Belt counties suggest that the Whig Party was back in the driver's seat. From what was then a historic high of 46.1 percent in the 1844 presidential election, the Democrats were held to just 39.3 percent in planter counties. This was even lower than their poor showing in 1840 when the Whigs took the White House. The strength of the Whigs' performance in the presidential election was subsequently magnified in the state elections of 1849. In that year, the Whigs took control of the State Senate.[48]

Eager to ride their winning message of selfless patriotism to future victories, the Whigs dropped their old party label and styled themselves "Unionists" for the 1851 U.S. congressional elections. They urged their base to disavow Southern Rights intransigence and commit instead to the Compromise of 1850.[49] Henry Hilliard typified the party's rhetorical strategy. He said of the compromise debate, "I desire to settle the question—not a part of the question, but the whole question—and to settle it completely."[50] Even William R. Smith, who decamped from the Whig Party over Clay's opposition to Texas annexation, sought and won the Unionist nomination for the Fourth Congressional District. In that contest, planter-heavy Tuscaloosa County gave Smith a 2-to-1 margin of victory. Overall the Whigs orchestrated a near-unanimous win in the congressional elections, with John Bragg and Sampson Harris being the only Southern Rights Democrats to win, and only then because they were mistakenly viewed as moderates.[51]

Alabama planters like others of their class tended to justify their support for unionism in terms that underscored their identity as businessmen in the wider national economy. Echoing the South Carolinian Armistead Burt's business-oriented argument against secession, one Alabama planter said, "Disunion will not give us a better price for cotton—will not increase the value of slave property—will not render them more secure—will not diminish taxation—but will be likely under the best imaginable state of affairs, to double taxation, diminish the price of staples, and reduce the value of negroes and land, fifty per cent."[52]

The resurgence of unionism chastened Southern Rights Democrats in Alabama. William L. Yancey's walk through the political wilderness is particularly telling of this moment in Southern Rights history. His fascinating "Address to the People of Alabama" reveals that he was ostracized from the Democratic Party for refusing to support the 1848 Democratic presidential nominee, Lewis Cass of Michigan, whose embrace of popular sovereignty, Yancey said, ran afoul of the Alabama Platform. At the 1848 Democratic convention, which was held in Baltimore in late May, Yancey walked out of the convention in opposition to the party's choice, the only member of the Alabama delegation who did so. That ostentatious rejection of party discipline was answered, he reported, "by the great majority of the democratic press with . . . a torrent of contumely—of personal abuse—of vindictiveness." Nor were his colleagues in the delegation amused, committed though they were to the same platform. "A portion of my co-delegates," he observed, "have also joined in the 'hue and cry' which has been raised to hunt down 'the rebel'—to drive 'the traitor' to his doom."[53]

As he began to pursue the formation of a secessionist third party, Yancey's close friends and allies privately counseled him against that course of action. Southern Rights cadres had gone as far as setting a date for the convention (July 12, 1848), at which point they intended to nominate a presidential ticket of Littleton Tazewell and Jefferson Davis. When Yancey persisted in this course over the objections of his fellow Democrats, U.S. senator Dixon H.

Lewis of Alabama killed the nascent organization by pulling his support in a letter dated June 29, 1848. In it, Lewis was gentle but firm. "It is natural that you should feel deeply the assaults that have been made on you," he wrote, "but does your personal honour or your party position require you to vindicate your sense of personal injury—by your present purpose of offering a new political organization?" "Would it not be the part of wisdom," Lewis pressed, "to wait for time and events to vindicate your course as a Delegate?"[54] With that polite missive, support for the third party evaporated and the shrillest of Democratic cadres retreated to the kind of conditional unionism evinced by David Hubbard above. After the 1848 presidential election, when the Alabama congressional delegation asked their state's governor, Henry Collier of Tuscaloosa, to declare his position on the Mexican Cession, Collier replied, "Our motto is the Union as it was adjusted by our fathers, a dissolution of the partnership as a lesser evil than degradation."[55]

Victory and Its Discontents

The Whigs thus played the role of savior to the slaveholding republic, but there were three contradictions in the Whig establishment's strategy, all stemming from the means of its ascent. First, the Whigs were not the only saviors of the Union, for the idea of breaking up the omnibus bill came not from the Whig Henry Clay but from the Democrat Stephen A. Douglas. Instead of understanding the late congressional impasse as an object lesson in the pitfalls of white settler colonialism, the Young America leadership of the Democratic Party—ever the advocates of Manifest Destiny— mistook the Compromise to be a blueprint for exploiting further expansion as a political issue. As one Democrat wrote, victory in the 1852 presidential election was assured "with Douglas and Cuba inscribed on our flag, as in 1844 we had Polk, Dallas, and Texas."[56] Instead of folding, the Democrats doubled down on expansion and would soon touch off yet another debate over the status of slavery in the western territories.

The second contradiction entails the unintended effects of Whig support for Zachary Taylor and the Compromise. Recall that General Taylor became the Whig presidential nominee in 1848 largely on the strength of southern delegations at the national convention; Taylor's floor generals only secured northern support in the last hours as the Connecticut delegation defected to Taylor to avoid a deadlocked convention. Sectionalism was therefore suppressed at the convention for the sake of party unity, but it remained a potential source of defection down the road.[57] Moreover, unity itself did not deliver what it promised to the Whigs, for the Compromise, while making Southern Rights Democrats like Yancey political pariahs, had the effect of cooling sectional tension in both parties and reuniting the Democrats. Thus, the Whigs inadvertently strengthened their adversaries and in doing so necessitated a counteroffensive in the future.

Third, that Southern Rights forces were defeated should not be mistaken to mean that they were dead. Yancey continued to advance the doctrine of secession with as much gusto as ever during unionism's ascendancy. In a letter dated May 27, 1851, he advised his colleagues to continue to organize and prepare for the next sectional crisis:

> The secession party . . . has every reason to persevere in perfecting its organization, by holding up to public scrutiny, the doctrine of secession. . . . And if we shall not have fully accomplished our aim before the arrival of another such a crisis, as that just passed, in which the feelings of the South shall again be outraged and disregarded, we shall, at all events, not have again to await the slow process of the disintegration of those old parties which have heretofore preyed upon the vitals of the South, and the formation of a resistance party, but thoroughly disciplined, and full[y] prepared, to meet the great emergency, with ranks swelled by the disaffection and irritation consequent upon such wrong and insult, the secession party will doubtless be enabled to place the State at once, in a position of independence and honor.[58]

Understanding better than anyone except perhaps the abolitionists that the slaveholding republic was fundamentally unstable, Yancey thus called upon his compatriots to prepare for the next crisis. He points out—rightly—that when the moment comes, Southern Rights forces will not have to wait for the party system to disintegrate or for their own party to take form, for in the event of a second sectional debacle the party system would be doubly compromised and Yancey's third-party insurgency would already be in position to exploit the crisis.

These then were the underlying conditions of party politics heading into the mid-1850s. They did not, however, make the secession crisis inevitable. For these seeds to bear fruit, certain events had to break Yancey's way. In the South, the course of the Whig Party could spell the doom of the Union or its preservation. The debate over the Mexican Cession had anointed the Whigs the single-biggest obstacle to secession in the South. We turn now to what the Whigs did at this pivotal moment in American history.

4

THE END OF THE
SLAVEHOLDING REPUBLIC

With the Compromise of 1850 signed and sectionalism reduced to a low hum, the Democratic Party met the new decade
with unity and vigor. In the 1852 presidential election their
candidate, Franklin Pierce, claimed the White House. President Pierce, like
his predecessor Polk, was an ardent imperialist, and his allies in Congress
redoubled their efforts to fulfill the promise of Manifest Destiny.[1]

Though Pierce, once in office, resorted primarily to the mechanism of patronage to maintain party unity, congressional Democrats galvanized their
caucus with an ambitious legislative agenda. Senator Augustus Dodge of Iowa
introduced a bill in December 1853 to organize the Nebraska territory. Not to
be outdone, Dodge's Democratic colleague Stephen A. Douglas announced a
bolder plan. Hoping not only to ensure that a transcontinental railway would
pass through his home state of Illinois, but also to burnish his credentials for
a future presidential run, Douglas introduced an alternative bill on January 4,

1854, to encompass the entire unorganized territory of the Louisiana Purchase from 36 degrees 30 minutes to the British North American (now Canadian) border.[2] Douglas's "Kansas-Nebraska" bill would become a political bombshell.

Kansas and Nebraska

To pass such a bill, Douglas knew he would need the support of southern legislators. Indeed, a bill to organize the Nebraska territory had failed in the face of southern opposition in the previous Congress. One southern senator, David Rice Atchison of Missouri, who roomed with three proslavery radicals in Washington, DC, informed Douglas that the price for southern support was the repeal of the earlier compromise of 1820, which prohibited slavery west of Missouri. Douglas was hesitant to offer that concession explicitly lest it alienate northern Democrats, so he reported a bill that was essentially silent on the question of slavery, specifying only that any resulting states would be admitted as free or slave depending on their constitutions. It was at this point that the outspoken anti–slavery-extension Whig William H. Seward of New York maneuvered to force Douglas into the position he was trying so delicately to avoid. Seward persuaded southern Whig senator Archibald Dixon of Kentucky to offer an amendment to the bill that explicitly repealed the Missouri Compromise. The move, Seward promised, would shore up Dixon's reputation in his section as a southern patriot and further strengthen the prospects of southern Whigs in general. At the same time, Seward hoped that the repeal would be so obnoxious to northern opinion that the bill would ultimately fail in the House, where Free Soilers held a clear majority. The call for repeal intensified southern pressure on Douglas, and Douglas bowed, reluctantly accepting Dixon's amendment. Accordingly, Kansas and Nebraska, once off-limits to slaveholders, were now at least accessible to them through the doctrine of popular sovereignty: either territory could become free or slave, the legislation said, depending on a vote of the people, though the timing of such a vote—whether as a territory or at the point of statehood—remained an open question.[3]

The political repercussions of the Kansas-Nebraska bill went according to Seward's plan by and large. On January 24, 1854, as the repeal began to take shape, Free Soil Democrats published a manifesto that excoriated the bill as "a gross violation of a sacred pledge; as a criminal betrayal of precious rights; as part and parcel of an atrocious plot" to organize the territories into a "dreary region of despotism, inhabited by masters and slaves." Far from unifying the party behind his leadership, Douglas had reinflamed sectional strife. Democratic congressman David Wilmot, author of the Wilmot Proviso, aptly predicted the fate of the Democratic Party. In a private letter to Pennsylvania governor William Bigler, Wilmot warned that the bill threatened his party "with annihilation in every free State" and "can only result in whittling away the democratic party into shavings."[4]

In the end, the amended bill passed the Senate 37 to 14 on March 4, with the promised southern support at its back. In contrast, the bill squeaked by the House by a vote of 113–100 on May 22 after weeks of rancorous debate, with northern Democrats splitting 44 in favor and 43 against, and southern Democrats overwhelmingly in favor, 69 to 9. Douglas had scored a Pyrrhic victory. He would later write that he returned to his home state of Illinois by the light of his own effigy. The Democrats endured losses all over the country in the aftermath of the bill's passage. To name just one example, everyone in the New York congressional delegation who had voted for the bill was defeated in the next election.[5]

If the 1854 Kansas-Nebraska Act whittled the Democratic Party into shavings, as Wilmot put it, then the ensuing debacle beginning in 1857 over the status of slavery in Kansas ground those shavings into sawdust. By then a new Democrat was in the White House, James Buchanan, but he, unlike his colleagues, was less committed to the doctrine of popular sovereignty. Buchanan's heterodoxy became apparent with Kansas's proslavery constitution. An assembly of territorial officials met at Lecompton, Kansas, in September 1857 ostensibly to settle the slavery question once and for all. But Free Soil advocates boycotted the meeting, while proslavery forces, who comprised the majority of territorial legislators, had no intention of submitting the constitution written there to a vote of the people (Free Soil voters outnumbered their Southern Rights counterparts). The decision was made to circumvent a referendum—the very heart of the Democrats' doctrine of popular sovereignty—by submitting the Lecompton constitution directly to the U.S. Congress for approval, a decision that President Buchanan supported. The

Lecompton constitution failed in Congress, but the English bill, a watered-down version, did pass. The latter ordered a referendum not on slavery but on the size of the land grant.[6]

The Kansas-Nebraska Act and the Lecompton constitution together left the Democratic Party in shambles. Douglas, possibly the most famous Democrat in America and the presumptive presidential nominee in 1860, broke with Buchanan over the subversion of popular sovereignty in the Lecompton fiasco. This meant that in addition to the Free Soil and Southern Rights Democrats who had reemerged during the debate on the Kansas-Nebraska bill, the party had spawned two additional factions: Buchanan Democrats and Douglas Democrats.[7] Secessionists, for their part, began their exodus from the Democratic Party and the Union. William Lowndes Yancey contradicted his earlier dictum that Texas and westward expansion guaranteed slavery's safety within the Union. Now, he said, "A Southern Republic is our only safety."[8]

Competing Whig Reactions

With the renewal of sectional infighting among Democrats, the Whigs sensed another opportunity.[9] William H. Seward and other Whigs who opposed the Kansas-Nebraska Act (so-called anti-Nebraska Whigs) hoped to become the main alternative to the Democrats in the North. Accordingly, they remained somewhat aloof from an emerging effort to fuse antislavery elements into a new "Republican" party. Thurlow Weed rebuffed the overtures of his fellow Whigs to abandon their party, saying, "Having found the Whig Party of the North, on all occasions, and in every emergency, the most efficient and reliable organization both to resist the aggressions of Slavery and to uphold the cause of Freedom, we concur . . . that it is best, now and ever, 'for the Whig Party to stand by its colors.' "[10]

But neither Weed nor Seward could have predicted that establishment or "Silver Gray" Whigs would build a competing party on top of a nativist third party. The "Know Nothings," so named because members were instructed to feign ignorance when asked about the organization, was founded in 1850 in New York City. Its formal name was the Order of the Star Spangled Banner. The order languished until 1853, when under the new leadership of a conservative New York City merchant, James W. Barker, the party undertook to build a tight, hierarchical national organization, spreading initially to the Northeast and Midwest, but eventually claiming some ten thousand local "lodges" across the country and upwards of one million members. The rapid growth of the Know Nothing or American Party was due largely to the organization's overt religious bigotry and hostility toward the two-party system. These dimensions of Know Nothing organizational culture were spurred on by the events of the day, in particular the Whig Party's pandering to Catholics in the presidential election of 1852 and what was broadly perceived as a Catholic attempt to undercut the public school system in 1853. Nativist public sentiment built to a crescendo after President Pierce's appointment of James Campbell, a Catholic, as U.S. Postmaster General and the visit of the pope's representative, Archbishop Gaetano Bedini, to the United States between June 1853 and February 1854. To the Know Nothings, these were signs of a Catholic conspiracy to infiltrate the republic and make it answer not to the people or president of the United States but to the pope in Rome. Such appeals were further strengthened by the Know Nothings' close connection with the temperance movement, which saw alcohol (and the immigrants who drank and peddled it) as the single-most corrosive influence on the country.[11]

After the 1852 election, the Democratic resurgence and the rapid ascendancy of nativism led former president Millard Fillmore and conservative Whigs to co-opt the Know Nothings. Though a majority of southern Whigs and many northern conservatives had already begun defecting to that organization, it was only after the Know Nothings scored major victories in Pennsylvania, Massachusetts, and New York that Fillmore and his allies moved to infiltrate. As Whig Party historian Michael F. Holt argues, conservative Whigs, hostile to their antislavery colleagues, sought "to convert the Know Nothing movement into the Union Party they had sought since 1853."[12]

The political debacle over Kansas and Nebraska thus led to two different counterreactions: anti-Nebraska Whigs led by William H. Seward and Thurlow Weed, who opposed the expansion of slavery on the one hand, and nativists led by Millard Fillmore, who hoped to unite northern and southern conservatives behind a unionist alternative on the other.

The two new factions exposed long-standing differences within the party between nativists and assimilationists: those who had always been suspicious of immigrants, and those who by contrast believed that immigrants could and should be allowed to integrate into the dominant Anglo society.[13] William H. Seward had long made a point of defending immigrant voters. As early as 1850, he wrote:

> I am in favor of the equality of men—of *all* men, whether they be born in one land or in another. . . . There is no distinction in my respect or affection between men of one land and of another; between men of one clime and another; between men of one race and another; or between men of one color and another; no distinction but what is based, not upon institutions of government, not upon the consent of society, but upon their *individual and personal merit.* (emphasis in original)[14]

Though this sentiment is complicated by his aforementioned collusion with Archibald Dixon to repeal the Missouri Compromise, the quotation is consistent with Seward's track record on black civil rights in New York. As a leading elected official, he refused to extradite to the South blacks who were accused of being runaway slaves. He also sent state officials to recover freed blacks who were kidnapped into slavery.[15]

Abraham Lincoln, who was an anti-Nebraska Whig before he became a Republican, likewise expressed hostility to nativism and married it to his critique of slavery extension. Amid the confusion of the mid-1850s, he said, "I think I am a whig; but others say there are no whigs, and that I am an abolitionist." Yet there was one thing of which he was certain: "I am not a Know-Nothing. . . . How can anyone who abhors the oppression of negroes, be in favor of degrading classes of white people?"[16]

Accordingly, when top Whig operatives like John P. Kennedy maneuvered to make the Roman Catholic Church a more feared specter than American slavery, assimilationist anti-Nebraska Whigs were already disinclined to merge with the Know Nothings and resistant to moderating their antislavery principles to strengthen southern Whigs. The "True friends of Freedom," one antislavery Whig insisted, "must never again allow political cooperation between Northerners and Southerners." Eventually Seward's, Lincoln's, and Weed's near-term objective would be to split antislavery northerners off from the Know Nothing Party and in doing so sink the latter's chances of becoming the main alternative to the Democratic Party.[17]

Nativism Divided

Though Fillmore and his lieutenants placed great stock in nativism as a unionist alternative in large northern states, they turned a blind eye to the fact that nativists in those states evinced a hostility toward slavery and the South. Indeed, in the authoritative account of the northern Know Nothing Party, Tyler Anbinder points out that a central component of the Know Nothings' mass appeal in the North was their reliable opposition to the expansion of slavery into the western territories.[18] Antislavery sentiment, nativism, and temperance were bound together in the Know Nothing imaginary. They, like their Protestant ministers, saw "rum, Romanism, and slavery" as the three evils cursing the nation.[19] Slavery and Catholicism in particular were seen as two sides of the same coin, for each sought to inculcate a slavishness that was incompatible with American values. Massachusetts congressman Anson Burlingame, for example, argued that

> Slavery and Priestcraft . . . have a common purpose: they seek [to annex] Cuba and Hayti and the Mexican States together, because they will be Catholic and Slave. I say they are in alliance by the necessity of their nature,—for one denies the right of a man to his body, and the other the right of a man to his soul. The one denies his right to think for himself, the other the right to act for himself.[20]

It therefore came as no surprise to Know Nothings that not one Catholic priest had signed a well-publicized antislavery petition to Congress in 1854 as the Kansas-Nebraska bill was before the people, a stark contrast to New England Protestant ministers who had signed the petition in their thousands. This was a powerful insinuation, and from 1854 to 1855 it led to the defeat of countless northern Democrats, whose base was among Irish Catholic voters. For instance, Democratic, Know Nothing, and independent newspapers alike blamed Democratic losses in Connecticut on both the "Nebraska iniquity" *and* antipathy to "Political Roman Catholicism."[21]

Southern Whigs-turned-Know-Nothings were likewise willfully ignorant of their northern colleagues' antislavery tendencies and opportunistically hewed to the twin issues of Catholicism and immigration as a way to save the national party and contain the Democrats' resurgence. South Carolina's George S. Bryan said southern Whigs' "only chance" was "a diversion—a change of names." Northern Whig attacks "against our section," he observed, had destroyed "the nationality of the Whig Party" and made it impossible for southern Whigs "to maintain brotherly relations" with them. Bryan's proposed solution was therefore "Fillmore & the Know Nothings—or whatever better than can be devised." Fillmore's lieutenant John P. Kennedy likewise held that the interests of the Whig establishment lay in cooperating "with the conservative National party of the South," because in Dixie, Know Nothingism was "thoroughly National and will enlist the support of the whole Whig party and, I doubt not, the National democratic party also." Conservative unionists from both parties and sections, Kennedy said, constituted in practice "one party" that would look with "extraordinary unanimity to Mr. Fillmore for 1856."[22]

As it turns out, Bryan and Kennedy grossly underestimated the effect of northern nativists' antislavery sentiment on the South. Fillmore should have known—in fact *did* know—better. In the early days of the nativist strategy, North Carolina Whig William A. Graham wrote to Fillmore explaining that southern Whigs saw their northern counterparts as "infested" by "Abolitionism or Free Soilism."[23] The clearest example of the challenges facing southern Whigs' nativist play was their defeat in the Virginia gubernatorial election of 1855, which was the first major test of Fillmore's strategy to frame the Know Nothings as the unionist alternative to the Democratic Party.

The cause of the defeat was what I call the "Wise attack," after the 1855 Democratic gubernatorial nominee in Virginia, Henry A. Wise. An important dimension of Wise's messaging was guilt by association: northern nativists had supported the election of two dyed-in-the-wool antislavery men, William H. Seward of New York and Henry Wilson of Massachusetts, to the U.S. Senate. This, the campaign said, proved that Virginia's Know Nothings were in league with abolitionists. Wise promised that Democrats would "defend the state against agrarianism, free-soilism and abolitionism, now threatening to invade the South from the Northern and non-slaveholding councils of Know Nothingism." That charge, which rapidly gained traction, prevented Virginia Whigs from joining the new party. One such Whig, William C. Rives, warned of southerners' belief that "all the New England States [are] strongly injected with the spirit of free-soilism & abolition." Accordingly, Rives reasoned, there "was very much . . . doubt whether the *order* can ever *nationalize* itself" (emphasis in original). News of the defeat went far and wide and so did the customary postmortems. Alabama's major Know Nothing newspaper, for example, reported that while immigrant voters had certainly hurt Virginia nativists, the latter also "had another enemy to fight—Massachusetts." Expecting accurately that southern nativists would see a repeat of the Wise attack if they did nothing, establishment Whigs descended on their party's national conclave in June 1855 determined to block their northern colleagues from passing an anti-Nebraska platform.[24]

On paper the June 1855 conclave was a southern nativist success. Fillmore emerged as the presumptive nominee of the party for the 1856 presidential election and the conservative majority passed a platform that promised to preserve the slaveholding republic. Sections Three and Twelve of the majority's report to the conclave kept the new party out of the slavery agitation business. Section Twelve was especially obnoxious to northern antislavery interests: it pledged Know Nothings "to abide by and maintain the existing laws upon the subject of slavery, as a final and conclusive settlement of that subject, in spirit and substance." In other words, it opposed any attempt to repeal the Kansas-Nebraska Act. Section Three of the platform praised "the maintenance of the union of these United States as the paramount political good" and advocated "uncompromising antagonism to every principle of policy that endangers it" and "the suppression of all tendencies to political division, founded on geographical discrimination, or on the belief that there is a real difference of views between the various sections of the Union."[25]

In practice the different factions of the party felt optimistic but for different reasons. Northern antislavery Know Nothings, who staged a walkout over Section Twelve, remained confident that they could pave the way for either a nativist antislavery party in the North or an exodus into the nascent Republican Party. Fillmore and his lieutenants were ecstatic that they had purged the Sewardites from the new party and thus enabled Fillmore's nomination. Southern Whigs fantasized that they had succeeded in preempting the Wise attack once and for all. By imposing a unionist platform upon the party, they had demonstrated beyond a shadow of a doubt their fidelity to southern interests. The Know Nothing *New Orleans Bee* hopefully editorialized, "the South may now stand upon this platform as a unit, if they wish to preserve the Union."[26]

Among the several factions, only the northerners' prognostications proved correct. Of the eight gubernatorial elections in 1855, the Know Nothings could claim only one victory—Kentucky. One after another Know Nothing candidate in the South fell to the Wise attack, namely, that the nativists were an antislavery fifth column weakening the South from within. That message was especially in evidence in Tennessee and Louisiana. In Tennessee, for example, nativist Whig William Collum attributed his defeat to "the cry of Abolitionist."[27]

The Wise attack was not the only source of anti–Know Nothing sentiment. Elsewhere the Whigs fell to internal conflicts, in which Whigs combined with Democrats to crush the nativist movement. Perhaps the worst instance took place in Georgia, where the infighting was so bad that the Whigs' most promising recruits left politics in disgust. Whig gubernatorial candidate Charles Jenkins wrote after the 1855 election, "I have concluded, therefore, that being neither a Democrat nor a Know Nothing, there is no place for me in this contest."[28]

The Birth of the Republican Party

If nativism led to the Whig Party's collapse in the South, then anti-Nebraska Whigs destroyed the party in the North. Above the Mason-Dixon line, antislavery elements across the political spectrum from Know Nothingism to abolitionism "fused" into the modern Republican Party, though the process differed by state. In Vermont and New York, fusion was complete by 1855; in Maine and Illinois, the Whigs were not entirely eliminated but had been torn apart; and in Massachusetts and Pennsylvania, the Whigs remained strong enough to hold off the Republican Party for another year. But overall, fusion ended as it did in New York. On September 26, 1855, the Whigs and Republicans of the Empire State held simultaneous conventions in Syracuse; when the Whigs were done passing a joint platform and slate,

Thurlow Weed marched them across town and into the Republican convention to thunderous applause.[29]

The battle between anti-Nebraska and Know Nothing Whigs thus obliterated the northern Whiggery. Seward himself, the staunchest and perhaps most prominent anti-Nebraska Whig in the nation, delivered a moving valedictory to the Whig Party on the steps of the New York state capitol in Albany on October 12, 1855:

> Shall we report ourselves to the Whig party? Where is it? "Gentle Shepherd" tell me where? . . . It was a strong and vigorous party, honorable for energy, noble achievements, and still more noble enterprises [yet] it was moved by panics and fears to emulate the Democratic party in its practiced subserviency. . . . It yielded in spite of your remonstrances and mine, and now there is neither Whig party, nor Whig, south of the Potomac. . . . Let, then, the Whig party pass. It committed a grievous fault, and grievously hath it answered [for] it. Let it march out of the field, therefore with all honors.[30]

Two developments in the spring of 1856 then pushed northern Know Nothings into a coalition with anti-Nebraska Whigs inside the Republican Party.[31] First, on May 21, proslavery "border ruffians" from Missouri ransacked the Free Soil settlement of Lawrence, Kansas. Then, on May 22, South Carolina representative Preston S. Brooks marched onto the floor of the U.S. Senate and used a walking cane to beat the abolitionist senator Charles Sumner of Massachusetts within an inch of his life. In a letter to Fillmore, the Massachusetts Whig Edward Everett wrote, "The late outrageous proceedings in Kansas and the assault on Mr. Sumner have contributed to strengthen the Republican Party."[32] When even establishment Whig support waned in advance of the 1856 election, some party leaders organized a late convention on September 17, 1856—the last Whig convention ever held. The forlorn gathering had 144 men in attendance, the smallest convention ever held by the antebellum republic's two major parties.[33]

Given the division of the Whig Party into southern Know Nothings, vulnerable to the Wise attack, and rapidly ascendant northern Republicans, the 1856 presidential returns turned out as might be expected. The Democratic nominee, James Buchanan, carried 45 percent of the popular vote and 174 electoral votes, a 58 percent majority in the Electoral College but a popular vote minority. The Republican nominee, John C. Fremont, carried 33 percent of the popular vote and 115 Electoral College votes, all from the North, where he carried eleven out of sixteen states. Fillmore ran a distant third, winning 21.6 percent of the popular vote but just one state, Maryland, for a pathetic 8 Electoral College votes in total. With this result, the Republicans, a purely sectional party hostile to the expansion of slavery, had replaced the Whigs as the main opposition to the Democratic Party in the North. The Republicans took three times the proportion of northern votes won by Fillmore and 4 percent more than Buchanan. Indeed, the Republican Party carried eight out of its eleven states with outright majorities in a heated three-way race; had they won just two more states, the Republicans would have captured the White House on their first try.[34]

Not only was the Whig Party dead, but now its hoped-for replacements—Seward's anti-Nebraska Whigs and Fillmore's Know Nothing Party—were dead, too, leaving the Republicans and Southern Rights Democrats to destroy the unionist rump of the political establishment. This led directly to the U.S. Secession Crisis. The destruction of the Whig Party allowed Republicans, instead of a different anti-Democratic alternative, to win the votes of northerners in 1860. The victory of Abraham Lincoln and the Republican Party in the 1860 presidential election, in turn, provoked the South into secession and war.[35] That Southern Whigs fell to the Wise attack was also decisive, for the Whigs in virtually every southern state comprised the stiffest opposition to immediate secession, while the Democrats were the vanguard of the secessionist cause.[36] Having thus fueled the opposition to itself in both the North and South, the Whig Party had, by its nativist turn, sowed the seeds of its own destruction and hastened its abdication as the leading alternative to secession in the South. By the late 1850s, not much stood in the way of the Southern Rights Democratic Party.

The Election of 1860, Secession, and War

It has been said that the counting of votes is merely the final ceremony of a long process. The votes taken in secession conventions across the South in the winter of 1860–61 comprise just such a ceremony, for each was enabled by the unanticipated political dynamics of compromise and the subsequent destruction of the two-party system. We see this most vividly in the key moments immediately prior to secession when the centrifugal forces of sectionalism overpowered the political establishment's will to preserve the Union. These moments include John Brown's abolitionist raid on Harpers Ferry, the 1860 Democratic National Convention[37] and presidential election, and South Carolina's attack on Fort Sumter.

John Brown's quixotic attempt to take the arsenal at Harpers Ferry, Virginia, and foment a slave rebellion in October 1859 was the last major event of national significance that had the potential to galvanize the forces of unionism. Though the raid itself was quickly suppressed, it became a media sensation, not least because John Brown's party of twenty-one rebels consisted of five African Americans. The Democrats hoped to unite their party in opposition to John Brown's brazen disunionism. Though the strategy resulted in modest political gains in 1859, the sectional interpretations of the raid prevailed. Antislavery forces in the North framed Brown as a martyr for freedom, while Southern Rights forces saw the raid as incontrovertible proof that the South would not be safe with the Republicans in power.[38]

Harpers Ferry and the Lecompton debacle formed the backdrop of the 1860 Democratic National Convention in Charleston, South Carolina. It is a misnomer to call it a convention at all, for the DNC was actually three separate meetings, each smaller than the last. The Charleston assembly in April ended abruptly when delegates from the Deep South bolted the convention and Stephen A. Douglas's floor managers called a recess.[39] When the Democrats reconvened in Baltimore in June, Southern Rights delegates left again to meet in a convention of their own and nominated Vice President John C. Breckinridge as their standard bearer.[40] The rump of the DNC then nominated Douglas for president.[41]

The same forces that disrupted the Democratic Party would go on to shape the 1860 presidential election. The election was a battle royal among the broken remnants of the party system: two unionist factions, the Douglas wing of the Democratic Party and the Constitutional Union Party, against two sectional factions, the Republican Party and Southern Rights Democratic Party. Douglas as always advanced a platform of limited government and popular sovereignty.[42] The Constitutional Union Party was a conservative, anti-Democratic coalition of Whigs and Know Nothings, mostly from the South, who made a last-ditch attempt to avert secession. They nominated two unionist Whigs: Senator John Bell of Tennessee for president and Edward Everett of Massachusetts for vice president.[43] The 1860 Republican National Convention nominated the seemingly more moderate and relatively less known Abraham Lincoln over the infamous anti-Nebraska Whig William H. Seward. The core of the Republican Party platform was free soil and free homesteads in the western territories. The Breckinridge faction was the preeminent choice of Southern Rights Democrats.[44]

The sectional parties prevailed. Lincoln held the advantage going into the election: to win, the Republican nominee only needed to add two states to his party's 1856 electoral map, Pennsylvania plus either Indiana or Illinois. He did precisely that, though his victory was a function of factionalism and the peculiarities of the Electoral College system. The Republicans increased their totals in Pennsylvania, New Jersey, Indiana, and Illinois, but they carried only 39 percent of the popular vote nationwide. The combined Douglas-Breckinridge totals actually increased Democratic vote share from 1.8 million (45 percent) in 1856 to 2.2 million (47 percent) in 1860, 400,000 more votes than the Republican Party, but factionalism decreed that those votes would never be joined. The Constitutional Unionists polled only 14 percent compared to the Know Nothings' 22 percent in 1856.[45] With Lincoln now the president-elect, the unionist establishment was too weak to prevent what happened next.

The spark to the flame was the decision to send federal reinforcements to Fort Sumter in South Carolina. Though the state militia had placed the fort under siege, President Buchanan, now seeing himself as the last-remaining thread holding the country together, refused to send troops.[46] Meanwhile, a few southern legislators attempted to craft a compromise that might stave off secession, but the unionist-secessionist split in those caucuses was so severe that even the staunch Democratic unionist, treasury secretary Howell Cobb of Georgia, saw these efforts as hopeless. He resigned, leaving one last southerner on the president's cabinet, Secretary of the Interior Jacob Thompson of Mississippi, who was a mole for proslavery radicals inside the administration. Under Thompson's watch, one million dollars mysteriously disappeared from the government's vaults.[47] Overcome with despair, President Buchanan declared a day of fasting and prayer on January 4, 1861.[48]

General Winfield Scott, the Whig presidential nominee in 1852, was not impressed. Having once again donned the colors of the U.S. military, he begged his commander in chief to send reinforcements to South Carolina, but the president was now intent on turning over the whole question to Congress.[49] As Buchanan vacillated between military, diplomatic, and legislative solutions to end the standoff, South Carolina governor Francis Pickens seized two forts, Moultrie and Pinckney, prompting General Scott to prevail once again upon the president to deploy troops.[50] At this point, the aforementioned mole, Secretary Thompson, urged Buchanan to show "generosity" and evacuate Sumter. Of course, generosity presupposed that the government was in control and could afford to take it easy on the enemy. Buchanan's newly appointed attorney general, Edwin M. Stanton, ridiculed Thompson's recommendation, pointing out that the government faced nothing less than a crisis of hegemony:

> Mr. President, the proposal to be generous implies that the Government is strong, and that we, as the public servants, have the confidence of the people. I think that is a mistake. No administration has suffered the loss of public confidence and support as this has done. Only the other day it was announced that a million of dollars had been stolen from Mr. Thompson's department. The bonds were found to have been taken from the vault where they should have been kept. . . . Now it is proposed to give up Sumter. All I have to say is, that no administration, much less this one, can afford to lose a million of money and a fort in the same week.[51]

Buchanan at last agreed to send reinforcements via the western merchant ship, the *Star of the West*. In a classic case of the pot calling the kettle black, Secretary Thompson resigned in a huff, calling the *Star of the West* a foul deceit. With Thompson's departure, Buchanan's cabinet consisted entirely of free-state men.[52]

By 1861 no institutional obstacle—not the Democratic Party, not the Whig Party, not Congress, least of all the White House—remained in place to arrest the momentum of the crisis. All that remained was the counting of votes. Several states voted to secede in rapid succession. By February 1, South Carolina, Mississippi, Florida, Alabama, Georgia, Louisiana, and Texas had voted to secede (Virginia, Arkansas, North Carolina, and Tennessee would leave the Union come spring). Southern militia seized Fort Pulaski in Georgia, Forts Morgan and Gaines off Mobile and the arsenal at Mount Vernon in Alabama, and Fort Pickens and other works at Pensacola in Florida.[53] On February 4, the seceded states met to form the Confederacy in Montgomery, Alabama. They nominated the former Democrat Jefferson Davis for president and the former Whig Alexander Stephens for vice president.[54]

Meanwhile, in Congress, Republicans and Southern Rights Democrats conspired to scuttle any and all eleventh-hour attempts at compromise. On January 4, 1861, for example, two weeks after South Carolina had seceded, Douglas gave an important speech exhorting his colleagues in the U.S. Senate to do all they could to preserve the Union. Though three more states, including Alabama, had seceded in the ensuing days, Douglas had reason to believe that as time ran out, his fellow Democrats would find it within themselves to avert catastrophe, as indeed they always had. But on January 16, the Republicans proposed to substitute the latest compromise bill with an inflammatory resolution that was expected to offend the South and get voted down. Once he detected the maneuver, Douglas, who was in the Senate anteroom, ran out to the floor to vote against the substitute, but by that point six Southern Rights Democrats had deliberately withheld their votes, allowing the Republicans to defeat the last real legislative fix to the crisis, 25 votes to 23.[55]

Douglas was furious. It was common knowledge that secessionists had been meeting with Republicans in their rooms, but now it was clear, at least to Douglas, that the two insurgent factions had been plotting to tear the country apart. In a sharp exchange with his Republican colleagues in the Senate, Douglas vented his frustration at being outmaneuvered by the sectional parties:

> Seven states are out of the Union, civil war is impending . . . commerce is
> interrupted, confidence destroyed, the country going to pieces, just because
> I was unable to defeat you. You can boast that you have defeated me, but you

have defeated your country with me. You . . . have triumphed over the unity
of these States. Your triumph brought disunion; and God only knows what
consequences may grow out of it.[56]

Here Douglas points out for all those still willing to listen that the Republican triumph came at a terrible price, and not just to his own political ambition. The Republican Party had defeated the last unionist candidate with sufficient stature to win the presidency, to be sure, but in doing so they also overthrew the slaveholding republic itself.

The political conditions did not improve during the transition between the Buchanan and Lincoln administrations. Lincoln's attempts at reconciliation fell flat in this context, though not in quite the same way as Buchanan's. As a congressman and Senate candidate Lincoln had steadfastly resisted compromise, in part because he believed that the threat of secession was merely a bluff and that southerners would never permit the Democrats to take them out of the Union. During the transition, the president-elect invited a southerner to join his cabinet, but he declined.[57] That was the last heard from his headquarters in Springfield, Illinois, before Lincoln assumed the presidency. Upon taking office on March 4, Lincoln was partial to the idea of reinforcing Fort Sumter, but again, believing there were sufficient grounds for reconciliation, he sent his envoys, Hurlbut and Lamon, to gauge the strength of unionism in the South (Hurlbut reported no such sentiment). Even at the very end, the president sent food—not troops—to South Carolina in hopes that by that sleight of hand he could do right by federal troops under siege inside Fort Sumter while averting military hostilities.[58] It is possible that Lincoln did so to gain public support for a military solution, since an attack from the South for so little reinforcement would necessarily justify a defensive response. However, his conduct up until that point appears to reject that hypothesis. As David M. Potter famously observed, "The fact that Lincoln's policy resulted in war does not necessarily mean that it was a war policy."[59] The mounting sectional conflict being what it was, South Carolina took Lincoln's delicate maneuver to be an aggressively hostile act. The nascent Confederacy bombarded Sumter, compelling the fort's commander, Major Anderson, to surrender. Sumter's capture inaugurated the American Civil War, and Virginia, North Carolina, Tennessee, and Arkansas at long last voted to secede.[60]

The Wise Attack in Alabama: Variation on a Theme

The sequence of partisan conflict in Alabama tracked with that of the nation. Like establishment Whigs elsewhere, Alabama Whigs reorganized as the Know Nothing or American Party after Democratic victories in 1852. The most prominent Whigs and Whig newspapers in Alabama declared themselves for the American Party. In 1855, all four Whig candidates for Congress, including William R. Smith, ran under the American banner.[61]

But Southern Rights Democrats in Alabama quickly pounced on the new Whig organization with a variant of the Wise attack. Recuperating the specter of the white slave, they accused the Know Nothings, whose northern chapters as we have seen were overtly antislavery and antisouthern, of conspiring with Republicans to maneuver the South into "submission." Secessionists thus articulated their efforts as a project to unmask the northern interests behind the Whigs' nativist play. On June 25, 1856, the *Advertiser*, the Democratic state newspaper, explained that the late "discord and dissension" among white southerners originated "from the day that Know Nothingism . . . dragged its slimy length into their midst," adding that "it came from the *North* and lapped the blood and warmed itself by the fire of blazing homes in the South" until at last it threw off "its mask of Black Republicanism" (emphasis in original). As the message gained traction and as the political stock of Southern Rights rose once more, the state Democratic Party as a whole began calling itself the "Democratic and Anti-Know-Nothing Party."[62]

Democratic attacks caused one after another Whig to defect from the American Party and thereby prove their credentials as southern men. Henry Hilliard, once the most important Whig in the state, worked to unite the South behind Buchanan's Democratic administration. In his published memoirs Hilliard justified his defection in this way: "The formidable display of strength by the anti-slavery party of the North made it plain that the interests of the Southern people demanded that any differences of sentiment as to other questions should be subordinated to resistance to this threatened aggression upon their rights."[63] Hilliard's public defection to the Southern Rights cause threw the Whigs into disarray. No one would accept the nomination of the American Party for any position. The old Whig organization exploded into multiple factions: a few held on in vain to nativism; some joined the secessionist William L. Yancey and his Southern Rights Democrats;

others hoped to resurrect the unionist cause by stumping for the Constitutional Union Party in the 1860 presidential election; and still others, the "Hooperites," who were named after the secessionist Whig Johnson J. Hooper, tried to beat Yancey at his own game by accusing the Democrats of being weak on Southern Rights.[64]

The Hooperites deserve some explanation. The Whigs' abdication of their position as the primary unionist alternative to secessionism ranged in practice from passive resignation to extreme Southern Rights activism. The extreme variant created an unprecedented dynamic in state politics. Yanceyites had never before needed an excuse to take the extreme position, but the Hooperites forced them to be ideologically purer. For example, in the spring of 1859, the Democrats dumped former congressmen James F. Dowdell and Eli S. Shorter—both Southern Rights men—because they had voted for the English bill in 1858, which as a reminder required a new referendum in Kansas as a way out of the Lecompton fiasco. In their place, the party nominated two uncontaminated Yanceyites, David Clopton and James L. Pugh. The Democrats in fact won by out-southernizing the Hooperites, but in doing so they pushed the state farther out on a limb.[65]

Qualitative and electoral return data suggest that the turn in Whig rhetoric toward Southern Rights began to resonate among the rank and file. For example, Tuscaloosa's elite benevolent societies, with few exceptions, had functioned unperturbed by sectional politics until 1857 when a religious tract proclaiming the moral evils arising from slavery occasioned protests from Southern Rights members.[66] A long-standing feud between Basil Manly and F. A. P. Barnard, the University of Alabama's president and its most illustrious professor, respectively, became sectionalized when Barnard came out publicly as a unionist.[67] As the nativists became increasingly identified with the Republican Party, Tuscaloosa Whig voters drifted to the Southern Rights Democratic Party. William R. Smith lost his first congressional race since winning the seat in 1851. His home county was a major weakness: landslides in Tuscaloosa County had always helped to put him over the top, but in 1857 Smith carried the county by only 156 votes.[68]

The Whigs had carried Tuscaloosa County in all but one presidential election since 1840, but the disorganization of the Alabama Whigs by 1857 and their prostration to Southern Rights principles allowed the Democrats to flip this planter stronghold by the widest margin in the party's history, capturing 54.4 percent of the vote. The Southern Rights presidential candidate, John C. Breckinridge, prevailed in 1860 despite the candidacy of Southern Unionist John C. Bell. Southern Rights Democrats in concert with the Hooperites had united the small farmer and herdsmen beats of the eastern half of the county with the planter beats of the once staunchly Whig southwest. Lexington, Foster's, Carthage, Hughes's, and the Court House in the town of Tuscaloosa itself, precincts that had universally rejected Texas annexation in 1844, posted majorities for the Southern Rights Democratic Party.[69]

In the 1860 presidential election the average Democratic vote share across planter beats in Tuscaloosa County broke the 50 percent barrier for the first time ever. Overall the trend in nonplanter beats from 1844 to 1860 is relatively flat, with the Democrats averaging about 70 percent of the vote. For planter beats, all Whig strongholds, the trend in Democratic vote share is U-shaped: planters defected to the Democrats in 1844 during the heyday of Manifest Destiny, were reabsorbed back into the Whig Party between 1848 and 1850, and then abandoned their party for good in the mid-1850s. With the Whig Party's collapse, planter and nonplanter precincts converged toward the Democratic Party.

There was a similar convergence toward the Democrats between the formerly Whig planter counties of the Black Belt and the rest of the state. The trend in nonslaveholding counties from 1840 to 1860 was relatively steady, with the Democrats fluctuating slightly but remaining comfortably above 60 percent in the two decades before the Civil War. For planter counties, the trend line is more erratic and tracks closely with the sequence of defection, reabsorption, and Whig collapse.

This is not to say that there were no unionist forces on the ground. Rather, the dynamics of the late 1850s prevented them from cooperating in the customary ways. A number of mainstream Democrats were turned off by Yancey's violent southernism. A case in point was John Forsyth, Buchanan's minister to Mexico. Frustrated at having insufficient resources to do his job, Forsyth broke with Buchanan and returned to Alabama to resume control of the *Mobile Register*, which he promptly turned into the state's leading

Douglas newspaper.[70] But whereas the Democratic establishment once had Whigs as a partner to contain its Southern Rights flank, the Whigs were now forced to prove their loyalty to southern principles. Accordingly, Democratic unionists became a solitary minority.

But Democratic unionists also actively participated in their own demise. As with the Kansas-Nebraska Act of 1854 at the national level, Douglas and his operatives in Alabama intensified the repercussions of the Whigs' disastrous counter-maneuvers at the state level. The offending act in this case occurred at the second 1860 Democratic National Convention in Baltimore. Yancey, who was a duly elected delegate of the Alabama Democratic Party, had been his usual troublesome self throughout the process. At the first convention in Charleston he exhorted his southern colleagues to resist the party's unionist platform even if it meant defeat in the presidential election:

> Go to the wall upon this issue if events demand it. Accept defeat upon it. Let the threatened thunders roll and the lightening flash through the sky, and let the dark cloud be pointed out by you, now resting on the Southern horizon. Let them know that our people are in earnest, and in accepting defeat upon that issue, my countrymen, you are bound to rise.[71]

Such rhetoric had been par for the course since 1848, but whereas in the past Yancey would have walked out of the convention all by himself, this time Douglasites provoked a mass revolt, in hopes that a southern withdrawal would get Douglas to the requisite two-thirds of convention delegates and win him the presidential nomination. Alabama Douglasites, John J. Seibels of Montgomery and John Forsyth of Mobile, unseated the legitimate Yancey delegation to the DNC and replaced it with a Seibels-Forsyth delegation that had no credentials or standing to be there. Douglas's forces thus refused to compromise with Yancey and in doing so left the country's most ardent secessionist without a party. This freed Yancey to lob his bombs from outside the organization that had once been the mechanism for his containment.[72]

The isolation and self-inflicted wounds of the Douglasites notwithstanding, by far the decisive factor, as Alabama historian Mills Thornton points out, was the defection of Whig voters to Southern Rights Democrats in the

Black Belt. One quarter to one third of the votes in those counties defected to Breckinridge on the urging of the Hooperites. The approximately 4,000 extra planter-county votes provided over half of Breckinridge's 7,200 margin of victory across the state. We see this dynamic even more clearly at the local level. In Tuscaloosa County, Hooperites infiltrated the town of Tuscaloosa, while the Yanceyites organized the subsistence farming areas, handing the county to the Democrats for only the third time in its history.[73]

Secession

Alabama's secession convention was held on a gloomy January day in Montgomery. It went as well as the unionists might have expected given the political winds. Southern Rights Democrats had so dominated the state by that point that the question was no longer whether Lincoln was right or wrong on slavery extension, but how to resist his administration. The convention consisted of fifty-three "immediatists," Southern Rights Democrats and Hooperites who wanted Alabama to secede from the Union at once, and forty-seven "cooperationists," mostly former cadres of the Whig Party along with a few Democratic unionists from northern Alabama who favored holding a convention of slaveholding states to decide the question.[74]

Even though the entire body favored the preservation of Southern Rights by one means or another, immediatists did not waste time in stigmatizing the cooperationist minority as treasonous at worst and surrendering at best. Thus, upon moving resolutions that charged "the Black Republican Party" with electing Lincoln "upon the avowed principle that the Constitution of the United States does not recognize property in slaves and that the Government should prevent its extension into the common Territories of the United States," George C. Whatley of Calhoun County said, "I offer these Resolutions for the purpose, in the outset, to ascertain the sense of this body upon the question of submission or resistance to Lincoln's Administration."[75] To this, the Whig-turned-cooperationist William R. Smith of Tuscaloosa objected: "It is true . . . that we are a minority. I am of that minority; but I do not associate with sub-missionists! There is not one in our company. We scorn the prospective Black Republican rule as much as the gentleman from Calhoun."[76]

Not to be outdone, Yancey then seemed to accuse Smith's fellow Tuscaloosan, Robert Jemison Jr., the leader of the cooperationist minority, of being a traitor. When pressed to clarify his remarks, Yancey explained that his accusation was aimed at certain portions of the state where the Ordinance of Secession would be resisted. The temperature rose considerably at that point. Jemison asked:

> Will the gentleman go into those sections of the State and hang all who are opposed to secession? Will he hang them by families, by neighborhoods, by towns, by counties, by Congressional districts? Who, sir, will give the bloody order? Who will be your executioner? Is this the spirit of Southern chivalry? Are these the sentiments of the boasted champions of Southern rights? Are these to be the first fruits of a Southern Republic? Ah! Is this the bloody charity of a party who seeks to deliver our own beloved sunny South from the galling yoke of a fanatical and puritanical abolition majority? What a commentary on the charity of party majorities! The history of the reign of Terror furnishes not a parallel to the bloody picture shadowed forth in the remarks of the gentleman.[77]

Jemison was expressing what was no doubt on the minds of other cooperationists and perhaps not a few immediatists. What would come from releasing themselves from a Union that had been the source of the slaveholding states' great wealth and power? One hypothesis, vividly articulated here, was that of a bloody witch hunt of traitors to the Confederacy, one that Jemison feared would put Robespierre's original Reign of Terror after the French Revolution to shame.

However stirring and plausible Jemison's prediction, the concrete fact of the matter was that he and his colleagues had not had the votes to stop the Southern Rights agenda since 1855. Any proposal to stop the immediatists now—so far downstream from the Whigs' glory days—was simply dead on arrival. Accordingly, before casting his own vote against the Ordinance of Secession, Smith sounded a passive-aggressive note of resignation, conceding defeat but predicting the destruction of their common country: "It is important to the State that you of the majority should be right, and that I should be wrong. However much personal gratification I might feel hereafter in finding that I was right on this great question, and that you were wrong, that gratification would indeed be to me a poor consolation in the midst of a ruined and desolated country."[78] The final vote was 61 ayes to 39 nays, with both delegates from Tuscaloosa and many of their erstwhile Whig colleagues voting in the negative. On the motion of William Lowndes Yancey, the perennial leader the Southern Rights democracy, the doors of the Alabama House of Representatives were thrown open to the public. The hall filled to capacity in an instant, and a giant flag, spanning the breadth of the room, was unfurled. It read, "Alabama: Independent Now and Forever."[79]

Logic of the Past

If the crisis sequence consists of (1) an unexpected challenge, (2) defection, (3) reabsorption, and (4) crisis, then the present chapter has shown how unionism backfired and precipitated the fourth and final episode, the crisis of hegemony.

The Whigs' reabsorption strategy began promisingly enough with the victory of General Zachary Taylor in the 1848 presidential election and the Compromise of 1850, but that triumph carried within it the seeds of its own reversal. Taking slavery off the table reunited Democrats who had earlier split over the status of slavery in the Mexican Cession. The resulting Democratic resurgence of 1852 and the party's passage of the Kansas-Nebraska Act in 1854 gave rise to two competing Whig counterreactions that then destroyed the Union. First, anti-Nebraska Whigs like William H. Seward and Abraham Lincoln formed the nucleus of the modern Republican Party. Second, Whigs-turned-Know Nothings like Millard Fillmore opened the southern half of the party to the Wise attack, causing one after another Whig to abandon their new party. Put another way, the Whigs inadvertently swept away the last institutional obstacle to secession in the South and then provided an anti-slavery specter—Abraham Lincoln and the Republican Party—that served as the pretext for secession.

In all of this, race was central. To begin, the downfall of the Whigs can be traced to the rise of nativism. Anti-immigrant sentiment—then as now—accuses foreigners of a conspiracy to undermine the sovereignty of the country and ultimately take it over. Establishment Whigs hoped to use nativism to build a new unionist alternative to the sectional parties. Similarly, factionalism in the Democratic Party turned on the politicization of landless whites, who dreamed of escaping wage dependency on farms and in sweatshops. Starting in the 1840s the Democrats promised that westward expansion would provide these less affluent voters with the chance to own land. The ensuing debate over the status of slavery in the western territories appeared to forestall that promise. Free Soil Democrats said that the expansion of slavery would prevent free white men from purchasing farms out West. Southern Rights Democrats claimed the same thing though with a twist: in addition to slavery being tied to the existing boundaries of the slaveholding states, the abolition of slavery would make whites equal to blacks. Last and most important, the crisis centered on whether to preserve or destroy the dominant social order of the day, the slaveholding republic, which was underpinned by the enslavement and elimination of people of color.

The sequence of partisan reactions and counterreactions flowing out of Martin Van Buren's defeat at the 1844 DNC and the accompanying pivot toward territorial expansion thus destroyed the generations-long agreement to avoid the politicization of slavery. It began innocuously as a battle for leadership succession in the Democratic Party but then exploded monumentally into a bitter debate over the status of slavery in the western territories. Via a sequence of triumphs and reversals, the Whigs then unwittingly destroyed the American two-party system and the slaveholding republic it held together.

Though the sequence of partisan reactions and counterreactions eventuated in this case in a crisis of hegemony, not all such sequences do. We turn next to a case in point. It was not at all clear looking forward from the Great Depression that politicians would respond with a solution that could preserve the existing power structure. If anything, the signals pointed to a deepening crisis, perhaps even a socialist revolution.

5

THE CONTRADICTIONS
OF THE NEW DEAL

The Great Depression was every bit as disruptive to the fabric of the republic as the political crisis over slavery, though of course in a different way. Those who lived through the 2008 recession will have firsthand knowledge of economic cataclysms, but the Great Depression, after which the most recent downturn is named, was a different order of magnitude altogether. The economy essentially collapsed. The stock market had begun to decline on October 21, 1929, and plummeted on the twenty-ninth. The trading value of stocks fell 40 percent in just one month. In a population that was one third what it is today, the number of unemployed grew from three million in 1930 to a staggering fifteen million by 1933. Factory payrolls were cut in half. Revenues in the construction industry tumbled precipitously from $949 million to $74 million. At U.S. Steel, the largest steel producer in the country, the number of employees went from 225,000 to zero.[1]

The winter of 1932–33 was particularly perilous. In that four-month period alone, the ranks of the jobless increased by two million people.[2] Meanwhile, the banking system went into cardiac arrest. It began with the collapse of the Detroit banks in February 1933; the State of Michigan declared an eight-day "bank holiday," tying up the deposits of 900,000 customers to prevent a run on the banks. The conflagration then spread to other cities. In Baltimore, people stood in interminable lines with satchels and paper bags to take away their gold and currency and stuff them in mattresses. The old order teetered on the brink. Recalling the roll call of secession conventions across the South in the winter of 1861, thirty-eight states had closed their banks by inauguration day, March 4, 1933. That morning, Richard Whitney announced the closing of the New York Stock Exchange, and the Chicago Board of Trade shut its doors for the first time since 1848.[3]

The sheer level of unemployment overwhelmed local governments and benevolent societies: in some cities, 90 percent of people were on relief. This precipitated a housing crisis of vast proportions. In 1932, a quarter of a million families lost their homes; in the first half of the following year, more than a thousand homes were being foreclosed on every day. Philadelphia, for example, averaged 1,300 sheriff's sales a month. Squatter settlements called "Hoovervilles" made of tents and cardboard shacks popped up under bridges, in parks, and on the main thoroughfares of American cities. The largest, in St. Louis, housed as many as one thousand people. On New York City's west side, squatters lined the shore of the Hudson River from 72nd to 110th streets. At least one million hobos roamed the country on railcars in search of work. The homeless and starving in the rural hinterland testified that they had, with grim interest, watched cows graze. One coal miner in Harlan County, Kentucky, wrote, "We have been eating wild greens . . . such as Polk Salad, Violet tops, wild onions, forget me not wild lettuce and such weeds as cows eat as a cow wont eat . . . poison weeds." The savage irony was that grain elevators were heaped to the brim with wheat: agribusiness simply refused to sell its produce at the market's low prices. This was a time of want amid plenty.[4]

The question then emerged, "Who was to blame for this catastrophe?" The near-unanimous reply, supplied by the press, politicians, and workingmen alike, was the businessman. The financier, once a folk hero for supposedly engineering the largest economic expansion ever, became the most hated man in America. His image was not helped by the congressional investigations into the collapse. A Senate inquiry led by Ferdinand Pecora revealed that CEOs were paying themselves astronomical salaries and bonuses, while paying nothing in income tax.[5]

Nor did the bosses' response to this heightened scrutiny rehabilitate their image. In a fit of aggressive irrelevance, John Edgerton, president of the National Association of Manufacturers, inexplicably blamed the Depression on workers. If they "do not . . . practice the habits of thrift and conservation," he said, "or if they gamble away their savings in the stock market or elsewhere, is our economic system, or government, or industry to blame?" Insensitive comments like this in a time of rampant starvation whipped the country into a fury. Senator Carter Glass of Virginia, a segregationist of the old school and not one for class warfare, went as far as racializing businessmen. He said, "One banker in my state attempted to marry a white woman and they lynched him."[6]

An uncanny and especially chilling parallel to the rise of ethnic nationalism in our own time was the call for a dictator. As we know in hindsight, Italy and Germany went precisely in that direction, but there was also a movement in the United States to draft a Mussolini to grab hold of the reins of government. The board of the venerable *Barron's* magazine editorialized that "a genial and lighthearted dictator might be a relief from the pompous futility of such a Congress as we have recently had."[7]

Workers and farmers for their part did not take this fiasco lying down. They were in open revolt. In the summer of 1932, the Farm Holiday Association, led by Iowa Farmers' Union leader Milo Reno, refused to ship produce to Sioux City until farmers were paid prices equal to the "cost of production." When fifty-five of their brethren were arrested for picketing, one thousand angry farmers stormed the county jail at Council Bluffs and forced their release. In Bucks County, Pennsylvania, three hundred farmers made authorities sell their friend's foreclosed property to them for $1.18 and then leased it back to him. Nebraska farmers carrying placards that read, "Be Pickets or Peasants," halted a train and took off a carload of cattle. And the dairy farmers of Wisconsin, irate at the prices being offered on the market, dumped milk onto the roadsides in defiance and fought pitched battles with police. All across the Midwest, the salt of the earth roadblocked highways with logs, smashed windshields, and slashed tires with pitchforks. Finally, to force the hand of Congress, Milo Reno called a national farmers' strike to begin on May 13, 1933.[8]

Striking and unemployed workers were every bit as mutinous. In February 1933, barter groups who had taken to exchanging services for food and other necessities reached their limit and seized a county building in Seattle. Ten thousand striking miners in southern Illinois organized a forty-eight-mile-long "Coal Caravan" to menace intransigent employers. And in Chicago several dozen workers were charged with dismantling an entire building and carrying the bricks away. Even the relatively conservative president of the American Federation of Labor, William Green, threatened a general strike if Congress refused to pass a bill that would establish a thirty-hour workweek and in doing so spread what little work there was among more workers.[9]

Though some, like Governor Floyd Olson of Minnesota, responded favorably to popular demands to halt foreclosure and other humiliations, more often the initial response to this uprising was violent repression. A case in point was the Harlan County, Kentucky coal strike of 1931. The precipitating issue, as with many labor disputes in this period, was the loss of work and the corresponding reduction in wages for those who still had jobs. Between 1930 and 1931, national coal production dropped by 100 million tons; whereas in 1924 there were 704,793 workers employed in the mines, by 1933 that number had dropped to 294,000. To make matters worse, coal operators in Harlan County then slashed the remaining workers' wages by 10 percent. The sheer magnitude of deprivation pushed public relief well past the breaking point.[10]

All of this led to a spontaneous walkout that the coal operators attempted to quell by force, prompting the miners to take up arms in defense in what became known as the Battle of Evarts. When workers then flocked to the United Mine Workers, the bosses fired the organizers along with the militant rank and file. From there the violence only escalated. When at last the Communist-led National Miners Union (NMU) joined the fray, management inaugurated an out-and-out reign of terror. Shootings were an almost daily occurrence, workers were blacklisted, and raids were conducted on miners' homes. There were arrests, dynamiting, beatings, and an attempt to starve the miners when the coal operators and authorities closed down relief kitchens.[11] The reign of terror was capped off by the so-called Evarts Battle Conspiracy Trials, in which 335 workers were brought up on charges of Communist conspiracy, though there was no evidence at all that the Evarts strike had been organized by any union, let alone the Soviet Union. In the end, fifteen trials were held, yielding seven convictions and life sentences, three acquittals, and five hung juries, though many, like Harry Simms, the lead NMU organizer, were simply shot to death in the streets and hollers of Harlan County. An editorial from the *Mount Sterling Gazette* reveals the attitude of political and economic elites in the area. The board wrote, "It is useless to send men and women of the stripe of the Harlan agitators to the penitentiary. They would be safer in a pine box six feet under ground."[12]

The severe economic contraction coupled with widespread insurrection gave many the impression that the entire system was in jeopardy. Alexander Sachs, economist for the Lehman Corporation, wrote a cabinet member in December 1932: "We are now faced in the United States . . . with the question of the solvency not of any part but of our whole system . . . The outstanding feature of this great depression is that the economic order . . . [has] come to be threatened, not by the destructive impact of external or natural forces, but by a spontaneous disintegration from within." Others expressed similar views during the Senate Finance Committee hearings in late February 1933. United Mine Workers president John L. Lewis told the committee that "the political stability of the Republic is imperiled," while Senator Robert Wagner testified, "We are not in a mere business recession . . . we are in a life and death struggle with the forces of social and economic dissolution." The newspaper man Morris Markey saw those same sentiments expressed by the Washington press corps. Referencing the main drags of the nation's largest cities, one reporter said: "Gentleman it's revolution. I'm telling you . . . I can see 'em now, howling up Fifth Avenue with blood in their eye, howling up Market Street and Beacon Street and Michigan Avenue."[13]

No Home for Labor

The situation was exacerbated by the fact that there was no natural home for organized labor in this moment. The Republican Party's prescriptions for the deepest recession in American history verged on irrelevance and to the degree that Republicans acted at all, they violently suppressed those who challenged their power. President Hoover, on whose watch the Depression began, cut a figure not unlike President Buchanan's as the republic hurtled toward secession and civil war. The Democratic Party for its part was locked in a deadly internal conflict, similar to that which tore the Whigs apart in the 1850s. Recall that establishment Whigs wanted to make the 1856 presidential election about immigration, while antislavery Whigs, who would form the nucleus of the Republican Party, wanted to debate the expansion of slavery into the western territories. Likewise, a faction led by the 1928 Democratic presidential nominee Al Smith and national committee chair John J. Raskob refused to politicize the Depression and instead hoped to make the 1932 presidential election about repealing the prohibition of alcohol. A competing faction led by Franklin Delano Roosevelt and "Progressive" Democrats wanted to turn the election into a referendum on the Republicans' mishandling of the economy and the resulting unemployment and backbreaking poverty of the "forgotten man." Amid the dysfunction of the party system, alternative third parties emerged, including the Communist Party, the Farmer-Labor Party, and the National Progressives of America, which recruited those workers and farmers who had had enough of the political establishment. The United States appeared to be heading for a classic crisis of hegemony, in which the great masses of the people withdraw their consent to be governed.

Public discourse in the initial years of the Depression was marked by contempt for Congress, political parties, and democratic institutions. The liberal Democrat William Dodd, future U.S. ambassador to Germany, wrote in 1932 to a colleague, "There is no doubt in the world that both political parties have been bankrupted." Indeed, in the lame-duck session of Congress between December 1932 and February 1933, in the very depths of the Depression, federal legislators failed to enact a single piece of economic legislation.[14]

Though there was a pox on both parties' houses, the Republicans were decidedly more unappealing. This was due not simply to the fact that the Depression had begun on a Republican's watch, but also to President Herbert Hoover's own hubris. Accepting the Republican presidential nomination at Stanford

Stadium in 1928, he blustered, "We in America today are nearer to the final triumph over poverty than ever before in the history of any land." He doubled down on this sentiment in his March 1929 inaugural address, declaring, "In no nation are the fruits of accomplishment more secure." Looking back on those pronouncements, the reporter Elmer Davis wrote that Mr. Hoover's promises "ran to that excess which above all things offended the Greek temperament, which seemed above all things to invite the corrective interposition of Nemesis. . . . Never in American history did a candidate so recklessly walk out on a limb and challenge Nemesis to saw it off."[15]

It is perhaps unfair to blame the president for not knowing that the worst economic cataclysm in history was just around the corner, but his reaction to the mass protests of this period were his own fault and evinced what contemporary observers saw as an utter lack of understanding for the art of governing. Wrote Willmott Lewis, Washington correspondent for the *London Times*, Hoover "can calculate wave lengths, but cannot see color. . . . He can understand vibrations but cannot hear tone." No episode captured both his hubris and lack of popular rapport than his mishandling of the Bonus Army.[16]

Veterans of World War I, like so many people at the time, were desperate for government assistance. Accordingly, they converged on Washington in June 1932 to petition for an advance on bonuses that the federal government had promised to give them in 1945. Veterans pitched tents in Anacostia Flats just outside the district and squatted in abandoned federal buildings near the White House. Though they did nothing more radical than carry signs that read, "Cheered in '17, Jeered in '32," President Hoover lost all sense of proportion, while his own secretary of war, Patrick Hurley, was convinced that a Communist uprising was imminent. The White House was put on lockdown and Pennsylvania Avenue cleared, creating the unwelcome impression that the president was further isolating himself from the people. He then dispatched General Douglas MacArthur to clear the Bonus Army. MacArthur led a detachment of cavalrymen with sabers drawn, six tanks, and a column of infantrymen with steel helmets and fixed bayonets across the bridge into Anacostia Flats. Unarmed veterans along with their wives and children fled pathetically before the troops, who proceeded to set the retired servicemen's tents ablaze. The general later justified the disproportionate response by calling the Bonus Army "a mob . . . animated by the essence of revolution," adding that had the president let the "insurrectionists" carry on for another week, "the institutions of our Government would have been severely threatened." Making matters worse, the Hoover administration then denied that the armed forces had fired the camps or committed any violence whatsoever, a lie that was exposed by the media.[17]

Nor were workers somehow predisposed to the Democratic Party. It is tempting to look back on the Depression and assume that FDR and the Democrats were somehow a match made in heaven, but several factors tend to contradict that assumption. First, ethnic urban workers had not reliably turned out in large numbers for either political party since the turn of the twentieth century. Moreover, the American Federation of Labor (AFL), especially under the leadership of Samuel Gompers, had pursued a pragmatic policy of occasionally endorsing "friends of labor" but overall steering clear of party politics for fear that partisanship might lead to internal bickering and ruin relationships with elected officials whom the AFL did not endorse. The latter prospect was particularly scary when workers were on strike. Other labor leaders were not so cautious and threw their support behind the Republican Party. Perhaps the most famous of these was John L. Lewis, who was president of the United Mine Workers (UMW), future president of the Congress of Industrial Organizations (CIO), and a lifelong Republican.[18]

The Democrats for their part were no class warriors. John J. Raskob, chair of the Democratic National Committee, was a former executive of the DuPont Company and insisted that the greatest question before the country was whether or not to continue Prohibition. Meanwhile, the 1928 Democratic presidential nominee, Al Smith, chastised Progressive Democrats like then–New York governor Franklin Delano Roosevelt, whose chief rhetorical appeal was to the "forgotten man." Smith said, "I will take off my coat and fight to the end against any candidate who persists in any demagogical appeal to the masses of the working people of this country to destroy themselves by setting class against class and rich against poor."[19]

It was not at all clear then, looking forward in time from 1929, that the Democratic Party would become the party of labor. Indeed, the conflict between the Roosevelt and Smith wings of the party escalated into an all-out war for the 1932 Democratic presidential nomination, the result of which was in doubt as late as the national convention itself. Though Smith, a Catholic, once confided to a colleague in 1930 that "there's no chance for a Catholic to be President," he came to feel that 1932 might be his second chance. Halfway through the primary season, rank-and-file Democrats started to look his way once again. By that point Roosevelt was running way ahead of the field, but then Smith trounced him in Massachusetts 3 to 1 and thrashed him across New England and Pennsylvania. Roosevelt, the vaunted candidate of the forgotten man, now looked as if he had no standing in the industrial Northeast. This was followed by Governor Roosevelt's stunning loss in delegate-rich California to native son and House Speaker John Garner, who was aided by the media mastermind William Randolph Hearst and California's U.S. senator William McAdoo. At the June convention in Chicago, the tally stood at 666 and 1/4 votes for Roosevelt, 201 and 3/4 for Smith, and 90 and 1/4 for Garner. Roosevelt of course held a simple majority, but then Smith did what so many Democratic candidates had done going back to the 1830s, namely, call the two-thirds rule. By that standard, the frontrunner still needed over one hundred delegates to clinch the nomination. Try as they might, Roosevelt's lieutenants were able to make only modest gains through the first two ballots and remained well shy of a supermajority. Faced with the prospect of a deadlocked convention, the governor's coalition began to crack, especially among southerners. It was only by the efforts of Louisiana's populist firebrand Huey Long that Mississippi stuck with Roosevelt; otherwise, that state would have touched off a mad rush out of the coalition to any number of candidates. After the third ballot, FDR's team had just a few hours to save their man's candidacy. But something happened then that no one had anticipated. On the fourth ballot, Senator McAdoo decided to pay Smith back for killing his presidential candidacy in 1924. McAdoo strode out onto the convention floor and said that he had not come to Chicago to deadlock a convention but to nominate a presidential candidate, and with that he threw California's forty-four delegates and the nomination to Roosevelt.[20]

Even then it was unclear whether FDR stood with the workingman or not. The Democratic platform was nearly identical to the Republican version, with a bit more social spending. Indeed, the Democrats of this period, including

Roosevelt himself, were fiscal hawks, and one of their principal attacks on Hoover was that he was a profligate spender. The major parties too remained insistent on fighting over Prohibition. As John Dewey observed, "Here we are in the midst of the greatest crisis since the Civil War and the only thing the two national parties seem to want to debate is booze." Nor did Roosevelt inspire confidence that he was going to do anything in particular to dig the country out of the ditch. For example, he vacillated wildly on fiscal policy. In Sioux City, Iowa, Roosevelt said in September 1932, "I accuse the present Administration of being the greatest spending Administration in peace time in all our history." Then in Pittsburgh the following month, he characterized "Federal spending" as "the most direct and effective contribution that Government can make to business." All of this flip-flopping led one New Dealer to reflect retrospectively on the campaign, "Given later developments, the campaign speeches often read like a giant misprint, in which Roosevelt and Hoover speak each other's lines." Walter Lippmann called Roosevelt the master of the "balanced antithesis," adding that FDR was "a pleasant man who, without any important qualifications for the office, would very much like to be President."[21]

In the absence of any obvious home for labor, third parties offered what at the time seemed a viable alternative. The Farmer-Labor Party in Minnesota regularly won state and federal offices throughout the 1920s and captured the governor's mansion in 1931 as the Depression became the central issue of the day. The Communist Party, as we have seen, was also on the move. In addition to organizing miners in the Midwest, Communists were also active in the Deep South, for instance in Alabama, where the party was an inter-racial coalition that pressed for voting rights, equal pay for equal work for women, and land for landless farmers. But the Communist Party was by far most visible in marches of the unemployed in the major cities of the North, notably in Detroit and Chicago.[22]

Co-opting Organized Labor

But if the alliance between the Democratic Party and the labor movement was not preordained, then a key question is how that alliance nevertheless materialized. The political establishment's co-optation of organized labor was a long and bumpy road, punctuated by epic industrial conflicts and the conscious attempt on the part of Progressive Democrats to establish industrial peace through the New Deal. Against those who have argued that the New Deal enabled the rise of militant industrial unions,[23] I argue the reverse: it was precisely the *inability* of the New Deal to address labor rights that led to labor militance. Labor militance in turn prompted the Democratic Party to do all that it could to channel the movement into mainstream politics and in doing so ensure the peaceful operation of the capitalist system.

The rhetoric of the New Deal was not an unsatisfactory beginning. We often remember FDR's first inaugural address on March 4, 1933, as the "Fear itself" speech. "First of all, let me assert my firm belief that the only thing we have to fear is fear itself," he declared. In this the new president brilliantly traced the source of the Depression to a mere feeling and therefore something the republic might conquer if only its citizens understood the weakness of the enemy. Less well remembered was that the speech was an attack on bankers. Americans were stricken with a "nameless, unreasoning, unjustified terror" caused by "rulers of the exchange of mankind's goods" who "have failed through their own stubbornness and their own incompetence, have admitted their failure, and have abdicated." "The money changers," he said, "have fled from their high seats in the temple of our civilization. We may now restore that temple to the ancient truths."[24]

In terms of concrete public policy, however, the New Deal was a hodgepodge of Roosevelt's lingering fiscal conservatism and a few progressive ideas. His first one hundred days began on March 9 with federal assistance to allow commercial banks to reopen. Complaining about FDR's opening salvo, one congressman said, "The President drove the money-changers out of the Capitol on March 4th—and they were all back on the 9th." On March 10, the new president sent his economy message to Congress, which sliced $400 million from veterans' pay and another $100 million from federal employees. Roosevelt then did the first of his many "fireside chats" over the radio on Sunday evening, March 12, calmly telling his listeners that it was now safe to return their savings to the banks. Though folks were still strapped for cash, deposits exceeded withdrawals in the ensuing days. Of the period between March 4 and 12, the American political economist Raymond Moley tellingly observed, "capitalism was saved in eight days."[25]

The president's next move was to buck up public morale by letting the masses drink again. On March 13, FDR asked Congress for an early end to Prohibition, starting with the repeal of the Volstead Act, which banned beer. Americans could now have a cold one so long as it did not exceed 3.2 percent alcohol. This workers did cheer: beer companies worked overtime in the ensuing weeks and could not meet demand. The people partied in the streets. In Milwaukee, there was a parade-like atmosphere, as ordinary citizens sang "Sweet Adeline" on Wisconsin Avenue.[26]

The next raft of legislation attempted to deal directly with the plight of farmers and workers. On March 16, the president issued his farm message, which resulted in increased farm prices and a moratorium on farm foreclosures. As such, FDR's agricultural policy tended to privilege property owners and did precious little for landless farmers like sharecroppers and farmworkers. The Agricultural Adjustment Act (AAA) paid political dividends for the Democratic Party, for the AAA succeeded in dividing rural America, making loyal Democrats out of a large-enough constituency to take the winds out of the sails of farmer-labor third parties.[27]

Work then began on the Home Owners' Loan Corporation (HOLC). Recall that in the first half of 1933 more than one thousand homes were being foreclosed on each day. Under the new program and its successor program, the Federal Housing Administration, bankers were assured that if they approved mortgages or refinanced them, the federal government would repay the loan even if the customer defaulted. HOLC helped to refinance and save one fifth of all urban homes in America, though as we shall soon see, it did so primarily for middle-class whites. The effect in June when Congress passed the legislation was nevertheless immediate. In Akron a double-column line stretched for three blocks down Main Street; when the doors opened, five hundred people pressed into the lobby to refinance their mortgages.[28]

But by far the most important legislation for workers and for organized labor was the National Industrial Recovery Act (NIRA). To address unemployment, the president initially opposed public works and wanted only a conservation corps to employ jobless youth in the nation's forests. However, labor secretary Frances Perkins along with Harry Hopkins, who headed the relief efforts in New York, and senators Robert La Follette Jr. of Wisconsin and

Edward Costigan of Colorado prevailed on him to propose a much-broader work program. On March 21, FDR sent an unemployment relief message to Congress with three pillars: the Civilian Conservation Corps (CCC), the Works Progress Administration (WPA), and half a billion dollars in direct federal government aid to the states for unemployment relief.[29]

Not included in that original message was its most controversial fourth pillar, the right to collective bargaining. Roosevelt's fellow New Yorker, Progressive Democratic senator Robert Wagner, persuaded the president that if business received concessions, labor must have a guarantee of collective bargaining. On May 10, FDR famously told a committee of his top aides to lock themselves in a room and come up with an omnibus bill. One week later, they had devised four major provisions: (1) the federal government would drop antitrust rules, thus freeing up business to fix pricing; (2) government, in return, would license businesses; (3) workers would receive the right to collective bargaining and codes that set a minimum wage and maximum hours; and (4) Congress would appropriate $3.3 billion in public works. The U.S. House of Representatives passed NIRA by a vote of 325 to 76; the Senate passed it by a seven-vote margin, and the president signed NIRA into law on June 16, 1933.[30]

The nation's most prominent labor leaders cheered the bill. AFL president William Green called it a "Magna Charta for labor," while UMW president John L. Lewis compared it to the "Emancipation Proclamation."[31] This was in large part because the AFL sought and won changes to the collective bargaining provision of NIRA, Section 7(a). This was the literal incorporation of labor's demands into the New Deal. On May 19, as NIRA was winding its way through Congress, Green proposed to the House Ways and Means Committee that after guaranteeing to employees the right to organize, Section 7(a) should continue, "and shall be free from the interference, restraint, or coercion of employers of labor or their agents, in the designation of such representatives or in self-organization or in other concerted activities for the purpose of collective bargaining or other mutual aid or protection." Green also recommended that the second clause ban company unions that answered to the boss: "No employee and no one seeking employment shall be required as a condition of employment to join a company union, or to refrain from joining a labor organization of his own choosing." Senator Champ Clark of Missouri proposed a proviso that opened the door to company unions but it was rejected. The final language of Section 7(a) was passed with the AFL's language intact.[32]

The problem with NIRA, however, was that it did not provide for any enforcement of its prolabor provisions, most importantly the right to organize. Employers across the land, including the largest companies, refused to comply with NIRA. When it became clear that the New Deal could not in fact provide for their collective rights, workers took matters into their own hands and organized the strike wave of 1933–34, one of the largest in American history. "Man-days" lost to strikes jumped dramatically from a total of 603,000 for January to June, to 1,375,000 in July, and then 2,378,000 in August. The total number of work stoppages in 1933 was the largest since 1921. Strikes were widespread, ranging from industries as diverse as coal, hosiery, and motion pictures, but the overriding issue was the same, namely, the fundamental right to collective bargaining.[33]

The pressure mounted in 1934 with 1,856 strikes involving 1,470,000 workers. In addition to the general economic despair of workers during the Depression, the key struggle was once again the broken promise of NIRA Section 7(a). The most heated industrial disputes were those of the Electric Auto-Lite Company in Toledo, the longshoremen's strike in San Francisco, the truckers' work stoppage in Minneapolis, and the cotton-textile strike in New England and the South. All of these led to violent confrontations between national guardsmen and management's paramilitary groups on the one hand, and largely unarmed workers on the other.[34]

The cotton-textile strike exemplifies the pitched battles of the 1934 strike wave. Francis Gorman, president of the United Textile Workers (UTW), called the strike on Labor Day weekend, 12:01 A.M. Saturday, September 1, possibly the worst time for textile employers, whose warehouses bulged with inventory. Workers struck the silk, woolen, and worsted industries in Providence, Rhode Island, Cohoes, New York, Philadelphia, and Greenville, South Carolina simultaneously. Gorman then sent "flying squadrons" to start strikes at nearby mills. The conflagration spread to North Carolina. Employers there refused to give their employees Monday, Labor Day, off. Gorman roused the workers on Sunday, and the next day 65,000 workers refused to report to work, crippling nearly the entire industry in that state. On Tuesday, September 4, cotton workers joined the strike in Georgia, Tennessee, Virginia, Massachusetts, New Hampshire, Maine, and New Jersey. Within just a few days, the strike swelled to 376,000 workers, the greatest single industrial conflict in the history of the U.S. labor movement to that point.[35]

The center of the strike in New England was Rhode Island. In Little Rhody, with its fifty thousand mill workers, the UTW struck every single mill. Governor T. H. Green, convinced that he was witnessing a Communist revolution, deployed the National Guard. At the Narrow Fabrics Company mill in Warren, troops equipped with tear gas bombs, clubs, and helmets menaced the strikers. Displays of force like this triggered violence. On September 11, 1934, two thousand workers descended on the mill in Saylesville; police shot five workers in the melee. Governor Green sent guardsmen in to reinforce the police, and the next day troops shot four more strikers. Enraged workers responded with two counterattacks, defying the guardsmen's tear gas and bayonets. Though management, the UTW, and the state agreed to rules for peaceful picketing on September 12, violence broke out again the next day in Woonsocket, where the National Guard opened fire, killing one striker and wounding seven others. Woonsocket declared martial law, while Green, who by now was clearly out of his depth, unsuccessfully petitioned the president for federal troops to crush the rebellion.[36]

Scenes such as these formed the backdrop of congressional hearings to discuss a replacement for NIRA, which in addition to being toothless in practice had meanwhile been declared unconstitutional by the U.S. Supreme Court. The leading sponsors of the new collective bargaining law, Robert Wagner in the Senate and William Connery in the House, justified passage of such a bill by making reference to the recent violence. Congressman Connery, addressing those who called him an enemy of business, said in a hearing on industrial strife: "They regard us as enemies of the employers, as actually being inimical to the employers, when we are not. What we are trying to do . . . is to save those corporations from communism and from bloodshed."[37] Similarly, Senator Wagner, the author of the National Labor Relations Act (NLRA), announced on the floor of the upper chamber that of the 3,655 new cases received by regional labor boards in the second half of 1934 and January 1935, "the issue of collective bargaining was paramount in 2,330 cases, or about 74 percent." He too addressed conservatives and intransigent business titans who called the concept of employer-employee negotiations "inopportune and hasty." Wagner stated that the proposed NLRA was "responsive to serious industrial disturbances of last summer, when blood ran freely in the streets and martial law was in the offing."[38]

There can therefore be no mistake, first, that the New Deal's *failure* to deliver on labor reform led to the strike wave of 1933–34, and second, that the strike wave in turn led to the passage of the NLRA or Wagner Act in 1935, which at last enforced collective bargaining through mechanisms such as "unfair labor practices" and adjudication of disputes by a state-appointed National Labor Relations Board (NLRB). If movement leaders had praised NIRA Section 7(a) in 1933 with their words, they then expressed their support of the Wagner Act and the Democratic Party with organizational muscle. The bloody battles of 1933 and 1934 had convinced them that they could not make the large corporations come to terms without the help of government.[39] Meanwhile, the Democrats, who were suffering the desertion of big business over their proworker stance, sought an even closer relationship with organized labor, especially the renegade industrial unions that had broken away from the AFL to form the Congress of Industrial Organizations (CIO).[40] The result of that increasingly intimate relationship was the founding of Labor's Non Partisan League, or LNPL, the thinly veiled arm of the Democratic Party within the movement, just ahead of the 1936 presidential election.

Paths Not Taken

In his capacity as a leading figure of LNPL, John L. Lewis devoted considerable time and energy to campaigning for Roosevelt in 1936. "The worker need only glance at the record," he once said, "to be convinced that he should support President Roosevelt. . . . His great reforms must be retained and maintained, and others equally important are yet to be secured." By contrast, Lewis called the Republican candidate, Alfred M. Landon of Kansas, "a little man out in Topeka" and a "bootlicker of plutocracy." Even the Communists jumped on the bandwagon, satisfied for the time being with infiltrating the CIO and guarding the left flank of the New Deal coalition.[41]

The founding of LNPL made independent labor parties less viable and created the conditions—via the marriage of Democratic and labor officialdom—for defeating subsequent waves of dissent. Arguably the last chance for an independent labor party was the spring of 1936, when the league had not yet decided internally to endorse Roosevelt for the presidency. The crucial first move came from Sidney Hillman, president of the American Clothing Workers of America (ACW), who convened a meeting on April 19 of his fifteen-member executive committee. In that meeting, Hillman warned that under a Republican administration,

> it would be silly to discuss organization in steel and the automobile industry. There would be no room for the CIO. . . . You talk labor party. But can you have a labor party without an economic labor movement? . . . I say to you that the defeat of Roosevelt and the introduction of a real Fascist administration such as we will have is going to make the work of building a labor movement impossible.

Speaking against an alliance with the Democratic Party were Joseph Salerno of the Boston ACW; Jack Kroll, secretary of the Ohio Farmer-Labor Party State Committee; and ACW cofounder and socialist Joseph Schlossberg. Hillman ridiculed the latter's efforts. Of Schlossberg Hillman said, "I listened to Brother Schlossberg . . . I have not heard him give any reason for opposing the policy proposed here other than that he has been a socialist for the last forty years and will not change now." With that, Hillman persuaded his executive committee to unite behind the Democratic Party. Later, at the May 26 ACW national convention in Cleveland, where the leading lights of the Democratic Party were the honored guests, the executive committee stifled labor party sentiment among the rank and file. Fresh off their victory, the Hillman-Democratic bloc traveled to Chicago four days later and put the proverbial nail in the coffin at a meeting of Farmer-Labor Party delegates from twenty-two states. The Roosevelt bloc was led by Hillman lieutenant J. B. S. Hardman, who introduced a resolution to table the call for a national convention and left the timing of that decision to the conservative wing of the Minnesota Farmer-Labor Party. It would never call a national convention.[42]

Even Lewis, a cofounder of the Non-Partisan League, could not gain traction with an alternative agenda when he broke with FDR over his neutrality in the "Little Steel" strike of May 1937. Roosevelt blamed both labor and management for the violence afflicting that dispute.[43] Condemning the president for his equivocation after courting the labor vote in 1936, Lewis famously said, "It ill behooves one who has supped at labor's table and who has been sheltered in labor's house to curse with equal fervor and fine impartiality both labor and its adversaries when they become locked in deadly embrace."[44] Lewis followed this scolding with an endorsement of the Republican presidential candidate, Wendell Willkie, in 1940. Speaking over the radio to some thirty million listeners, Lewis announced that if his proposed course was not vindicated, he would resign as president of the CIO, effectively making his members choose between FDR and him.[45]

The workers chose FDR. Roosevelt won reelection in a landslide, carrying 400 Electoral College votes to Willkie's 82. When Lewis returned to his office in Washington after the election, he found signs that said, "Resignation accepted" and "Lewis phooey." From that point forward, Lewis was a diminished man, and the cause of his fall from grace was unquestionably the termination of his relationship with the president.[46] In sum, organized labor, due in large part to Lewis's own efforts as a leader of LNPL and to the help of the Communist Party, was so thoroughly incorporated into the machinery of the New Deal and the Democratic Party that workers overthrew their own leader in favor of a politician.

The chances for an independent labor party worsened further after that. The separation of the left-led industrial unions (CIO) from the relatively more conservative craft unions (AFL) divided a labor vote that might have otherwise been united behind a third party. The Communist Party had taken its partnership with the Democratic Party to such extremes that it endorsed the Kelley-Nash machine in Chicago (which was directly responsible for the massacre of steelworkers in that city) and the antiunion boss Frank Hague in New Jersey.[47] Likewise, the rise of the Non-Partisan League and the virulence of the AFL's redbaiting of the CIO meant that the Farmer-Labor Party (FLP) lost the backing of organized workers in the big industrial states. The key moments in the FLP's downfall were the defeat of Thomas Amlie in the 1938 FLP primary for mayor of Milwaukee; the routing of the party's statewide candidates in former FLP strongholds like Iowa and Wisconsin; and ultimately the merger in April 1944 of the only substantial FLP, in Minnesota, with the Democratic Party under the leadership of Hubert Humphrey.[48] Perhaps the last viable third-party alternative of the period, the National Progressives of America (NPA), founded in 1938 by Wisconsin governor Philip F. La Follette, the younger son of Robert M. La Follette, similarly fell to the Democratic juggernaut. Critical to the demise of the NPA was the weakness of Governor La Follette himself in Wisconsin. Although a majority of progressives supported his organization, a vocal minority refused to endorse it. Even the Madison *Capital Times*, an organ of the Wisconsin Progressive Party, editorialized, "If repudiation of Pres. Roosevelt is to be a requisite of joining this new venture, the Capital Times is frank in saying that it will not go along." Eleven Progressive leaders, including Paul Alfonsi, speaker of Wisconsin's lower house, held that the NPA tended "to split the unity of the people," adding, "While making no attack on Wall Street monopolies," National Progressives make "sharp attacks on the standards of organized labor and on relief and the W.P.A." When at last Roosevelt was nominated for a third term in 1940, the NPA fell apart.[49]

The relationship between the Democratic Party and organized labor was both liberating and co-optive of workers. It was liberating in the sense that it shifted control of the workplace to varying degrees from management to labor, but it was nevertheless co-optive because the rank and file was subjected to the legal and political control of the state and union leaders. This is not to say that workers stopped fighting. In fact, in 1946, ten years after the founding of Labor's Non-Partisan League, the movement, then led by Walter Reuther and the United Auto Workers, touched off the largest strike wave in U.S. history, with 4.6 million workers walking off the job. But in the aftermath of that conflict, the federal government clamped down further on labor militance with the Taft-Hartley amendments to the NLRA, which banned sympathy strikes, secondary boycotts, and mass picketing, required anticommunist pledges, outlawed political contributions, authorized the president to seek injunctions to order strikers back to work, and made unions legally liable for unauthorized or "wildcat" strikes. Essentially, with Taft-Hartley, the only thing workers could do was engage in a highly bureaucratized form of collective bargaining. The labor movement, which in the United States and elsewhere had once been a diverse array of organizations, including unions, third parties, revolutionary organizations, and cooperative enterprises, was reduced to a trade union movement, concerned above all with its relationship to the Democratic Party and the smooth operation of industrial capitalism.[50]

Racial Contradictions of the New Deal

As we prepare to leave the Depression and return to our own time, we would do well to remind ourselves of the connective tissue that ties the New Deal to Barack Obama's New New Deal (beyond the obvious). Because the Depression happened on their watch, Republicans spent the ensuing generation in opposition. During that time, Republicans who had success at the ballot box tended with a few notable exceptions to cop to the terms of debate set by the Democratic Party. But then a new generation of Republicans—neoconservatives like Ronald Reagan, some of them former Democrats—capitalized on the New Deal in a different way: they argued that the Democrats had betrayed the New Deal's promises to white people.

Though Franklin Roosevelt was not overtly segregationist in his implementation of welfare state policies, a variety of New Deal programs contained racial loopholes that excluded workers and property owners of color. This was due to northern Democrats' long-standing coalition with southern segregationists and western farm states.[51] For example, the 1935 National Labor Relations Act legalized collective bargaining for the first time in American history, but it exempted employers from the domestic and agricultural sectors where workers of color were disproportionately concentrated.

Likewise, the Federal Housing Administration (FHA) and the GI Bill made home buying more affordable to select people. Federally backed mortgages helped some sixteen million World War II veterans purchase homes; the rate of home ownership increased from 44 percent in 1940 to 62 percent in 1960, such that for the first time in history a majority of Americans became property owners. However, FHA-backed home loans were only available to whites buying single-family homes in all-white suburbs. The FHA's own underwriting manual read, "If a neighborhood is to retain stability, it is necessary that properties shall continue to be occupied by the same social and racial classes." Together the FHA, GI Bill, and NLRA ensured that whites had first dibs on the best property, public schools, and jobs of the postwar era.[52]

This new white suburban middle class, whose membership consisted increasingly of upwardly mobile union members, became the core constituency of the New Deal voting bloc, but their preeminent, if counterintuitive partner was the African American community. The Democratic Party mobilized blacks in two distinct phases, each of which reflected the centrality of white voters to its political strategy and the secondary status of black voters. The first phase, 1932–65, began as southern blacks migrated to pivotal areas in populous battleground states. Truman administration official Clark Clifford observed, "The Negro vote today holds the balance of power in Presidential elections for the simple arithmetic reason that the Negroes are geographically concentrated in the pivotal, large, and closely contested states such as New York, Illinois, Pennsylvania, Ohio, and Michigan."[53]

The Democratic strategy for recruiting black voters evolved from symbolic gestures to civil rights, but stopped short of addressing residential segregation, which was a core principle of New Deal home finance. The 1936 Roosevelt campaign named African American delegates to the Democratic National Convention for the first time in party history. In 1940, blacks were mentioned in the party platform—again for the first time. In 1948, Harry Truman went so far as to endorse the findings of his Committee on Civil Rights, which decried racial discrimination. Finally, in the 1960s, symbolic gestures flowered into a full-blown platform of civil rights when pollsters predicted that the loss of white votes in the South would be offset by support among northern and newly enfranchised southern blacks as well as racially moderate whites. Robert F. Kennedy admitted that his late brother had hesitated to press civil rights for fear that it would cost him votes "even in the suburbs." But in 1963 the pollster Louis Harris predicted that whereas Jack Kennedy had lost 4.5 million votes with his qualified support for civil rights, he would gain 11 million votes from those who had voted for Richard Nixon in 1960.

The pollsters were vindicated spectacularly in the 1964 presidential election when Lyndon B. Johnson, running on a civil rights platform, carried all but six states in the entire Union, including the upper South.[54] Having thus captured the White House in a landslide, Democratic elites began to push the progressive agenda to its logical conclusion, calling not only for civil and political rights such as the right to vote, but also for the desegregation of housing, education, and employment.

It was this later move to address the lingering structural inequalities of the New Deal that the Republican Party used to fuel a white backlash and return to power. The violent campaign of "massive resistance" to desegregation in Mississippi and Alabama, which was anchored in old-fashioned biological racism, is of course famous. On every Martin Luther King Day, Americans bear witness to Bull Connor's police and German Shepherds as they attacked a nonviolent protest in Birmingham, Alabama. But the more general form of resistance in both the North and South was relatively moderate in nature.[55] Advocates of a colorblind approach to race relations supported civil rights but framed the desegregation of white neighborhoods, schools, and workplaces as "anti-democratic" or "reverse racism." In 1968 Richard Nixon used the metaphor of "the silent majority" to engineer a defection among the Democrats' white suburban middle-class constituency. He did so in part by insisting that while legally enforced or de jure segregation was certainly illegal, no one could be blamed or punished for the supposedly preexisting or de facto segregation that occurred under the FHA. The Republican Party's appeal to colorblindness was also central to the rise of Ronald Reagan: one could not wage a war on black people, who were equal under the law to whites, but one could wage a war on "welfare" and "drugs" that just so happened to devastate communities of color disproportionately. Reaganism became so dominant that Democratic president Bill Clinton also adopted a colorblind posture: distancing himself from the progressive wing of his party, he signed so-called welfare reform into law, which in the ensuing years dramatically reduced the amount of cash payments to welfare recipients from $20.4 billion in 1996 to $9.6 billion in 2011. President Clinton also signed a federal "three strikes law" in 1995, which imposed harsher penalties on offenders with two prior arrests and accelerated the mass incarceration of black people.[56]

At the same time, Republicans married the white backlash to neoliberal economic policies, chief among these being government deregulation and free trade. Deregulation entailed the retreat of the state from the market and thus the return of the freewheeling capitalism of the pre–New Deal era. It consisted in lower taxes, the privatization of state-owned firms, the busting of unions, and less government regulation. Free trade entailed the reduction and elimination of tariffs on imported goods. The GOP held that multilateral free trade agreements were good for business. If the United States and its trading partners did not tax each other's imports, then American corporations would gain unprecedented access to foreign markets. American manufacturers could also produce their goods in nonunion workplaces abroad for lower wages, since those goods could now flow freely between countries without the impediment of tariffs. Finally, Republicans argued, freer trade fostered greater international cooperation and thus could stop the spread of communism and, later, terrorism. The Democrats, not to be outflanked, also adopted the Republican position. Importantly, the bipartisan Washington Consensus on trade emerged at roughly the same historical conjuncture as Nixon's colorblind civil rights policy, the late 1960s and early 1970s.[57]

Neoliberal economic policy and colorblind racism are not just two separate pillars of the same political project, however: they are linked by deindustrialization, the outsourcing of heavy manufacturing jobs overseas. Deindustrialization made the distinction between individual civil rights and structural inequality all the more vital to electoral politics. To win the votes of whites, the major parties promised to preserve their privileged access to social benefits. As more and more white union members joined the ranks of the unemployed, taking up a greater proportion of both welfare benefits and service sector jobs, there was a simultaneous push to remove unemployed *black* workers from the welfare rolls and the labor market. According to a report from the Congressional Budget Office, the poorest fifth of American households consumed 54 percent of social benefits in 1979; by 2011 they consumed only 36 percent, while the lion's share went toward "maintaining the middle class from childhood through retirement."[58] Simultaneously, law and order initiatives from Nixon to Clinton inverted the proportion of white and black inmates in America's prisons. Whereas the inmate population in the middle of the twentieth century was 70 percent white, reflecting the percentage of whites in the general population, in 2009 only 30 percent of inmates were white. Much of the increase in black inmates is due to drug use, possession, and dealing, even though whites are five times more likely to use illicit drugs and 45 percent more likely to sell drugs. The dispossession of unemployed blacks deepened further as states passed laws stripping ex-convicts of their right to vote, denying them access to social benefits such as interest-free college loans, and limiting their access to the job market by mandating that job applicants list whether they have ever been convicted of a crime.[59]

Though these policies made American society profoundly unequal for all people, mainstream American politics through the turn of the twenty-first century had become a fight over who could best safeguard the racial and economic privileges of *whites* under increasing pressure from deindustrialization and free trade. Far from addressing the problem of mounting inequality, this political program, which I call postracial neoliberalism, allowed inequality to grow and fester until at last it erupted in a social and economic cataclysm.

6

THE MISEDUCATION OF
BARACK OBAMA

As if to punish the establishment's hubris, postracial neoliberalism unleashed the Great Recession, the worst economic calamity in eighty years. Between May 2007 and October 2009, eight and a half million people lost their jobs, and the national unemployment rate more than doubled from 4.4 to 10 percent. The long-term unemployment rate (among those who could not find a job for twenty-seven consecutive months) was the highest recorded in the postwar period. These numbers had a devastating impact on other areas of social life that are tied to unemployment. The percentage of uninsured people in America increased by one third. The poverty rate increased from 12.5 percent in 2007 to 15.1 percent in 2010, while the wealth of all people plummeted by double digits due to the home foreclosure crisis and the stock market crash.[1]

Although the negative effects of the Great Recession were widespread, each demographic group suffered differently. Men took the brunt of joblessness relative to women: the decline in employment in 2008 happened mainly in historically male-dominated occupations like construction and natural resource extraction, which experienced a sharp drop of 1.2 million jobs. At the same time, women suffered more than men in the area of housing. One 2015 study found that women were 25 percent more likely than white men to receive predatory "subprime" loans and were foreclosed on at higher rates. The young were poorer than the old: almost a quarter of those aged eighteen to twenty-four lived below the poverty line, whereas a tenth of those aged fifty-five to sixty-four did. People with less education were hit harder than those with more; because of the overlap in education and social class, poorer people took it on the chin while the affluent were relatively unscathed. For example, the unemployment rate for folks who did not graduate high school was 10.6 percent compared to 3.3 percent for those with a college degree. However, of all forms of inequality, one's race was by far the most powerful predictor of how well one did during the recession. In late 2008, the unemployment rate for whites, Latinos, and blacks was 6.3, 8.9, and 11.5 percent respectively. Though all groups lost assets in the recession, wealth fell by 16 percent among white households, 66 percent among Latino households, and 53 percent among black households.[2]

As shocking as some of these numbers might be, none compare to the heartbreaking stories of real people. Poverty became visible again during the Great Recession. Tent cities resembling the Hoovervilles of the Great Depression sprung up across the country from Sacramento, California, to Tampa Bay, Florida. Having lost their jobs and homes, people hung tarps off chain-link fences next to railroad tracks, camped under highway overpasses, and lived on toxic waste dumps where others refused to live. Tammy, a resident of a tent city in Reno, Nevada, told a *Guardian* reporter, "We eat things that other people throw out. . . . It's really embarrassing to say, but that's the way it sometimes is out here."[3]

The recession changed people's lives overnight. As consumer spending decreased sharply, so too did private sector employment. Companies, fearing the worst, laid workers off in droves and without warning. Before the recession, Patrick Robbins of Chicago was a sportswear buyer at Mark Shale earning $110,000 a year. Within a week of being laid off, his family was on Medicaid and food stamps. Robbins told the *Chicago Tribune* how that felt: "From middle class to poor. Immediately."[4]

As these realities set in, people turned their attention to those responsible for the Great Recession. Chief among these were Wall Street investment bankers, who traded "exotic" securities like high-risk adjustable-rate mortgages on the stock exchange. Though low- and middle-income consumers could afford these home loans in the short term (they were low-interest mortgages often requiring no down payment), subprime interest rates were designed to balloon in the long term, making it impossible for some to continue mortgage payments. Tens of thousands of people defaulted on their loans, and banks moved in to foreclose. The resulting glut in the housing market caused property values to plummet, and homeowners who had bought at the top of the market now found themselves "under water," owing more to the banks than their homes were worth. Once it became clear that mortgage securities were toxic assets, the public eye pivoted to the "predatory" lenders, Countrywide Financial and others, who sold these mortgages on the quick in order to turn around and sell them in prepackaged bundles to Wall Street traders for a profit.

Moreover, because these toxic assets infected the portfolios of big banks, one had to wonder whether the latter had enough capital to continue doing business. Some of the largest and oldest investment concerns, which held vast amounts of the country's wealth, teetered on the brink of collapse. Some did collapse. In September 2008, Lehman Brothers found themselves with $600 billion in assets but just as much in debt, leading to the largest bankruptcy filing in American history. Faced with such widespread uncertainty, banks stopped lending and cut off small- to medium-sized businesses in the "real economy" that relied on bridge loans on a month-to-month basis to make payroll. Lending also dried up for new entrepreneurs, whose start-ups were often financed by home equity loans and second mortgages.

It was not long before media, politicians, and think tanks began connecting the dots from bankers and lax regulatory oversight to the economic collapse. Once they did, Wall Street and the Bush administration became the object of fierce public scrutiny. Targeting the Troubled Asset Relief

Program, or TARP, through which the government bought and thereby cleared the banks' balance sheets of high-risk mortgage securities, journalist Gretchen Morgenson fumed: "And you also know that we should steel ourselves for heavy losses as the TARP gets pulled over our eyes. Never mind that it was the banks, with their reckless lending and monumental leverage, that drove us into this ditch. Such is our lot today: They break it. We own it."[5] Even prominent conservative politicians piled on. Asked on the television program *60 Minutes* whether the American people should be frightened about the financial collapse, the 2008 Republican presidential nominee John McCain said, "I think they should be deeply concerned about the fact that innocent Americans that don't work on Wall Street and don't work in Washington are the victims of the greed, the excess, and, yes, in some cases, corruption."[6]

On the left, the criticism was predictably pointed. In the second presidential debate, then-senator Barack Obama struck a note of incredulity at Mr. McCain's newfound animus toward Wall Street. Refusing to let his opponent cast himself as anything other than a friend of the big banks, Mr. Obama said, "Let's, first of all, understand that the biggest problem in this whole process was the deregulation of the financial system. Senator McCain, as recently as March, bragged about the fact that he is a deregulator."[7] The liberal think tank Center for Public Integrity wrote that 80 percent of subprime lenders were financed by the likes of Lehman Brothers, Merrill Lynch, J.P. Morgan, and Citigroup. Far from being the "unwitting victims of an unforeseen financial collapse," Public Integrity held that these institutions were in fact "enablers that bankrolled the type of lending that has threatened the financial system."[8]

Reassembling the New Deal Coalition

Barack Obama promised to end the daily indignities of the Great Recession and bring to account those who were responsible. Though he rarely challenged racial inequalities at a structural level, his agenda did challenge the model of unregulated free market capitalism that had brought so many to ruin. Obama Democrats made their claim to the presidency by advancing a revisionist and postracial history of the New Deal.[9]

Mr. Obama's personal narrative, so much a feature of his campaign, contained numerous idealized allusions to New Deal policies, especially the FHA, which had historically made home mortgages more accessible to white workers; the GI Bill, which in addition to providing low-interest, long-term mortgages to white veterans also paid for a college education; and deficit-spending programs that put the unemployed back to work. In El Dorado, Kansas, his white grandparents' ancestral home, then-candidate Obama said, "I am standing here today because my grandfather got the chance to go to school on the GI Bill, buy a house through the Federal Housing Authority [*sic*], and move his family west."[10] In Indiana, Mr. Obama equated his own plans with that of President Eisenhower's embrace of New Deal deficit-spending programs: "Now, back in the 1950s, Americans were put to work building the Interstate Highway system and that helped expand the middle class in this country. We need to show the same kind of leadership today."[11] Later, in a speech in nearby St. Louis titled "An Agenda for Middle Class Success," he alluded to his future legislative agenda in this way: "We sent my grandfather's generation to college on the GI Bill, which helped create the largest middle-class in history. And that's what this country will do again when I am President of the United States."[12] Throughout his campaign, Mr. Obama asserted that New Deal liberalism, or at least an updated version thereof, was the answer to the Great Recession. He framed himself as the very product of the aspirations and policies of the New Deal. Significantly, he evoked a putative golden age of the American economy without any mention of Jim Crow segregation.[13] On both race and the economy, Mr. Obama's candidacy was positively Rooseveltesque.

President Obama's 2009 inaugural address was not a "Fear itself" speech, but it did hit on the New Deal themes of deficit spending, government regulation, and jobs:

> The state of our economy calls for action, bold and swift. And we will act, not only to create new jobs, but to lay a new foundation for growth. We will build the roads and bridges, the electric grids and digital lines that feed our commerce and bind us together. . . . This crisis has reminded us that without a watchful eye, the market can spin out of control. The nation cannot prosper long when it favors only the prosperous.[14]

In this, the first speech of his young presidency, Mr. Obama previewed his plans to maneuver the American economy onto a "new foundation for growth." He promised to keep a "watchful eye" on the market to prevent it from spinning out of control, to reinvest in the country's ailing infrastructure, and to create new jobs.

The American public thus had good reason to expect FDR's second coming. In a postelection op-ed, titled "Franklin Delano Obama?" the Princeton economist Paul Krugman wrote, "Suddenly, everything old is New Deal again. Reagan is out; F.D.R. is in."[15] *Time* magazine's November 24, 2008, cover featured Barack Obama's likeness photoshopped onto a famous image of a smiling FDR driving a Cadillac with his trademark fedora and cigarette filter. The cover story by Peter Beinart was titled, "The New New Deal."[16] Similarly, of the 2009 American Recovery and Reinvestment Act (President Obama's thinly veiled answer to the 1933 National Industrial Recovery Act), the journalist Michael Grunwald wrote:

> It was the biggest and most transformative energy bill in U.S. history, financing unprecedented government investments in a smarter grid; cleaner coal; energy efficiency in every imaginable form; "green-collar" job training; electric vehicles and the infrastructure to support them; advanced biofuels and the refineries to brew them; renewable power from the sun, the wind, and the heat below the earth; and factories to manufacture all the green stuff in the United States. . . . It authorized a high-speed passenger rail network, the biggest new transportation initiative since the interstate highways, and extended our existing high-speed Internet network to underserved communities, a modern twist on the New Deal's rural electrification. It updated the New Deal-era unemployment insurance system and launched new approaches to preventing homelessness, financing infrastructure projects, and managing stormwater in eco-friendly ways.[17]

Not surprisingly, Grunwald also titled his book *The New New Deal*. While some on the left may insist that Barack Obama was no progressive and too far to the right to even "sell out," I want to suggest that his initial candidacy broke, if not with preexisting civil rights policy, then certainly with the economic policy of the previous forty years.

Of course, it is one thing to argue that Barack Obama campaigned on the promise of a New New Deal and quite another to demonstrate that his message gained sufficient traction on the ground to reassemble the New Deal coalition of white suburban middle-class and black voters. In fact, news reports suggest that white suburban voters were central to the 2008 Democratic coalition nationally. The Democrats carried fifteen of the fastest-growing one hundred counties, compared to just three in 2004. Obama also ran ahead of Senator John Kerry, the 2004 Democratic presidential nominee, in ninety-four of those counties.[18]

This dynamic was especially at work in Indiana and North Carolina, which the Democrats had not carried since 1964 and 1976 respectively. County-level electoral data from these states reveal three patterns. First, John McCain carried the rural counties of both states with 60 percent of the vote or more. Second, the Democrats predictably offset the rural vote by carrying the major cities. But third, the Obama campaign's advantage was made possible by black voters in urban centers and white middle-class voters in suburban areas, especially the high-growth suburbs that had given the Republican Party supermajorities in previous election cycles.

The returns of two white suburban counties in Indiana are a case in point. Hamilton and Hendricks were then Indiana's only entrants in the one hundred fastest-growing counties in the United States. Both were affluent suburbs of Indianapolis and were over 90 percent white.[19] The Democrats increased their share of the popular vote in each of these key areas. Although the Republicans carried Hamilton and Hendricks, as they typically do, their margin of victory dropped by a combined total of 32,504 votes relative to 2004. The loss of what are routinely bankable Republican votes in the suburbs was therefore decisive given the urban-rural stalemate between the parties and the fact that the Democratic margin of victory in Indiana was a mere 28,391 votes.[20] Additionally, while black turnout was far more important in North Carolina, as we shall soon see, there was nevertheless a net gain to the Democratic Party of 11,534 black voters in Indiana from 2004 to 2008.[21]

U.S. Census data and the local paper of record, the *Indianapolis Star*, provide important clues about who voted for Mr. Obama, especially in Hamilton County. To begin, although both counties remain overwhelmingly white, the U.S. Census estimates a drop in the percentage of whites from 2000 to 2009 and therefore an increase in the percentage of people who are more likely to vote Democratic. Next, the Obama campaign benefited from some 240,000 newly registered Democrats but primarily in "defecting" counties—the twelve counties that President Bush carried in 2004 but were carried by Senator Obama in 2008. Demographic shifts and voter registration notwithstanding, a closer look at Hamilton County suggests that the Democrats' 13.5 percent improvement over their 2004 performance appears to be due largely to the defection of already-registered Republican voters. An important component of the Obama campaign's county organization was a chapter of "Republicans for Obama" (RFO). One sure sign of RFO's effectiveness was the relatively enthusiastic turnout for Republican governor Mitch Daniels: whereas Senator McCain carried Hamilton by 30,000 votes, Daniels carried it by 80,000. Indiana Republican Party chair Murray Clark called the disparity "jaw-dropping."[22]

Nor was Indiana an isolated case. The Republican Party witnessed defections in high-growth counties across the nation, while the Democrats ran up the score with new registrations among African American voters in cities. The Obama campaign's strategy to rebuild the Democrats' strength in the very suburbs the party had brought into existence through the FHA and to expand turnout among traditional Democratic voters reconfigured the electoral map and put in play states the party had not carried since it *was* the party of the New Deal.

North Carolina is a good example. The Tar Heel State had not given its electoral votes to a Democrat in thirty-two years, but like Hendricks and Hamilton counties in Indiana, all four of North Carolina's high-growth counties either flipped for the Democrats or saw unprecedented erosion in the Republican base. These were Wake County, which houses metropolitan Raleigh and the so-called Research Triangle; Mecklenburg County, which contains the city of Charlotte and its suburbs; Union County, a Charlotte exurb; and Brunswick County, a suburb of Wilmington at the southernmost tip of the state. White voters were the supermajority in all four districts.[23]

County-level electoral returns report that the Democrats carried North Carolina by expanding their share of the black vote in cities and their share of white votes in the suburbs. George W. Bush carried Wake County in 2000 and 2004, but in 2008 the Democrats surged dramatically, improving on their 2004 showing by eight percentage points. Mecklenburg County had been trending Democratic since 2000, yet it too witnessed a higher-than-expected twenty-point Democratic margin of victory in 2008. The Democrats lost Union and Brunswick counties, but not without shaving several percentage points off the 2004 Republican advantage. Finally, Democrats increased their already formidable advantage in the African American community. According to the *New York Times*, 22 percent of North Carolina's electorate in 2008 was black, compared to 18.6 percent in 2004.[24] The net gain due to increased black turnout was 156,816 votes from 2004 to 2008.[25] In a state where the Republicans lost by just 14,177 votes, the Democrats' expansion in city centers and suburbs was sufficient to flip the state from red to blue for the first time since 1976.[26]

U.S. Census data and local newspapers offer valuable clues as to who voted for Mr. Obama and why.[27] In a precinct-by-precinct analysis of how "whites boosted Obama" in Mecklenburg County, the *Charlotte Observer* reported that although the GOP still managed to carry heavily white Republican precincts, the Democrats dramatically improved on their 2004 performance. For example, in the Charlotte suburb of Huntersville, which was then 88.4 percent white, Mr. Obama took 41 percent of the vote to Mr. Kerry's 28 percent. A similar pattern was found in Charlotte's neighboring counties, which voted heavily for Mr. McCain, including Union County. At the same time, the article described "a massive turnout among African Americans" in which "a number of first-time voters said they came to the polls solely because of Obama." In the predominantly black precinct of Barringer Elementary School in west Charlotte, where Democrats are accustomed to overwhelming margins of victory, Senator Kerry defeated President Bush 723 to 36, while Obama defeated McCain 1,617 to 16.[28] In Wake County, the story seemed to center more on the forty-seven thousand newly registered Democratic voters, but many of these were former registered Republicans. Eleven precincts that voted for President Bush in 2004 flipped for Mr. Obama in 2008, including heavily Republican Brier Creek Community Center in northwest Raleigh.[29]

There can be little doubt then that the Obama campaign touched off a defection from the postracial neoliberal establishment in 2008. Though increased black voter turnout helped Mr. Obama, to be sure, the defection of white suburban middle-class voters from the Republican Party added to his margins in key states where Democrats had not been competitive for a generation. Overall, the Democrats carried 52 percent of independent voters and 50 percent of suburban voters.[30] President-elect Obama had reassembled the New Deal coalition.

Reabsorption from the Left

If the history of political crises teaches us anything, however, it is that the political establishment does not take a challenge to its power lightly. Just as the rise of secessionism and militant trade unionism prompted the mainstream party system to reassert itself through the Compromise of 1850 and the New Deal, so too did establishment Democrats and Republicans attempt to absorb Barack Obama's challenge to the status quo.

At the end of the preceding chapter we learned that the Republican Party married free trade and deregulation with the claim that desegregation betrayed the New Deal's promise to white people. The GOP thus advanced a new political project, one that was simultaneously colorblind and neoliberal. Having been beaten with this formula by Richard Nixon, Ronald Reagan, and George H. W. Bush, the Democrats, led by Bill Clinton and the conservative Democratic Leadership Council, struck the same colorblind posture on race relations and embraced neoliberal economic policy. In what some consider the defining moment of the 1992 presidential campaign, Bill Clinton distanced himself from the progressive wing of his party by denouncing the rapper Sista Soulja for allegedly inciting the violence that led to the Los Angeles riots.[31] And just as Ronald Reagan famously declared that "government is not the solution to our problem; government is the problem" in his 1996 State of the Union address to Congress, President Clinton announced, "The era of big government is over." Barack Obama's repeated references to New Deal policies signaled that he was about to upset the apple cart, and the establishment of both parties moved in to contain him.

The Clintonites' infiltration of the Obama administration was partly the unintended result of the president's own preoccupation with educational pedigree and high-level government experience. The only Democrats who met these criteria were Clinton Democrats, as they had been the most recent party cadres to occupy the White House. This structural reality together with Mr. Obama's insistence that his administration be a model of meritocracy created a dynamic in which former Clinton administration officials simply moved one step up from where they had been a decade before: deputy assistant secretaries became assistant secretaries, former heads of small agencies became the heads of large agencies, and so on. Though a small coterie of Mr. Obama's non-establishment friends and allies formed part of the administration, their numbers were few and their placement within the bureaucracy at a lower profile compared to establishment neoliberals—so called FOBs (Friends of Bill)—who occupied cabinet positions and top-shelf appointments in the White House.[32] Once in place, Clintonites systematically undercut the New New Deal and preserved the neoliberal underpinnings of the American economy.

The process began just after Mr. Obama won the Democratic nomination with the appointment of John Podesta as head of the candidate's secret transition team. While the nominee thought he was simply picking the best-credentialed person for the job, members of the Obama campaign worried that Podesta would end up "building the architecture for a new quasi-Clinton administration." That is in fact what happened. Podesta recruited Carol Browner, former head of the Environmental Protection Agency under President Clinton, to lead the policy team on energy and the environment. He then staffed the economic transition team with other Clintonites, including Clinton commerce secretary Bill Daley, who chaired the team and would later become Mr. Obama's second White House chief of staff, and Clinton budget director Jack Lew, who would become the president's third chief of staff. The only non-Clintonite on the economic transition team was Robert Greenstein, founder of the liberal Center for Budget and Policy Priorities. Reflecting back on the secret transition team, one Obama aide told the journalist Michael Grunwald, "That's when the old guard started taking over."[33]

The transition team then moved into the governing apparatus. Given the backdrop of the Great Recession, the most fateful appointments were to the economic team that presided over the economic recovery and bank regulation. To head the National Economic Council, President Obama appointed Harvard economist and former Clinton treasury secretary Larry Summers, who had become infamous for deregulating markets in the 1990s. For treasury secretary, the president chose Timothy Geithner, head of the New York Federal Reserve and a friend of Wall Street. To direct the Office of Management and Budget, Obama picked Clinton senior economist Peter Orszag, a deficit hawk of the old school. The only exceptions to the recycling of Clinton appointees were the president's appointments to the Council of Economic Advisors (CEA), which became an in-house White House think tank and an outpost for "Obama people." To head it, Obama chose Christina Romer, then a Harvard economic historian (now at Berkeley) who was known for arguing that FDR's stimulus package was too small and was abandoned too soon to be effective.[34]

Housing New New Dealers and neoliberals under one roof led to opposing plans for the economic recovery. The New New Dealers led by Romer proposed a stimulus plan with a price tag of at least $800 billion and as high as $1.2 trillion, much of it actual stimulus that would have pumped money directly into the economy with funding for infrastructural improvements, public works jobs, and cash transfers to the unemployed. The neoliberals—Summers, Geithner, Orszag, and Lew—advanced much smaller packages ranging in price from $175 billion to $800 billion, which were structured to provide an initial stimulus in the short term and return to a program of "austerity" or spending cuts in the medium term.[35]

The neoliberals won this battle with two kinds of palace intrigue. First, neoliberals used backroom strategies, sometimes to isolate the president from non-Clintonites and at other times to water down progressive policy proposals. Rahm Emanuel in his position as White House chief of staff thus worked to get the Obamas' longtime friend Valerie Jarrett to fill the president's vacant Senate seat, not out of any admiration but in order to get Jarrett out of the White House. Similarly, when Elizabeth Warren called for a government agency to protect consumers from the predations of Wall Street,

Timothy Geithner called a meeting to develop an "Elizabeth Warren Strategy" that would neutralize the Harvard professor. Unbeknown to Warren herself, Geithner said he would only support the creation of the agency if Warren were not the head of it. Neoliberals also employed inside dealing to protect the banks from so-called conditionalities, in which the government would only agree to recapitalize the banks if they took hits like a moratorium on CEO bonuses. The president became angry when he heard that AIG and other firms had given their executives $18 billion in bonuses during the depths of the recession. Provoked by the president's anger, U.S. senator Chris Dodd inserted an amendment in the nearly completed American Recovery and Reinvestment Act to dramatically curtail such bonuses at banks that had received government bailout money. Geithner moved swiftly to weaken the amendment; just prior to the vote, he convinced Dodd that the rule should apply only to bonuses given after the bill's passage.[36]

Second, Summers and Emanuel worked to "filter" the range of competing proposals that reached the president. Summers persuaded Obama that it was faster for him to read dissenting arguments on economic policy than to have competing actors debate the issues in the Oval Office. Emanuel decided which agenda items were politically feasible and formulated the strategy for their execution. As early as two months into the administration, Summers and Emanuel had formed a back channel that positioned them as the ultimate gatekeepers on politics and policy.[37] In an especially poignant Oval Office meeting on restructuring the banks and setting the price of the stimulus, Rahm Emanuel exploited a break when the president left to have dinner with his family. The chief of staff took over, saying, "Let me be clear—taking down the banking system in a program that could cost $700 billion is a fantasy. With all the money that already went to TARP, no one is getting that kind of money through Congress, especially with this AIG bonus disaster. The job of everyone in this room is to move the president, when he gets back, toward a solution that *works*" (emphasis in original).[38] Looking back at that meeting, CEA chair Christina Romer reflected, "This was the crisis that we should not let go to waste . . . [but] right there, Rahm killed it." Once the president returned to the Oval, Summers explained the "team's" decision in this way: "We had this very good discussion at the beginning of the meeting, but while you were away,

Rahm made the point that there's no chance of Congress approving any more TARP funds. So a broader, systemwide solution doesn't seem possible. But it's absolutely possible, Mr. President, to do Citi, just Citi."[39]

In the end the recovery act would cost $787 billion, including over $200 billion in tax cuts that would not provide much stimulus at all.[40] From there the Obama administration would slam the brakes on the stimulus and call for fiscal discipline and further tax cuts. In due course, Mr. Obama started to sound every bit the centrist President Clinton had been, and copped to the Republican line that what the economy needed above all was tax cuts. In his 2010 State of the Union address, the president said:

> Let me repeat: we cut taxes. We cut taxes for 95% of working families. We cut taxes for small businesses. We cut taxes for first-time homebuyers. We cut taxes for parents trying to care for their children. We cut taxes for 8 million Americans paying for college. As a result, millions of Americans had more to spend on gas, and food, and other necessities, all of which helped business keep more workers. And we haven't raised income taxes by a single dime on a single person. Not a single dime.[41]

With the containment of Obama accomplished and Clinton Democrats now entrenched at this critical stage of the policy-making process, other New New Deal initiatives suffered. Three areas bear mention as they were central features of the original New Deal. First, the president's economic advisors rejected direct government hiring for public works projects despite Mr. Obama's open support for such initiatives during the campaign. Second, in the area of housing and foreclosure, which were central to the first New Deal, congressional Democrats proposed a bill that would have allowed judges to modify homeowners' mortgage debt when they filed for bankruptcy. Though Mr. Obama expressed support for the proposal in 2008, the administration chose not to endorse the bill and it failed. Third, whereas Mr. Obama had voted as senator in favor of the Employee Free Choice Act to make it easier for workers to join unions, as president he yielded to the antiunion lobby and let the measure go. In sum, the neoliberal Democratic establishment had managed the president well. As Larry Summers once said to Peter Orszag, "We're home alone. There's no adult in charge."[42]

Reabsorption from the Right

The media has characterized the right-wing strategy to contain Mr. Obama as nothing less than complete intransigence. The "party of no" was much more complex than that, however, involving at least two more-or-less uncoordinated organizations, the Republican congressional leadership and the Tea Party, each pursuing its own objectives and for different reasons.

The Republican congressional leadership sought to frustrate President Obama's postpartisan message, which they viewed as a strategy to build a bipartisan consensus that could push through the New New Deal and engineer a Democratic realignment. At a private December 2008 meeting, new House minority whip Eric Cantor suggested that the strategy going forward was to deny the president-elect the ability to create postpartisanship. He said, "We're not here to cut deals and get crumbs and stay in the minority for another 40 years. . . . We're not rolling over. We're going to fight these guys. We're down, but things are going to change." The Republican caucus thus sought to deny the president the postpartisan route to a legislative victory, and in doing so hurt his approval ratings by insinuating that it was the president's extreme hard-left agenda that was making a unified postpartisan government and society impossible.[43]

Perhaps the surest sign of this strategy was that Senate minority leader Mitch McConnell and his caucus blocked bills that had wide bipartisan support prior to Obama assuming office and that McConnell himself had supported. In October 2008, the leaders of both parties supported the Troubled Asset Relief Program (the so-called bailout) to keep the economy from collapsing, but McConnell worked to gum up the distribution of TARP funds in January 2009, just three months after he had voted to authorize them. McConnell also aggressively employed Senate rules to undercut the will of the majority. Republicans filibustered even uncontroversial bills, including the Public Land Management Act for the protection of parks in nine states, which was introduced on a bipartisan basis before Mr. Obama's inauguration.[44]

Though the Republicans did not have the numbers to completely halt the agenda until 2010 when they recaptured the majority in the House, the successive procedural delays to the passage of legislation gave the GOP time to tarnish the Democratic agenda in the court of public opinion. Of the huge battle over the Affordable Care Act, or "Obamacare," Republican senator Robert Bennett said, "The fact that Obama's health-care bill did not pass by the dates he kept putting on it was not an accident . . . McConnell knew the places to go . . . we finally ran out of options by Christmas Eve. But in the process of that yearlong journey, the Republicans won the public-relations battle."[45]

The reason the Republican congressional leadership gave the public for its obstructionism was that the Obama administration's agenda for "Europeanizing the country" was so extreme that it could not in good conscience go along. The implication was that it was the Democrats' fault—that if it hadn't been for them, the GOP would not have adopted their oppositional posture. Addressing a crowd in Beattyville, Kentucky, in October 2010, McConnell said of Obama's liberal government:

> It's running banks, insurance companies, car companies, nationalized the student-loan business, took over our health care, passed a financial-services bill that not a single banker in Kentucky thought was a good idea. They've got people at the FCC trying to take over the Internet. People at the National Labor Relations Board trying to get rid of the secret ballots for labor-union elections. They passed a budget that puts us on a path to double the national debt in five years and triple it in 10. This is Big Government liberalism on display.[46]

Once the president was boxed in, McConnell's short-range goal was to make the president tack right, but his end goal was to put Obama out of the White House by 2012. In an interview with the *National Journal*, McConnell said, "The single most important thing we want to achieve is for President Obama to be a one-term president." When asked to clarify whether in the meantime that meant "endless, or at least frequent, confrontation with the president," McConnell said, "If President Obama does a Clintonian backflip, if he's willing to meet us halfway on some of the biggest issues, it's not inappropriate for us to do business with him," adding, "I don't want the president to fail; I want him to change."[47]

With the help of neoliberal infiltration from within, Republican intransigence from without *did* change the president. Then in the 2010 midterm elections, the GOP reversed the Democrats' recent gains, carrying independent voters by 18 percent, compared to Mr. Obama's four percentage-point edge in 2008 and congressional Democrats' 18-point advantage in 2006. To suggest that the Republican leadership was solely responsible for this victory, however, would be to ignore a second conservative force that worked to contain Barack Obama's challenge to postracial neoliberalism: the Tea Party.

The Tea Party began its strange career as a straightforward, if hardline agent of the status quo. On the one hand, it sought to maintain white people's privileged access to social benefits; on the other, it worked to preserve the orthodoxies of neoliberal economic policy: lower taxes, free trade, and government deregulation. The Tea Party was therefore not a reaction to the economic crisis as such but rather a mobilization against Barack Obama's *response* to the crisis.

Concern mounted among these constituents with the costly bailouts of the banks and auto companies and then boiled over with the American Recovery and Reinvestment Act. The latter led to the initial call to arms on February 19, 2009, when CNBC reporter Rick Santelli condemned the proposed foreclosure relief plan for "rewarding bad behavior" and invited America's capitalists to a "Chicago Tea Party."[48]

From there the Tea Party developed into an assemblage of three moving parts: the grassroots movement, political elites, and the conservative media. The racial contradictions of the New Deal lived on in the attitudes of grassroots activists and are perhaps their most distinguishing feature. In 2009, politicians reported being told at town-hall meetings to keep the government's hands off Medicare, even though Medicare is a government program. A closer look at Tea Party attitudes reveals a solution to this puzzling policy position: race. A poll conducted by Public Policy Polling found that two-thirds of those identifying as Tea Party supporters favored increasing the payroll tax to sustain Social Security. However, Tea Party activists also distinguish between benefits that people have "earned" and other benefits for low-income people that place a burden on hardworking taxpayers to bankroll freeloaders. One popular Tea Party bumper sticker reads, "You are not ENTITLED to what I have EARNED." The question of course is just who these feckless freeloaders are. In a survey of seven states the University of

Washington found that Tea Party supporters were more likely than other respondents to rate blacks and Latinos less hardworking and less trustworthy. One Tea Party activist told researchers that a "plantation mentality" was keeping "some people" on welfare. The implication is that it is unjust for the government to shift resources away from hardworking white people who deserve social benefits toward lazy nonwhites who never paid into the system.[49]

Political elites connected to the Tea Party were neoliberals who sought to pour the new grassroots energy into the old bottles of smaller government and free market orthodoxy. FreedomWorks, which founded the Tea Party Patriots and was run by former Republican House majority leader Dick Armey, is a multimillion dollar organization advocating "Lower Taxes" and "Less Government." Perhaps even more famously, the Koch brothers rode the Tea Party to prominence after years of being minor players within the Republican Party despite their enormous wealth. Though founded in 2004, their policy group, Americans for Prosperity, picked up steam from 2009 to 2011, raising money to block passage of the Affordable Care Act and undercut collective bargaining through right-to-work laws.[50]

Finally, the Tea Party forged strong ties to the conservative media giant Fox News, which became the media outlet of choice for the rank and file. Indeed, Fox was a prime mover of the Tea Party in its early days. On April 9, 2009, just weeks after President Obama's inauguration, Fox News icon Glenn Beck told viewers, "This year, Americans across the country are holding tea parties to let politicians know that we have had enough." Broadcast transcripts from April 2009 show that the news outlet regularly advertised "Tax Day" rallies, occasionally reaching fifty mentions a day, while Fox's competitor, CNN, rarely mentioned the rallies at all. No wonder that a CBS/*New York Times* poll conducted one year later revealed that 63 percent of Tea Party supporters watched Fox News, compared to 11 percent of all respondents.[51]

The combination of grassroots mobilization, elite support, and free media became a formidable operation. In the November 2010 midterm elections, the Tea Party helped Republicans win six seats in the Senate and sixty-three more seats and the majority in the House of Representatives, the largest congressional seat change since 1948. In the initial stages of the relationship, then, the Republican Party and the Tea Party appeared on the surface to be one well-oiled machine. The dramatic decline in Tea Party protests in the lead-up to the Republican takeover provides further evidence of the overlap between the two sets of organizations.[52] By 2010, with the help of establishment Democrats inside the White House, the Republicans had effectively killed the New New Deal.

Warning Signs

The co-optation of Barack Obama turned out to be a Pyrrhic victory, for the neoliberal center began to show signs of weakness soon thereafter. Progressives in the Democratic Party began to break away from their more conservative counterparts as early as 2011 when Vermont senator Bernie Sanders and his chief surrogate, Cornel West, urged a primary challenge to President Obama in advance of the 2012 election. In an astonishing ninety-minute speech on June 28, 2011, titled "Dear Mr. President," Mr. Sanders spoke to concerns that Obama was simply "yielding to the incessant, extreme Republican demands" on tax cuts and federal spending. Later, in a July 2011 interview on the *Thom Hartmann Program*, Mr. Sanders said:

> I think there are millions of Americans who are deeply disappointed in the president; who believe that, with regard to Social Security and a number of other issues, he said one thing as a candidate and is doing something very much else as a president; who cannot believe how weak he has been, for whatever reason, in negotiating with Republicans and there's deep disappointment. So my suggestion is, I think one of the reasons the president has been able to move so far to the right is that there is no primary opposition to him . . . I think it would be a good idea if President Obama faced some primary opposition.[53]

Sanders's interview is significant for two reasons. First, there was "deep disappointment" that the president allowed the Republicans to undercut the progressive agenda of the 2008 campaign. Second, Sanders, previewing his own presidential bid, pins the rightward drift of the Obama administration on the fact that Mr. Obama had not faced opposition from the left flank of his party.

One month later, Princeton professor and Sanders surrogate Cornel West likewise made reference to the neoliberal co-optation of the Obama administration. In an interview with Amy Goodman on *Democracy Now*, he said: "It's very clear that President Obama caves in over and over again. He punts on first down. If you're in a foxhole with him, you're in trouble, because he wants to compromise, you want to fight. . . . Unfortunately, Tim Geithner and his economic team . . . have indifference toward the poor and working people . . . he's rightly associated much more with the oligarchs than with poor people."[54] Asked whether he was alluding to another candidate running for president, Professor West added, "It would be a Bernie Sanders-like figure who is fundamentally committed to . . . putting poor and working people at the center."[55]

Given that skepticism of Mr. Obama's "change" agenda was growing even on the left, it should come as no surprise that the president did not do as well in the 2012 election as he did in 2008. Whereas he carried Indiana and North Carolina in his first campaign, largely on the strength of the revived New Deal coalition of black and white middle-class suburban voters, he lost both states in 2012: Indiana by a ten-point margin, and North Carolina by a two-point margin. Further, exit-polling data reveal that with few exceptions Mr. Obama's margin of victory decreased ominously across all demographic groups, including the base. After winning the suburban vote by two percentage points in 2008, he lost it by the same margin in 2012. And whereas Senator John McCain carried the white vote by 12 percent, Governor Romney beat Obama by 20 percent. Among blacks, another historic constituency of the New Deal voting bloc, the president's margin of victory dropped by four percentage points.[56] Finally, in Wisconsin, Michigan, and Pennsylvania, states that were supposed to guarantee Democratic presidential victories in perpetuity, the Democratic advantage declined by almost half from 1.7 million votes in 2008 to 1.07 million votes in 2012.

The 2012 election in turn led to open conflict between the Tea Party and Republican establishment, culminating in the government shutdown of October 2013. The origins of the shutdown can be traced to January 2013 when House Republicans convened in Williamsburg, Virginia, to reverse course after Mitt Romney's defeat in the 2012 presidential election. The leadership put forward a plan in which the Republican majority would force fiscal concessions from the Democrats when the limit on the debt ceiling (the dollar amount of debt the federal government could legally take on) was due to expire in late spring 2013. But Tea Party Republicans wanted to act earlier, seeing the approaching negotiations over a continuing resolution (CR) to extend federal spending as an opportunity to prevent the Affordable Care Act from going into effect on October 1. Said Jeff Duncan, a Tea Party congressman from South Carolina: "We always seemed to be kind of kicking the can to the next fight. And we felt like, 'We've got two fights here, the CR and the debt ceiling—we're willing to have it sooner rather than later.' "[57]

The clash of the two plans set up a showdown between the Republican establishment and the Tea Party, with each side casting aspersions on the other. Raul Labrador, a hardline conservative, blamed Republican failures on House Speaker John Boehner's cautious approach to negotiating with the White House: "Boehner is informed by his background. And his background is being a bartender—going into a negotiation thinking, you know, 'My job is just to get both sides to like each other and pay the tab.' And, at the end of the day, they're both going to be happy because they're going to be drinking, and they're going to leave me a big tip."[58] Establishment Republicans bristled at this and other patronizing insults, many of which were carried out by Tea Party-affiliated organizations like Heritage Action, which used scorecards to evaluate representatives on their commitment to conservative values. Centrist representative Adam Kinzinger of Illinois denounced these practices in the following terms:

> The vast majority of us are pro-life, all of us vote to repeal Obamacare, we all like smaller government. But what's happened is these outside groups that raise money on trying to say that they're the defender of liberty and purity—they don't spend any of that money really on anything but overhead and attacking Republicans. My voter ID says Illinois 16th district—it doesn't say Heritage Action on it. There are some people that are so eager to do what these groups say, you may as well just let all your staff go and just take your vote recommendations from Heritage Action. You could save the taxpayers some money.[59]

Kinzinger's allusion to Tea Party groups has some empirical basis. In September the Tea Party caucus created a "toolkit" to inoculate those who were fearful of shutting down the government. Heritage Action, to which Kinzinger refers, funded a nine-city "Defund Obamacare" tour and trained some six thousand volunteers to descend on meetings and challenge their elected representatives; the aforementioned scorecards made all but the most conservative congressional Republicans the target of attacks from the far right. David Wasserman of the nonpartisan *Cook Political Report*, which tracks House races, said that the proof of far-right organizational influence was that "a freshman member of Congress from North Carolina" was "able to round up a gang of 80 that's essentially ground the government to a halt."[60]

With the additional urging of freshman Texas senator Ted Cruz, who told conservative House Republicans to "buck Boehner," the Tea Party caucus voted against a continuing resolution and shut the government down from October 1 to October 16, disrupting vital public services and furloughing some 800,000 federal employees.

The government shutdown would come to define President Obama's second term, for even after it was resolved in the Democrats' favor, the debacle represented an underlying stalemate among the proliferating factions of the party system. The various right-wing groups that comprised the Republican Party became further emboldened, while the left flank of the Democratic Party found a standard-bearer. Faced with disappointment from progressive Democrats and intransigence from the opposition, Barack Obama gave up on a legislative program. Instead he took to issuing a series of executive orders. By the end, the president was not even able to nominate a judge to the U.S. Supreme Court, though it was his constitutional prerogative to do so.

The mass discontent that the stalemate fomented became palpable as the American people entered the primary season. In 2015, the Gallup Poll asked Americans, "How much of the time do you think you can trust government in Washington to do what is right—just about always, most of the time, or only some of the time?" Only 19 percent of respondents said either always or most of the time, the lowest percentage recorded since pollsters began asking the question in 1958.[61] What America's political class faced in 2016 was not just an election but a systemic collapse in public confidence.[62]

7

THE ELECTION OF DONALD TRUMP

Hillary Clinton's mother, Dorothy Rodham, was abandoned by her family at a young age, but she persevered and built a life for herself and her family. Throughout the 2016 presidential campaign, Mrs. Rodham's memory was called upon to remind voters of the candidate's tenacious blue-collar background, and she would anchor the victory speech that Secretary Clinton planned to give on election night. In her address, the candidate imagined herself traveling back in time to tell her frightened eight-year-old mom: "Listen to me. You will survive. You will have a good family of your own, and three children. And as hard as it might be to imagine, your daughter will grow up and become the President of the United States."[1] Hillary Clinton would never deliver that speech, but neither she nor her staff had prepared a concession. In her autobiographical account of her defeat, she wrote: "I felt shell-shocked. I hadn't prepared mentally for this at all. There had been no doomsday scenarios playing out in my head in the final days, no imagining what I might say if I lost."[2]

Clinton watched as two constituencies turned against her, though in different ways. First, white working-class precincts seemed to be energized in the wrong direction. In Michigan, Pennsylvania, and Wisconsin, in particular, she writes, "we were getting killed in heavily white, working class rural and exurban areas." This meant that the Democrats would have to run up the score in the big cities, especially Philadelphia, Pittsburgh, Detroit, and Milwaukee. But second, Black and Latino voters had not turned out in the numbers she had hoped, and it became clear as the night wore on that there would not be enough votes from that quarter to overcome her opponent's lead. At 2:29 A.M., the Associated Press called Wisconsin for Donald Trump, and not long after, the president-elect took the stage to give his own victory speech. In this moment, Clinton looked around the dining room of her hotel suite and observed that the people she loved and trusted "were all in as much pain and shock as I was."[3]

Shock is a quintessential reaction to crises of hegemony. It is not every day that the people withdraw their consent to be governed by the establishment, and when they do the sense of surprise and dread hangs heavily on the political class. Indeed, even Senate majority leader Mitch McConnell, who was as well acquainted with the Republicans' internal polling as anyone was, expressed surprise at the results. In an interview with Kentucky Educational Television in December 2016, Mr. McConnell said, "I didn't think Trump had a chance of winning."[4] Similarly, when asked why the Republicans were in such disarray despite controlling all three branches of government, Senator Pat Toomey (R-PA) confessed, "Look, I didn't expect Donald Trump to win, I think most of my colleagues didn't, so we didn't expect to be in this situation."[5] But the rarity of such crises is not the only thing that makes them shocking or surprising. A crisis of hegemony creeps up like a thief in the night, because it originates in relatively small events that build by twists and turns to monumental outcomes.

Reabsorption Backfires on the Right

If the Republican establishment thought it had found in the Tea Party a vehicle for its revival, then it was sorely mistaken. An analysis of the ideological shift between the 111th House of Representatives in 2010 and the 112th House in 2011 reveals a sharp rightward lurch in the Republican caucus. One study found that 77 percent of newly arriving Republicans that year, including dozens of Tea Party-backed Republicans, were more conservative than the typical Republican in the previous Congress—and many were to the right of nearly all continuing Republicans.[6]

This was by design. Despite the appearance of cooperation with the Republican establishment early on, the Tea Party ran a competing slate of candidates in the primaries to accelerate the Republicans' rightward drift. The Tea Party Express (TPE) raised $2.7 million to fund Tea Party-aligned candidates against moderates in the 2010 congressional primary elections. TPE was behind Scott Brown's shocking win in Massachusetts for the U.S. Senate seat once held by liberal lion Ted Kennedy, and behind Christine O'Donnell's campaign against Mike Castle in Delaware, as well as insurgencies against key establishment figures like Alaska senator Lisa Murkowski, Indiana senator Richard Lugar, and Maine senator Olympia Snowe.[7]

After sending its cadres to Washington, the Tea Party trained its representatives to block compromises between the Republican congressional leadership and the Obama administration. Following its 2010 victory, FreedomWorks chief Dick Armey held a retreat in Baltimore for incoming GOP House members on how to hold fast to small-government principles and avoid being co-opted by the Republican leadership. The Tea Party and allied groups also introduced scorecards to gauge how faithful Republican congressional representatives were to the conservative cause, and it punished moderates accordingly.[8]

These efforts drove a wedge between the Republican leadership and the right wing of the caucus. Tea Party Republicans viewed McConnell with contempt. The Senate leader's nemesis until 2013 was no Democrat (though the president remained his permanent target), but rather South Carolina senator Jim DeMint. DeMint campaigned hard for Tea Party candidates and disrupted the party's national congressional election strategy, including in McConnell's home state of Kentucky, where Rand Paul embarrassed the Senate majority leader by roundly defeating his handpicked choice for the state's other U.S. Senate seat.[9] Even a leader as conservative and intransigent as McConnell was too far to the left for the Tea Party, and so were the majority leader's allies. For instance, Utah senator Bob Bennett, whom journalist Michael

Grunwald calls "a loyal soldier in McConnell's army of No," was pilloried by Tea Partyers as "Bailout Bob" for his support of the bank and auto bailouts and was not allowed to defend his seat in the 2010 primaries.[10]

The Tea Party was therefore a double-edged sword for the GOP. Its multiple and overlapping organizations galvanized the base and breathed new life into a party that some pronounced dead after Barack Obama's victory in 2008. However, the Tea Party also fractured the Republican Party, belittled its leadership, and created room for the emergence of extreme right-wing candidates and activists.

The "birthers" are a case in point. Though racist conspiracy theories about Barack Obama's birthplace emerged as early as 2004 during his run for the U.S. Senate, the Tea Party gave voice and organization to birtherism. According to 2010 American National Election Study (ANES) data, close to half of all Tea Party Republicans identified as birthers, compared to 37 percent of other Republicans and 22 percent of all those polled. The same survey found that upwards of 80 percent of Tea Party supporters evinced negative racial attitudes toward blacks. Indeed, an NAACP report published in the same year as the ANES data observed that racist organizations like the Council of Conservative Citizens had infiltrated the Tea Party.[11]

Donald Trump's alliance with the birthers started in 2011 as he flirted with a presidential bid. On the talk show circuit, he said of President Obama, "I want him to show his birth certificate. There is something on that birth certificate that he doesn't like." Though he decided not to run in 2012, Mr. Trump continued to press the issue in media appearances and social media. A YouGov poll from that year would report that 41 percent of respondents either believed that Mr. Obama was born outside the United States or were not sure.[12]

Although the Republican Party seemed once again on an upward trajectory, the conditions were thus set for organizational division later on. The Tea Party emerged as a challenger instead of an ally to the congressional leadership. It also encouraged the proliferation of antiestablishment right-wing factions like the birthers, some of which were unapologetically racist. Democrats, of course, reacted to these developments with a mixture of glee and horror, but they were hardly in a position to crow, for problems were emerging in their own backyard.

Reabsorption Backfires on the Left

Divisions on the American left emerged in successive waves of revolt, each of which was critical of Barack Obama for abandoning a progressive agenda. The first of these was Occupy Wall Street, a spontaneous grassroots movement that began in New York City with a twenty-thousand-person occupation of Zuccotti Park in the fall of 2011. It was joined by some thirty-nine organizations including the city's largest labor unions and MoveOn.org. The movement touched off 1,600 other occupations in the United States and around the world. Encampments spread not only to Boston, Chicago, Seattle, Houston, Tampa, and Nashville but also to London, Sydney, Cape Town, Tokyo, and São Paolo.[13] Though the various occupations addressed issues that were specific to their context, the common thread tying the worldwide movement together was a rejection of both mounting economic inequality under neoliberalism and the collusion of political and economic elites in the maintenance of that system. New Yorkers Against Budget Cuts (NYABC), one of the organizations that formed the nucleus of the original occupation, put it this way: "We hear it every day: There's no money. No money to keep our senior centers open, pay our teachers, serve the homeless or help college students graduate. There's no revenue to pay for vital services or invest in creating jobs. Well, people across this country have had enough. There is no revenue crisis; there is an inequality crisis."[14]

Because neoliberalism's fundamental assumption is that the market—not the state—will provide, the approach of most Western democracies to the Great Recession was to cut government spending, regulations, and interest rates until the market got back on its feet. NYABC took aim at spending cuts and insisted that the state had more than enough revenue to address the real problem of inequality. Nor was this a matter of movement rhetoric: Occupy's critique of the "1 percent" and defense of the "99 percent" seeped into public discourse and put class inequality on the agenda where it had once been taboo. According to one Nexis survey, within Occupy's first seven weeks the term "income inequality" was cropping up nearly six times as often as it had one week prior to the encampment in Zuccotti Park.[15]

There was of course an empirical basis to the Occupiers' claims. For many regular people, the New New Deal never materialized. Though unemployment had decreased from 2010 until the end of the Obama administration and while the stock market had rebounded, not much had changed for people in the real economy. Median income in the United States was lower in 2017 than it was in 2007 before the Great Recession. Perhaps worse still, labor's (as opposed to Wall Street's) share of gross national product hit a record low during the Obama years: after averaging 70 percent of GNP from 1947 to 2001, labor's share averaged an unprecedented 63 percent from 2010 to 2014.[16]

To the Occupy movement, Barack Obama came to signify all that was wrong with the political and economic system. It signaled this sentiment in two ways: first in expressing disappointment with the president, and second in policing the Democratic Party's attempts to co-opt the movement. As many have observed, a core constituency of the Occupiers were unemployed young people, many of them college graduates with hefty student loan debt. That demographic had gone heavily for Mr. Obama in 2008: 66 percent of voters under thirty years of age voted Democratic in that year—the largest share of the youth vote won by any party since youth exit polling began in 1972.[17] Todd Gitlin observes that this constituency may well have occupied Wall Street sooner but gave "Obama the benefit of the doubt" until they were "dazed by disappointment." As Occupy activist Jeremy Varon said: "This is the Obama generation declaring their independence from the administration. We thought his voice was ours. Now we have to speak for ourselves."[18]

The distrust of President Obama and his party also manifested itself in the Occupiers' "co-optation phobia." Occupy Wall Street declined to wade into the 2012 presidential campaign and routinely rejected politicians seeking to be associated with the grassroots movement. They shooed away not only mainstream Democrats like Representative John Lewis of Georgia or House Speaker Nancy Pelosi but also putative renegades like Elizabeth Warren of Massachusetts. The refusal to associate with the Democratic Party was, for Occupiers, a badge of honor. After Nancy Pelosi publicly urged Democrats "to mobilize the 99 percent," Occupy's Matt Smucker wrote, "The fact that establishment Dems are clamoring to figure out how to co-opt this energy is a serious victory."[19]

The second progressive backlash to the Obama administration came from the Black Lives Matter (BLM) movement, which emerged in 2013 after the killer of unarmed black teenager Trayvon Martin was acquitted. The movement must be understood in relation to Barack Obama's postracial posture. Fully 80 percent of people polled in 2008 believed that the Obama presidency would benefit minorities and the poor, and two-thirds of all eligible black voters cast a ballot in the 2008 presidential election, the highest turnout for that demographic since 1968. But with the high-profile murders of unarmed black men in 2013 and 2014, BLM activists became critical of the president's rhetoric and policies. Rachel Gilmer, associate director of the African American Policy Forum, and Ashley Yates, cofounder of Millennial Activists United, criticized President Obama's "My Brother's Keeper" initiative, which challenged local communities to alleviate their own disadvantage by improving access to vocational training. Gilmer and Yates slammed the initiative for assuming that the violence perpetrated against people of color could somehow be remedied by "fixing" communities of color themselves instead of addressing the wider systemic problem of social inequality.[20]

Mr. Obama's nonsystemic policy prescriptions were consistent with his rhetoric. As early as the 2008 NAACP annual convention, then-senator Obama had lent credence to white stereotypes about the promiscuity of blacks by urging his audience to tell young black men that "responsibility does not end at conception . . . what makes them men is not the ability to have a child but the courage to raise one."[21] Unjustified black anger was another theme in Mr. Obama's message on race. In his response to the killing of Michael Brown in Ferguson, Missouri, in 2014, for instance, the president said that the conflict "requires we listen, and not just shout."[22]

Black Lives Matter activists reacted strongly to Mr. Obama's rhetoric of "Black Blame," which calls upon black people to take responsibility for their own lives, but does not ask the same of whites.[23] In the week after a grand jury failed to indict Michael Brown's killer, an activist and artist from St. Louis, Tef Poe, sent a letter to the president condemning his response:

I speak for a large demographic of us that has long awaited our Black president to speak in a direct tone while condemning our murders. From our perspective, the statement you made on Ferguson completely played into the racist connotations that we are violent, uneducated, welfare-recipient looters. . . . When the president your generation selected does not condemn these attacks, you suddenly begin to believe that this system is a fraudulent hoax—and the joke is on you.[24]

As Tef Poe's scolding suggests, BLM's resistance to Mr. Obama grew more oppositional and evinced a deepening sense of betrayal. In February 2016, Aislinn Pulley, a cofounder of Black Lives Matter Chicago, snubbed President Obama's invitation to the White House. Instead of a constructive dialogue, "what was arranged was basically a photo opportunity and a 90-second sound bite for the president," she said, explaining, "I could not, with any integrity, participate in such a sham that would only serve to legitimize the false narrative that the government is working to end police brutality."[25] That summer, ABC News hosted a town hall on racism and police brutality with the president. When Clifton Kinnie, a nineteen-year-old BLM organizer from Ferguson, Missouri, asked how communities of color could be kept safe, the president exonerated the police, saying, "The police feel as if they are being attacked because we haven't provided them situations in which it's easier for them to do their jobs." BLM cofounder Patrisse Cullors, who attended the town hall, called the event a "shit show" and added that "it was all about apologizing about the cops, it was a mess."[26]

If the Republican establishment's absorption of the New New Deal had inadvertently welcomed extreme factions into its party, then Clinton Democrats' infiltration of the administration alienated those who had voted for Barack Obama in 2008. Younger voters, joined by progressive trade unionists and MoveOn.org, expressed their alienation through Occupy Wall Street, while people of color expressed their break with the Democratic Party through Black Lives Matter. The resulting factionalization formed the backdrop of the 2016 primary elections.

The Republican Primaries

The fight for the Republican nomination began with a crowded field of seventeen candidates. Though the primaries typically dwindle down to one candidate well ahead of the party convention in late spring and early summer of election year, in 2016 the Republican contest became a three-way race with no one clinching a majority of delegates until the bitter end. The leading candidates were Governor John Kasich of Ohio, a moderate and the lone representative of the Republican establishment; Senator Ted Cruz of Texas who represented the social conservative wing of the party; and Donald Trump, the hotel magnate from New York, whose coalition included the Tea Party, birthers, and the white ethnic nationalists of the so-called alt right. Senator Marco Rubio of Florida was a consequential figure, not so much because he was a viable frontrunner but because he was sufficiently popular to draw votes away from his opponents in a highly competitive field; this made him a prospective junior partner in an anti-Trump ticket.

Governor Kasich's claim to the nomination was his experience. Throughout his campaign, which lasted longer than any other candidate's except for Donald Trump's, he touted his long years of public service. As the buzzer sounded on his closing statement at a Republican primary debate in February 2016, the governor said:

> I was chairman of the House Budget Committee and one of the chief architects the last time we balanced a budget, and it was the first time we had done it since man walked on the moon. We had a $5 trillion surplus and we cut taxes. I spent ten years in the private sector, actually learning how business works. And now I'm the governor of Ohio, and I inherited a state that was on the brink of dying. And we turned it all around with jobs and balanced budgets and rising credit and tax cuts, and the state is unified, and people have hope again in Ohio.[27]

A remarkably disciplined candidate, he pivoted consistently to his expertise even in the face of attempts to pull him off message. Asked to speak on immigration, one of Mr. Trump's signature issues, Kasich first admitted that "Donald Trump is hitting a nerve in this country" but then returned to the rationale for his candidacy. "You know, look, I balanced the federal budget as one of the chief architects when I was in Washington," he reminded a debate audience in Cleveland, continuing, "I took the state of Ohio from an $8 billion hole and a 350,000 job loss to a $2 billion surplus and a gain of 350,000 jobs."[28]

Senator Cruz, in contrast to those whom he called "campaign conservatives," billed himself as the only true social conservative in the race. He promised repeatedly to shut down Planned Parenthood, a provider of abortion services, and vowed to preserve the religious liberty of Christians. In Manchester, New Hampshire, he put his religious devotion on display, announcing, "I am blessed to receive a word from God every day in receiving the scriptures and reading the scriptures. And God speaks through the Bible." Offering his own recipe for victory in the next presidential election, Mr. Cruz said: "If we're going to win in 2016, we need a consistent conservative.... And I have been proud to fight and stand for religious liberty, to stand against Planned Parenthood, to defend life for my entire career. And I will be proud to continue to do so as president of the United States."[29]

Donald Trump's message was one of American victimization: the country, like the white constituents he sought to recruit, was being taken advantage of and systematically exploited. Where former president Ronald Reagan called America a "Shining City on a Hill," Mr. Trump repeatedly called the United States a loser. At the first Republican primary debate in August 2015, he ended his closing remarks by saying: "Our country is in serious trouble. We don't win anymore. We don't beat China in trade. We don't beat Japan, with their millions and millions of cars coming into this country, in trade. We can't beat Mexico, at the border or in trade. We can't do anything right."[30]

At the March 2016 primary debate in Detroit, Michigan, he reused the theme of haplessness to agitate on immigration and crime. "I'm playing to the fact that our country is in trouble, that we have a tremendous problem with crime. The border is a disaster, it's a like a piece of Swiss cheese."[31] In the area of national security, America was also the big loser. "Our military is depleted," he said, and yet "we take care of Germany, we take care of Saudi Arabia, we take care of Japan, we take care of South Korea. Saudi Arabia was making a billion dollars a day, and we were getting virtually nothing to protect them." The solution to America's epic decline was Mr. Trump: only he would renegotiate or end the trade deals and treaties that have made America a shadow of its former self. In his closing remarks at the February 2016 primary debate in New Hampshire, he told voters, "Our country that we love so much doesn't win anymore," but when he became president, "we will win, and we will win, and we will win."[32]

The differences among the candidates did not, in and of themselves, make a Trump victory inevitable, but the factionalism they at once signaled and intensified made it difficult to consolidate into one anti-Trump alternative. There were in fact numerous and varied attempts to unite the party against a Trump nomination. As early as the fall of 2015 Republican strategists Alex Castellanos and Gail Gitcho attempted to establish a so-called super PAC with the help of top-shelf donors like casino magnate Sheldon Adelson and hedge fund manager Paul Singer. In February 2016, Maine governor Paul R. LePage urged his colleagues at a governors' meeting to draft an open letter to the American people renouncing Donald Trump.[33]

Meanwhile the campaigns reached out to one another in a bid to join forces, but in each case no candidate recognized the other's authority to lead the party. Senator Rubio, for instance, made an overture to Governor Christie of New Jersey that went awry. According to one person familiar with the meeting, Mr. Christie "took the message as deeply disrespectful and patronizing, questioning why a '44-year-old' was telling him about his future."[34] Ted Cruz likewise approached Mr. Rubio with the idea of a unity ticket in early March, but Rubio rebuffed his Senate colleague. In a bitter postmortem of the encounter, Doug Deason, a Cruz supporter who volunteered to make the approach, said: "Rubio was too pompous to act on it. He believed his own internal polls and there was no swaying him away from staying in the race through the Florida primary."[35]

Among the strongest indications of the establishment's despair was their appeal to Mr. Kasich, their very own candidate, to drop out of the race in order to give Ted Cruz, their nemesis in the Senate, the clearest possible path to the nomination. But Kasich insisted that he could win the Ohio primary on March 15 and unite the party behind his campaign if Marco Rubio lost his home state of Florida on the same day. Republican lawmakers, including Senate majority leader Mitch McConnell, privately vented over Mr. Kasich's intransigence at Senate luncheons. Said one senior Republican senator, "He's just flailing his arms around and having a wonderful time going around the country, and it just drives me up the wall." McConnell himself reportedly thought Kasich's campaign "irrational because he has no plausible path to the nomination."[36]

As the foregoing strategies faltered, Republican elders mounted a last-ditch one-hundred-day campaign in March to deny Mr. Trump the 1,237 delegates needed to clinch the nomination outright. It began with Mitt Romney's speech at the Hinckley Institute on March 3, 2016, twelve days ahead of the Ohio and Florida primaries:

> If the other candidates can find some common ground, I believe we can nominate a person who can win the general election and who will represent the values and policies of conservatism. Given the current delegate selection process, that means that I'd vote for Marco Rubio in Florida and for John Kasich in Ohio and for Ted Cruz or whichever one of the other two contenders has the best chance of beating Mr. Trump in a given state.[37]

When the March 15 primaries left only two alternatives to Mr. Trump, Governor Kasich and Senator Cruz, so-called war councils convened to unite behind one of the candidates. But in a sign of persistent factionalism Republicans could not come to a consensus. Conservative activists were uneasy with the party establishment, while Republican elites, who tended to favor Mr. Kasich, were turned off by the activists' ideological purism.[38] Accordingly, the councils advised the two candidates to get out of each other's way in the respective states where one had a clear advantage over Mr. Trump, and the campaigns agreed among themselves to do so. The strategy appeared to work at first, with Senator Cruz winning Wisconsin as planned, but Kasich later broke the pact by campaigning in states like Indiana and Utah where Cruz was meant to go head-to-head with the frontrunner.

Amid the turmoil of the three-way race for the Republican nomination, still another faction prepared to nominate a third-party candidate who might deny Donald Trump the presidency in the general election. William Kristol, editor of the conservative *Weekly Standard*, circulated a memo detailing a strategy to get an independent candidate on general election ballots across the country. In an interview, Mr. Kristol said, "I think the ballot access question is manageable," but "the big question is, who's the candidate?" In this, the ballot effort seemed to favor former Oklahoma senator Tom Coburn and former Texas governor Rick Perry. Offering his own party as a prospective vehicle for such a strategy, Nicholas Sarwark, executive committee chairman of the national Libertarian Party, hinted that there might be a "late entrant" in that convention.[39]

The sum total of these myriad maneuvers suggests a Republican establishment in crisis. Party elders were unable to impose a candidate on the field and instead were forced to propose a plan whereby two to three alternative candidates might deny Mr. Trump a majority of party delegates. When this strategy, too, failed, conservatives attempted a third-party strategy. Fred Malek, finance chairman of the Republican Governors Association, offered this analysis of the situation: "There's no single leader and no single institution that can bring a diverse group called the Republican Party together, behind a single candidate." South Carolina senator Lindsey Graham likewise remarked, "There's this desire, verging on panic, to consolidate the field," but "I don't see any movement at all."[40]

Mathematically speaking, a unity ticket could have denied Donald Trump the nomination as late as May 2016, a fact that observers both in and outside the party were keen to point out.[41] Together Ted Cruz, John Kasich, and Marco Rubio amassed over 15 million votes, compared to Mr. Trump's 13.3 million votes.[42] Moreover, in the first half of the primary season, from February 1 to mid-April, Mr. Trump's average vote share across thirty-three states was only 34.06 percent. He also tended to lose head-to-head contests. From late April on, however, as the other candidates began to run out of time and money in a stubbornly divided field, Mr. Trump's vote share jumped dramatically to 65.56 percent. The latest research on the Republican primaries demonstrates that although Mr. Trump was the plurality winner (he received less than 50 percent of the total primary vote), he could have been beaten in several pairwise contests.[43] The problem was not electoral math but the factionalization of a once-unified Republican Party.

The Democratic Primaries

Though the Democratic primary field consisted initially of three candidates, including former Maryland governor Martin O'Malley, the race for that nomination very quickly became a head-to-head contest between self-avowed socialist Senator Bernie Sanders of Vermont and Secretary Hillary Clinton of New York. The clash between Sanders and Clinton centered on two reoccurring themes. The first was whether or not Hillary Clinton represented the neoliberal establishment. At first, the Vermont senator was content to blame the establishment without naming names. On January 25, 2016, in a debate at Drake University in Des Moines, Iowa, Sanders said, "The crises that we face as a country today . . . are so serious that we have got to go beyond establishment politics and establishment economics."[44] But just ten days later in Durham, New Hampshire, the senator sharpened his attack. To a question about Clinton's lopsided advantage in endorsements from elected officials, he said: "Yes, Secretary Clinton does represent the establishment. I represent, I hope, ordinary Americans, and by the way, who are not all that enamored with the establishment."[45] In response, Secretary Clinton sought to deny Sanders's claim to the mantle of insurgent. Clinton said, "Senator Sanders is the only person who I think would characterize me, a woman running to be the first woman president, as exemplifying the establishment." She then explained why she was winning the race for endorsements: "People support me because they know me. They know my life's work. They have worked with me and many have also worked with Senator Sanders. And at the end of the day they endorse me because they know I can get things done."[46]

Beyond the subject of endorsements, the theme of establishment politics also became tied to the issue of campaign finance. At a debate in Milwaukee, Wisconsin, on February 11, 2016, Mr. Sanders told viewers that he was "the only candidate up here . . . who has no Super PAC." Instead, his campaign reached out to "working families." In an appeal for donations, he said, "Look, we know things are tough, but if you want to help us go beyond establishment politics, and establishment economics, send us something." This was in direct contrast to Secretary Clinton who, Sanders said, "received 25 million dollars last reporting period, 15 million dollars from Wall Street."[47] To this, Clinton insinuated that by criticizing her use of Super PACs to fund her campaign, Mr. Sanders was in effect criticizing President Obama, who enjoyed widespread support among Democratic primary voters. She responded:

The real issue, I think, that the Senator is injecting into this is that if you had a Super PAC, like President Obama has, which now says it wants to support me . . . if you take donations from Wall Street, you can't be independent. I would just say, I debated then Senator Obama numerous times on stages like this, and he was the recipient of the largest number of Wall Street donations of anybody running on the Democratic side ever.[48]

The second major source of division between the two candidates was trade policy. Senator Sanders uniformly criticized international trade deals like the North American Free Trade Agreement (NAFTA). Secretary Clinton was more supportive of such deals but equivocally so. In Des Moines, Senator Sanders said: "I have understood from day one that our trade policies have cost us . . . millions of decent-paying jobs. I didn't have to think hard about opposing the Transpacific Partnership [TPP]. It took Hillary Clinton a long time to come on board." In Durham, New Hampshire, a debate moderator asked Secretary Clinton to explain why she supported NAFTA in the 1990s, opposed NAFTA in the 2008 presidential race, and then seemed to change her mind on TPP. She responded: "I voted against a multinational trade agreement when I was a senator, the CAFTA [Central American Free Trade Agreement] agreement, because I did not believe it was in the best interests of the workers of America. . . . I did hope that the TPP, negotiated by this [Obama] administration, would put to rest a lot of the concerns that many people have expressed. . . . Once I saw what the outcome was, I opposed it."[49]

Mr. Sanders seemed to press his advantage by highlighting his consistent opposition to past trade agreements and, by implication, Secretary Clinton's inconsistency and disregard for American workers. In Durham, he recalled his reaction to the rising chorus of free trade advocates in the 1990s:

We heard all of the people tell us how many great jobs would be created. I didn't believe that for a second because I understood what the function of NAFTA, CAFTA, PNTR with China, and the TPP is, it's to say to American workers, hey, you are now competing against people in Vietnam who make 56 cents an hour minimum wage. I don't want American workers to compete against people making 56 cents an hour. . . . So do I believe in trade? Of course, I believe in trade. But the current trade agreements over the last 30 years were written *by corporate America, for corporate America*, resulted in the loss of millions of decent-paying jobs, 60,000 factories in America lost since 2001.[50] (emphasis in original)

By the March 6 debate in Flint, Michigan, the Clinton campaign seemed to pivot to a different strategy, one that attacked Sanders's opposition to the 2009 bailout of the big three automakers. When Sanders once again criticized Secretary Clinton for supporting "virtually every one of the disastrous trade agreements written by corporate America," Clinton fired back, taking advantage of Michigan's historic relationship with the auto industry. "In January of 2009, President-Elect Obama asked everybody in Congress to vote for the bailout," she said, pointing out that Sanders "voted against the money that ended up saving the auto industry." Secretary Clinton also stopped running away from NAFTA, suggesting that "in the 1990s, we got 23 million new jobs and incomes went up for everybody."[51]

Sanders's attack on the status quo gained traction in key states that comprised the Democratic establishment's so-called Blue Wall. Bernie Sanders carried both Michigan and Wisconsin, industrial states that should have responded favorably to Clinton's auto bailout pivot. Michigan exit polls revealed that out of 1,601 respondents, Sanders won 55 percent of men, 56 percent of whites, and 54 percent of those earning $30,000–$50,000 a year. Sanders was even more dominant among the same demographics in Wisconsin: there he carried 64 percent of men, 59 percent of whites, and 58 percent of the $30,000–$50,000 income bracket. It bears mention that both Michigan and Wisconsin are "open" primaries, meaning that voters need not be registered Democrats to participate. To the degree that primary election exit polling is predictive, they arguably presage general election dynamics better than "closed" primaries in Blue Wall states like Pennsylvania, where Clinton prevailed.[52]

In addition to foreshadowing weakness in Michigan and Wisconsin specifically, the primary vote tally suggested that the Clinton campaign would have trouble with three constituencies nationally in the general election. First, Bernie Sanders carried 71 percent of voters under the age of thirty, more than the historic 59 percent Mr. Obama won in 2008. Sanders also won the endorsement of the remnants of Occupy Wall Street, whose base as we have seen was among recent college graduates.

Second, the 2016 Democratic primaries gave rise to competing approaches to mainstream politics within the Black Lives Matter movement. One was a critical engagement with the Democratic Party, while another rejected party politics altogether in favor of grassroots mobilization. In a panel organized by the progressive magazine *In These Times*, R. L. Stephens, founder of Orchestrated Pulse and a Minneapolis-based organizer, publicly split with Alicia Grazer, cofounder of the Black Lives Matter Network over the latter's relationship with the Democratic Party. Grazer began the conversation by commending BLM activists for pressing Hillary Clinton in the run-up to the 2016 election on her involvement in the "hyper-incarceration" of black people during her husband's administration. Stephens interjected, "But who cares whether Hillary Clinton feels bad or has a personal reflection about her old policies? Politics is not about a change of heart . . . it's about power here, and I'm not seeing, in any of the rhetoric or any of these examples, real power being built at the ground level for marginalized people."[53] In the end, the Black Lives Matter Network drifted to a position of political independence and refused to endorse any presidential candidate in 2016, firm in the belief that withholding a high-profile endorsement would put pressure on the establishment to address mass incarceration and police brutality.[54]

Third, local unions, state labor federations, and a handful of national unions broke with the wider labor movement and endorsed Bernie Sanders instead of Hillary Clinton. This included the 700,000-member-strong Communications Workers of America (CWA). Although Secretary Clinton could claim the support of the largest unions, including the Service Employees International Union, the American Federal, State, County, and Municipal Employees, and both teachers' unions, it is significant that organized labor began to speak out against their party's leadership. Don Trementozzi, president of CWA Local 1400 in New Hampshire explained his endorsement of Mr. Sanders by alluding to the two-party system's support of neoliberal trade deals: "In our union's recent campaign against the Trans-Pacific Partnership, Bernie was not on the fence—he was helping us lead the fight against a job-killing trade bill backed by Democrats and Republicans alike."[55]

Thus, while the Democratic Party was not beset with a three-way race for the nomination, it was nevertheless weakened by antiestablishment dynamics akin to those roiling the Republican Party. Secretary Clinton's alliance with the party establishment and with corporate America was a central theme in the Democratic primary debates and gained traction in Blue Wall states like Michigan and Wisconsin where Senator Sanders scored surprise victories. Indeed, 2016 was a year in which an avowed socialist became a serious contender for the Democratic nomination. Moreover, dynamics on the ground suggested that Democratic Party support was softer than usual among key constituents in its base, namely young people, African Americans, and union members. If Hillary Clinton enjoyed an advantage over Donald Trump going into the general election, then that advantage would be precarious.

The General Election Campaign

The 2016 presidential race began with two very tense party conventions. The Republicans gathered in Cleveland from July 18 to July 21. Unlike previous conventions, this one could not showcase its past presidents. In a sign of the establishment's break with Donald Trump, the Bushes, who had mounted the party's last two successful White House bids, decided to skip the event. Even dissident factions managed to register their disapproval. Ted Cruz, hardly an establishment figure, refused to endorse the presumptive nominee. Instead, he ominously advised his fellow Republican delegates to "vote their conscience." Though a brokered convention never came to pass, Donald Trump himself gave voice to his isolation from the rest of the Republican field. In his acceptance speech, the hotel-magnate-turned-politician said, "No one knows the system better than me, which is why I alone can fix it." Observers called the speech "dark"; its imagery spoke of a prostrated, humiliated people at risk of losing what little they had left. He said, "Our convention occurs at a moment of crisis for our nation. . . . The attacks on our police, and the terrorism in our cities, threaten our very way of life. Any politician who does not grasp this danger is not fit to lead our country."[56]

The Democratic National Convention in Philadelphia just one week later was a sharp contrast in tone, but its levity masked a similar underlying factional tension. The Democratic establishment was out in force. Presidents

Clinton and Obama had big speaking parts and sat high atop the convention hall, directly facing the podium; President Carter addressed the convention via satellite. The lively optics of the first woman nominee of a major party compared favorably with the opposition's "midnight in America" message. Secretary Clinton reminisced of how much farther she had traveled than her mother in just one generation. "Standing here as my mother's daughter, and my daughter's mother, I'm so happy this day has come," she said, proudly observing, "When any barrier falls in America for anyone it clears the way for everyone." But the Democrats' convention, like the Republicans', was divided. Though Bernie Sanders went out of his way to announce his withdrawal from the race (he was the one who nominated Clinton for the presidency at the convention), factionalism persisted. On Tuesday, July 26, Sanders delegates and supporters from across the United States walked out of the convention, chanting, "This is what democracy looks like!"[57] There might well have been an even bigger showdown had the Clinton campaign not made a series of policy concessions to Sanders ahead of the convention, such as including the abolition of the death penalty on the party platform.[58]

Having accepted their respective parties' nominations, Donald Trump and Hillary Clinton embarked on a general election campaign that can only be described as scandal-ridden. Mr. Trump was the main object of scrutiny in the first month of the race. On August 1, just days after the convention, the Republican nominee picked a fight with a Muslim Gold Star family whose son had been killed in the line of duty. The following week, Mr. Trump seemed to suggest that "second amendment people" assassinate Hillary Clinton for trying to take away their guns. And at the end of August, Donald Trump met with Mexican president Peña-Nieto only to return to the United States to give a strident anti-immigrant speech in Arizona—the diplomatic equivalent of a slap in the face.

Criticism then shifted abruptly to Hillary Clinton. On September 2, the Clinton e-mail controversy resurfaced for the first time since FBI director James Comey exonerated the Democratic nominee on July 5. Once again, Clinton was being asked why she had used a private server to conduct the business of the government as secretary of state. A week later, Hillary Clinton compounded her troubles by making an apparently elitist remark about

Trump supporters: "You know, to just be grossly generalistic, you could put half of Trump's supporters into what I call the basket of deplorables. Right? The racist, sexist, homophobic, xenophobic, Islamophobic—you name it. And unfortunately, there are people like that. And he has lifted them up." Two days later, Clinton, who was then suffering from pneumonia, stumbled at a 9/11 ceremony, giving rise to sexist insinuations, including from Trump himself, that she was physically unfit to be president.[59]

Finally, those expecting an "October Surprise" were treated to two. The first was the release of a 2005 Access Hollywood tape in which Mr. Trump, not knowing he was being recorded, said: "You know, I'm automatically attracted to beautiful women. I just start kissing them. It's like a magnet. You just kiss. I don't even wait. When you're a star they let you do it. You can do anything. Grab 'em by the pussy. You can do anything."[60] The revelation brought fresh denunciations from political elites in both parties, women's groups, and voters on the ground. But just as Mr. Trump's demise seemed imminent, the FBI—on October 28—announced that it would review a new cache of Clinton e-mails from the laptop of Anthony Weiner, the estranged husband of Clinton aide Huma Abedin. Though the FBI reported no wrongdoing on November 7, the day before the election, the media firestorm revived charges of dishonesty and corruption.[61]

All of this was punctuated by three presidential debates, each of which occasioned its own wave of commentary. The first debate, which took place on September 26 in Hempstead, New York, was the most watched presidential debate in American history with some eighty million viewers tuning in. Arguably the most famous exchange was one in which Mr. Trump took Ms. Clinton to task for her support of NAFTA:

TRUMP: All you have to do is look at Michigan and look at Ohio and look at all of these places where so many of their jobs and their companies are just leaving, they're gone. And, Hillary, I'd just ask you this. You've been doing this for 30 years. Why are you just thinking about these solutions right now? . . .

CLINTON: I think my husband did a pretty good job in the 1990s. I think a lot about what worked and how we can make it work again . . .

TRUMP: He approved NAFTA, which is the single worst trade deal ever approved in this country.

CLINTON: Incomes went up for everybody. Manufacturing jobs went up also in the 1990s . . .

TRUMP: Your husband signed NAFTA, which was one of the worst things that ever happened to the manufacturing industry.

CLINTON: Well, that's your opinion. That is your opinion.

TRUMP: You go to New England, you go to Ohio, Pennsylvania, you go anywhere you want, Secretary Clinton, and you will see devastation where manufacture is down 30, 40, sometimes 50 percent.[62]

The second presidential debate, which was held in St. Louis on October 9, was notable for the way the Republican nominee responded to the Access Hollywood controversy. Prior to the debate, Mr. Trump held a press conference with women who claimed that Bill Clinton had sexually harassed them. Perhaps undercutting his denial of the harassment charges, Trump then followed Clinton around the debate stage and threatened to throw her in prison.

The third and last debate took place in Las Vegas on October 19 and was true to the freewheeling ethos of the venue. Donald Trump, pressing his anti-immigrant message, said, "We have some bad hombres here and we're going to get them out."[63] Trump ended the debate refusing to say whether he would concede if he lost the election.[64]

The steady onslaught of scandals, while certainly reinforcing the Democrats' unfavorable impression of the Republican nominee, spoke directly to those who harbored "politically incorrect" sentiments. The attack on the Khan family was a sure sign that Mr. Trump was anti-Muslim; the double-crossing of Peña-Nieto and the allusion to "bad hombres," a clear signal that he was anti-immigrant; and his sexual aggression toward woman, proxy locker-room talk with frustrated straight men in the mass electorate. His Nixon-like allusions to "law and order" in the inner city and his attacks on trade deals like NAFTA rounded out the picture, as these stoked working-class and antiblack sentiment in the nation's suburbs and exurbs. Hillary Clinton only served to confirm these resentments by calling all of the above a "basket of deplorables."

If any of the aforementioned examples were infelicitous slips of the tongue, taken as a whole they nevertheless aligned with the Trump campaign's overall messaging. A Harvard University study of Donald Trump's seventy-three campaign speeches found that immigrants, including undocumented immigrants and Muslim refugees, were described negatively seventy-four times and positively only twelve times. Indeed, immigrants were the group mentioned most during the course of the campaign, with a total of 364 mentions. Allusions to workers were the next most frequent with 217 mentions, and his references to them were overwhelmingly positive.[65]

The Returns

It is one thing to point out the respective parties' messaging and internal divisions but quite another to show that these dynamics translated into shifting voting patterns on the ground. To bridge this gap we now turn to an analysis of the 2016 electoral returns, with a special emphasis on the youth vote, African Americans, and union members, among whom the election was won and lost.

The youth vote's allegiance to Bernie Sanders came back to haunt the Democratic nominee in the general election: though Clinton bested Trump in this demographic, both candidates did poorly overall, as one in ten young voters bucked the establishment and cast their ballots for either Green Party candidate Jill Stein or Libertarian Gary Johnson. Clinton herself observes that Stein carried more votes than the margin of victory in three once reliable Democratic states: Michigan, Wisconsin, and Pennsylvania. For example, the Green Party won 31,000 votes in Wisconsin where Mr. Trump's margin of victory was only 23,000.[66]

In 2008 the Democrats enjoyed a twenty-point advantage among union households, an advantage that slipped slightly as the New New Deal did not materialize in 2012. As the reabsorption of the Obama agenda gave way to a full-scale revolt on the left and right, however, the Democratic advantage among union households fell precipitously. Until 2004, people in union households were much more likely to vote Democrat than those in nonunion households; by 2016, the difference between the union and nonunion household vote decreased to a historic low of 5 percent. This is partly because union density itself is shrinking. Compared to 1964, when unionization rates were well over 30 percent in the Rust Belt, now they are roughly 10 percent, due most recently to "right to work" laws that incentivize workers not to join unions.[67]

Though organized labor still delivered a majority of its ballots to the Democrats, the effect of this defection, especially in the Rust Belt where union density is high relative to the rest of the country, was disastrous for the Democratic Party. The Democrats' electoral advantage from 2008 to 2016 in Wisconsin, Michigan, and Pennsylvania vanished. Barack Obama had defeated John McCain in those states by 1.7 million votes in 2008 and Mitt Romney by 1.07 million; in 2016, Donald Trump carried all three states by a combined total of 77,000 votes.

Given the tight margin, the defection of the union vote was decisive. In Michigan, Hillary Clinton carried union households by sixteen percentage points—considerable, but less than half of the thirty-three-point margin that a weakened Obama posted there in 2012. Especially critical was the vote in Macomb County, a white United Auto Workers suburb. Tracking with the overall sequence of defection, reabsorption, and crisis, Barack Obama carried Macomb 53–45 percent in 2008 and 52–48 in 2012, while Mr. Trump carried it 54–42, or by 48,000 votes. In a state where Trump won by just 10,000 votes, the dramatic vote shift in Macomb was cataclysmic to the Clinton campaign.

The outcome of the 2016 election was in part a class revolt in the upper Midwest. Most of the country came home to their respective parties—fully 91 percent of those who cast ballots in 2016 voted by party identification— but a few dozen midwestern counties defected.[68] Defecting counties had distinctive class profiles. Nationally, the counties that Secretary Clinton carried accounted for most of the country's gross domestic product, whereas the counties that Mr. Trump won accounted for a much smaller share of GDP. This is reflected in the sixteen-point swing from the Democrats to Republicans among those earning less than $30,000 a year, compared to those earning between $100,000 and $199,000 annually, who swung decisively to Secretary Clinton. Indeed, 2016 marked the first time in the history of the modern two-party system that Republicans fared better among poor white voters than they did among affluent whites.[69] Specifically, two types of counties shifted their allegiance from the Democratic to the Republican Party: the few rural counties that were not already solidly Republican, and postindustrial counties. The decline in support from Barack Obama in 2012 to Hillary Clinton in 2016 in eight Rust Belt counties is particularly telling. Macomb County, Michigan, and Lackawanna County, Pennsylvania, both traditional Democratic white working-class strongholds, saw a 15 percent drop in support between 2012 and 2016.[70]

Hillary Clinton's defeat in the upper Midwest also turned on a revolt in the African American community. Black turnout saw a double-digit decline across the Rust Belt. In some cases, like Milwaukee and St. Louis (anchor city to the suburb of Ferguson), the drop was well over 20 percent. Nationally, the black voter turnout rate in a presidential election declined for the first time in two decades. After reaching a record high of 66.6 percent in 2012, turnout fell sharply to 59.6 percent. Meanwhile Latino turnout did not make up for the decline among African Americans: turnout in that sector dropped slightly from 48 percent in 2012 to 47.6 percent in 2016.[71] Black and white poor and working-class midwestern voters thus rejected Ms. Clinton but in different ways. Black folks stayed home, while white folks switched allegiance. The Cooperative Congressional Election Study shows that fully 12 percent of Trump voters had voted for President Obama in 2012.[72]

Survey and polling data suggest that the Republicans' emphasis on trade contributed to the defection. National exit polling reveals that a slightly higher percentage of voters (42%) thought that trade deals took away American jobs rather than created them (39%). Mr. Trump carried 64 percent of those who had an unfavorable opinion of international trade. But the Republican advantage on trade was even larger in the industrial Midwest. A poll conducted by *Politico* and Harvard's Chan School of Public Health in late August and early September reported that midwestern voters were twice as likely (53%) as voters from other regions (roughly a quarter each in the Northeast, the South, and the West) to say that free trade hurt their communities. Donald Trump won these voters by large margins. In Pennsylvania, which had not given its electoral votes to a Republican nominee in a generation, Mr. Trump carried two-thirds of those who were critical of global trade.[73]

Donald Trump's emphasis on race relations also contributed to the defection. The Voter Studies Group, which tracked eight thousand voters between the 2012 and 2016 elections, found that the decisive factors in President Trump's victory were "attitudes about immigration, feelings toward black people and feelings toward Muslims." The American National Election Studies (ANES), the gold standard of survey election research, similarly found that resentment toward these same groups was a strong predictor of Mr. Trump's success. According to the ANES, those who switched their vote from Barack Obama in 2012 to Donald Trump in 2016 on average held more negative views of undocumented immigrants than those who either did not switch parties or switched from the 2012 Republican nominee, Mitt Romney, to Hillary Clinton in 2016. Qualitative data from defecting counties corroborate these findings. Democratic Party pollster Stan Greenberg conducted postelection focus groups in the white UAW suburb of Macomb County, Michigan, whose defection from the Democratic Party was five times Mr. Trump's margin of victory in that state. The key themes of those focus groups, Greenberg found, were "frustration with elites and a rigged political system, and a desire for fundamental change, but also anger at immigrants who compete with them for jobs and don't speak English, fear of Muslims, and resentment of minorities who are seen as collecting more than their fair share of government benefits."[74]

The Question

Rather than tackle the underlying inequalities of our social and economic system head-on, Donald Trump has succeeded in pitting one group of neoliberalism's victims against other victims. Nor is Mr. Trump the only architect of division. The Far Right is on the move elsewhere, from Islamists and Hindu Nationalists in Turkey and India, to neo-Nazis in Europe and the United States. Now that we find ourselves swept up in a global wave of ethnic nationalism, what is to be done? Historians are fond of joking that the future is not their period of expertise, but as scholars and citizens of this world we are bound by duty, if not to predict the future then to help change the path we are presently on if indeed we believe that the times require it. I turn now to the international stage and to the importance and possibility of a coherent progressive alternative to ethnic nationalism.

8

THE PATHS OUT OF CRISIS

In *What Happened,* Hillary Clinton's autobiography of the 2016 election, the Democratic nominee is clear-eyed about the importance of Mr. Trump's election. What is at stake, she writes, is "whether we can heal our democracy and protect it in the future."[1] Interestingly, she looks to the Civil War for guidance on how to press on. Clinton begins her book with a quote from the abolitionist and former slave Harriet Tubman, who gave this advice to travelers on the Underground Railroad:

> If you are tired, keep going.
> If you are scared, keep going.
> If you are hungry, keep going.
> If you want to taste freedom, keep going.[2]

It is perhaps no accident that at this critical moment in American history the leader of the Democratic Party turned to an unsung hero of the movement against slavery. At a personal level, it is an exhortation to persevere through the humiliation of defeat, but at the level of historical significance, it equates 2016 with 1861 as twin crises in the ongoing struggle for freedom.

Since the 2016 election, others have drawn similar parallels between these two moments, but what unites these stories beyond the symbolic is the reactive sequence of events leading to political crisis. In this I break with linear stories that either connect the dots from economic interests to big events, or insist that earlier events lead logically and inexorably to later events. Van Buren's defeat at the 1844 Democratic National Convention did not lead directly to the U.S. Secession Crisis. It was the complex sequence of partisan reactions and counterreactions flowing out of that moment that led to secession and then to the war. Polk's victory in the 1844 Democratic nominating contest was a mandate for Manifest Destiny, an agenda of aggressive colonial expansion that promised landless whites cheap land and a life of economic independence out West. The colonization of what was still northern Mexico then touched off a divisive debate over whether slavery would be permitted in the conquered territories, thereby leaving northern and southern whites alike in landless limbo. This gave the Whig Party an opportunity to contain the dangers posed by Manifest Destiny to the slaveholding republic. The Whigs framed themselves as the champions of the Union and demonized abolitionists and secessionists for threatening to tear the Union apart. However, the Whig reabsorption strategy had the unintended effect of benefiting the Democrats as much as it did the Whigs, and subsequent Democratic victories led the Whigs to overreact and reorganize as the nativist Know Nothing Party. This is when things took a dramatic turn. Antislavery Whigs in the North reorganized as the Republican Party to stop the nativists from distracting the country from the scourge of slavery, while secessionist Democrats stigmatized the Know Nothings as a northern antislavery party. Whigs in Alabama and across the South then abandoned their party to prove their loyalty as southern men. With this stunning act of collective abdication,[3] the Whigs not only removed themselves as the lone obstacle to secession in the South, but also gave rise to the Republican Party, which would make war on the southern rebellion and end the institution of slavery.

Similarly, Hillary Clinton's defeat in 2008 did not lead directly to the election of Donald Trump in 2016. The latter might have been averted had the

Obama administration fulfilled its promise of a New New Deal. Instead, the political establishment absorbed the challenge to postracial neoliberalism and achieved its Pyrrhic victory, on the left with the infiltration of the Obama administration from Clinton Democrats, and on the right with the reactionary obstruction of congressional Republicans and Tea Party operatives. In the years that followed, through action and counteraction, the major parties split into myriad factions and created just enough room for Donald Trump to step into the breach and unite the fragments of the party system with the political program of economic nationalism. That program, together with the Democrats' damaged prestige among young voters, African Americans, and union members, precipitated a defection in the Rust Belt that handed the presidency to a white ethnic nationalist.

These sequences are not just "one damn thing after another": they share a logic and represent a *crisis sequence*, a series of triumphs and reversals whose outcome turns on the failure of the establishment to absorb an existential challenge to its power. The sequences also share a racial logic. For what sets the United States down the road toward crisis in each case is the failure to deliver on the promise of white privilege. In the nineteenth-century debate over whether the colonized western territories would become free or slave, each political party accused the other of denying free white men access to land and a life of economic independence. Likewise, the dispossession of the white working class is a powerful theme in contemporary American politics, because both the New Deal and the postracial neoliberal establishment had promised to maintain whites' privileged access to the best jobs, neighborhoods, and schools. As a result, what is called into question with each crisis of hegemony is a racialized economic order that distributes power and resources unevenly across social groups.

Ethnic Nationalism around the World

The lessons of American politics are applicable outside the United States. As we know, Donald Trump is but one instance of a worldwide phenomenon, though on the international stage we have seen ethnic nationalists form not only successful right-wing parties but also failed and left-wing organizations.[4] In India, the all-important prelude to the rise of Hindu nationalism was the Emergency. In response to growing unrest due to rising food prices and inflation, Indira Gandhi's Congress Party suspended elections from 1975 to 1977, effectively outlawing opposition to its Nehruvian socialist program. The Bharatiya Janata Party (BJP) and its organizational ancestors grew out of that historical moment and pushed the Congress Party out of power, first in 1977 and then in 1998. The Congress Party's center-left coalition attempted to reabsorb the Hindu nationalist challenge by harnessing the energy of the lower castes, whose silent revolution at the turn of the twenty-first century demanded the expansion of affirmative action in government hiring among other so-called reservations. Although the Congress Party was able to take back power from 1999 to 2009, the dynamics of absorption, like those in the United States, eventuated in a BJP-led backlash that framed the Congress's play as an irresponsible populism, one that created a spate of social welfare initiatives even as it dispossessed the poor through a simultaneous program of neoliberalization. Since 2014 the BJP has been the dominant party in India, while the left remains fractured.

Bolivia has likewise experienced a failure of the establishment, but the crisis sequence in that case has led to social democracy. In the 1980s and 1990s, Bolivia's regime undertook a structural adjustment program imposed by the International Monetary Fund and World Bank that reduced the role of the state in stabilizing markets, privatized state-owned industries in oil and gas, and initiated draconian cuts in government spending. This led to an extended period of military dictatorships, mass unrest, civil war, and hyperinflation. Against this backdrop, Evo Morales's Movimiento al Socialismo, or MAS, forged a coalition of indigenous farmers and nonindigenous progressives by promising to end structural adjustment, reform land rights, and thereby "decolonize" the state. Neoliberals attempted to absorb the indigenous challenge by circumventing the MAS through federalism, devolving power down to the states where the old elite still held sway. However, the federalist ploy has thus far failed to arrest the enormous outpouring of support for a progressive response to years of political and economic turmoil.

In Canada, the political establishment absorbed the Reform Party's right-wing challenge. Pierre Elliot Trudeau and the Liberal Party dominated

Canadian politics from the late 1960s to the early 1980s through a distinctive brand of federalism that included multiculturalism, bilingualism (English and French), and a strong social safety net. When Brian Mulroney and the Progressive Conservative Party promised a neoliberal alternative, right-wing constituents in the western provinces of British Columbia and Alberta joined the coalition enthusiastically and helped to elevate Mulroney to power in 1984. But western conservatives broke with the coalition in 1987 as Mulroney appeared to endorse Trudeau-style federalism while also attempting to incorporate Québec as a "distinct society" with certain rights and privileges. The Reform Party campaigned to end any so-called favoritism to linguistic and racial minorities and return the government to the people. Though they saw some success in the 1990s, the mainstream party system systematically blocked the Reformers' expansion into the more populous "must-have" political strongholds of Ontario and Québec. After polling in the single digits in the eastern provinces for over a decade and despite repeated attempts to rehabilitate their image for a more moderate audience, the Reformers merged into and adopted the political program of the Conservative Party in the early 2000s.

These are but three examples of a worldwide phenomenon. We have seen similar challenges to mainstream party systems across Europe, the former Soviet Bloc, and the Middle East. Though ideological orientation and outcome vary, the career of ethnic nationalism in each case turns on the establishment's ability to absorb a challenge to the status quo.[5] Ethnic nationalism, like any insurgent political project, unfolds in sequences of partisan struggle. As the examples suggest, such sequences typically begin with a dominant political project like Nehruvian socialism in India or neoliberalism in the United States that is disrupted by some contingency, often political and economic turmoil. This leads to a challenge to the status quo that the establishment then attempts to absorb. The dynamics of this last stage of partisan struggle are decisive in explaining the rise and fall of what we might call the political center. Where the establishment fails or if its reabsorption strategy backfires, the center falters. Where the establishment suppresses or co-opts the ethnic nationalist challenge, the center holds.

It is of course possible for a country to lurch directly from an unexpected challenge to a brand-new social order, but political elites tend to be more resilient than that. They can be counted on to contain the situation whether through violence or persuasion. Think of the suppression of Islamist groups like the Muslim Brotherhood in Egypt after the Arab Spring revolutions. Assuming that the political class is typically unwilling to relinquish its power after a single challenge (even one so impressive as Tahrir Square), then the dynamics of reabsorption become critical to understanding the origins of ethnic nationalist ascendancy.

Three Paths out of Crisis

Neither the success nor failure of the establishment is the end of history. Life continued after the Civil War, and life will go on long after Donald Trump leaves the White House. This is not to dismiss fears of a protofascist world order but rather to anticipate the road ahead in a constructive and hopeful way. The Italian intellectual Antonio Gramsci once described times like ours as moments of frightening transition. He wrote, "The crisis consists precisely in the fact that the old is dying and the new cannot be born; in this interregnum a great variety of morbid symptoms appear." Some have taken liberties to translate the last phrase more ominously as, "Now is the time of monsters." Americans are living through just such an interregnum now, for if postracial neoliberalism is in crisis, it remains unclear what if anything will replace it.

There are three paths out of crisis. The first is what Gramsci called "Caesarism," which is the path that Italians notoriously took on the way to World War II. This path entails the rise of a charismatic leader, whom people follow in the absence of any other alternative. Such leaders arise when none of the competing political camps have the consent of the people to rule. The second path is one in which the establishment reexerts its influence over the masses by some sleight of hand, whether by changing party names, leaders, or programs, while keeping the underlying political and economic system in place. The third path is a new political program that can unite the broken fragments of the party system behind a progressive alternative.

We do not yet know which path the American people will take. There is of course evidence of the first path. Donald Trump's ego and his thinly veiled sexism and racism pull for a comparison with Mussolini and other fascist strongmen. We have heard this kind of impressionistic analysis from liberal pundits, but it is more telling that conservative analysts have written explicitly in favor of a Caesarist presidency. This suggests that at least for some in the Republican camp, Mr. Trump represents an unavoidable way out of the impasse of contemporary American politics. In an interview with former Bush speechwriter David Frum, the conservative *New York Times* columnist Ross Douthat said:

> I've wondered if the "pre-existing conditions" are now bad enough that there simply isn't going to be, say, a recovery of congressional effectiveness or a return to a healthy left-right dynamic without a kind of Caesarist interlude ... in which a dangerously strong president reshapes his party and the political process in ways that make it possible to pursue the common good again. In other words, Trump is the wrong kind of Caesar, but some version of what he represents, some authoritarianism-skirting leader, might in fact be a necessary figure for our polarized and increasingly dysfunctional politics.[6]

For Douthat, an opinion-maker in the Republican Party, Caesarism is not only a symptom of but also a potential solution for polarization, political dysfunction, and congressional ineffectiveness.

Nor is this point of view isolated to conservative elites like Ross Douthat. Liberal journalist Peter Beinart, in a story about why conservatives are falling for Trump, documented the views of anonymous online writers for the now defunct *Journal of American Greatness*. One contributor, writing under the pseudonym "Decius," wrote: "Caesarism is not tyranny. It is rather a sub-species of absolute monarchy, in which the monarch is not an unjust usurper but the savior of a country with a decayed republican order that can no longer function. . . . Have we not degenerated to the point that we are ready for Caesar?"[7]

Congressional Republicans appear to have made peace with the Caesarist interlude. Despite losing the U.S. House of Representatives to the Democrats in the 2018 midterm elections, the GOP shows no signs of deserting its leader.[8] Even after an embarrassing special election loss in a Pennsylvania House district that went heavily for Mr. Trump in 2016, the GOP blamed its candidate, Rick Saccone, for running a lackluster campaign instead of pinning the loss on voter disenchantment with the president. If anything, the party line went, the president's efforts prevented a more embarrassing loss. Former House Speaker Paul Ryan, who had had public spats with Donald Trump over his racist remarks, went as far as to say, "The president came in and helped close this race and got it to where it is right now."[9]

Conservative support for Caesarism notwithstanding, there is also evidence that the political establishment has succeeded thus far in containing the Trump presidency in certain policy domains. Prior to reaching a compromise on NAFTA with Canada, thirty-six Republican senators, alarmed at early plans to scrap the trade pact altogether, signed a letter urging the president to retain it. The letter reads" "Mr. President, your leadership has jump-started our economy. The recent tax reform bill is already leading to economic success across all industries and the stock market is at record highs. . . . The next step to advance the economy requires that we keep NAFTA in place."[10] The Senate majority whip, Republican John Cornyn of Texas, who signed the letter, explained why he and his colleagues pressed the president on trade. "We wanted to make that point," he said, "because we don't want all the good economic news that's been coming out lately as a result of the regulatory rollback and the tax bill to be negated by economic shock caused by some misstep on NAFTA."[11] Though the president nearly scrapped NAFTA in April 2017, he has thus far refrained from doing so.

The president has bowed to pressure from his party in other policy domains as well. His recent statements on gun control, which appeared to reverse conservative opposition to comprehensive background checks and age limits, have been largely contained.[12] The same can be said of Mr. Trump's unorthodox positions on foreign policy. Though he sought a diplomatic rapprochement with Russia, he stopped pursuing the objective in the face of stiff resistance from the State Department and Congress.[13] All of this is to say nothing of neoliberals occupying high-profile positions in the administration: the (deposed) secretary of state and former ExxonMobil CEO Rex Tillerson, treasury secretary and former Goldman Sachs partner Steven Mnuchin, Council of Economic Advisors chair and Goldman Sachs president Gary Cohn, and commerce secretary and private equity billionaire Wilbur Ross.[14]

The third path out of the crisis is murkier than the other two. The perennial question for the left in the United States has been something like, "What political vehicle can gather the poor, the marginalized, and the oppressed under one progressive banner?" Since the Great Depression, the answer to that question—for the labor movement, the civil rights movement, the antiwar movement, the women's and LGBT movements, and the environmental movement—has been the Democratic Party.

That alliance has no doubt yielded historic victories, but I want to propose another path: a path of political independence. By this I do not mean getting out of institutional politics altogether, but rather focusing on mass mobilization. What if instead of aligning with just one party the American people built a grassroots movement that made the party system as a whole align with their demands for equity and justice? We have already seen an example of what this might look like in the #RedForEd strike wave. Teachers have made state and local legislators across the political spectrum prioritize public education. They did not door-knock or phone-bank for either major party to realize their goals—they went on strike. They built a grassroots movement of rank-and-file teachers to demand not only large wage increases but also a greater commitment to the public sector in general, reversing the trend toward further neoliberalization.

Assuming that the recent strike wave can be replicated on a larger scale, two questions remain unanswered. What will this movement's message be, and who has the capacity and resources to lead?

Economic Democracy

To forge a new hegemonic bloc that can challenge ethnic nationalism, progressives must do two things that they are not currently doing. First, they must offer a vision of society that is neither postracial neoliberalism nor ethnic nationalism. For too long, postracial neoliberalism has avoided the problem of social inequality in all its forms. Neoliberalism's false promise has been that if everyone has individual rights on paper, then everyone should be able to prosper in the market so long as they work hard and take personal responsibility for their own lives. We know that to be patently untrue. Women have the right to vote, but they still earn a fraction of what men make despite having the same qualifications, and they still endure sexual harassment on the job. On paper, black people have the right to due process under the law, but their lives are all too often cut short by a criminal justice system that is stacked against them. There is no law barring queer people from working, but some employers do not offer domestic partner benefits and still others do not include gender identity in their nondiscrimination clauses. Workers have the right to join a union, but employers have broad leeway to intimidate workers into opposing the union, while "right to work" laws deprive workers of the dues money their unions need to rent office space, buy computers, pay staff, and represent their interests effectively.

Ethnic nationalism's answer to the problem of inequality is just as problematic. Donald Trump promises, first, to cancel or modify trade deals like NAFTA that outsource American jobs abroad and, second, to deport undocumented workers who are supposedly stealing jobs from American citizens. The issue of borders and immigration is tied to the alleged influx of terrorists across the American border with Mexico. To the degree that there is a problem with crime, it is not with the police but with the disorder caused by people of color. Mr. Trump has also maintained the innocence of men, including himself, who have been accused of sexual harassment. And the only explicit course of action that Mr. Trump has recommended with respect to the LGBT community is the exclusion of transgendered persons from the military.

The problem with these precepts is twofold: first, they promise to empower only straight white men to the exclusion of all others, and second, even working- and middle-class white men are unlikely to benefit in the long term. Ethnic nationalism assumes that white men are much stronger as a force unto themselves than they would be by working in solidarity with everyone else. Together white men are strong, just as other unified groups can be, but mathematically, as a force for social justice, they are at a disadvantage in comparison to diverse coalitions of multiple groups working toward a common objective.

An alternative to postracial neoliberalism and ethnic nationalism is economic democracy. Economic democracy is the idea that none of us can be free unless all of us have power in the workplace and are key stakeholders in the economy. Today most workplaces are dictatorships: when you go to work, you serve at the will of your employer. Being an "at will" employee forces workers to make tough choices: put up with low wages, disrespect, harassment, homophobia, and racist jokes, or lose your job. More broadly, when workers do not have a seat at the table, the U.S. economy gets structured in such a way that the three richest men have more wealth than the entire bottom half of American society combined. This will only get worse under the new tax plan, which redistributes wealth to the rich in an already profoundly unequal society.[15]

If we are serious about moving beyond neoliberalism and stopping ethnic nationalism in its tracks, then we have no choice but to build another mass movement. In this, the labor movement has an important role to play. The 2016 election turned partly on the disaffection of white and black working-class constituents in the Rust Belt: those who have felt left behind and taken for granted by a Democratic Party that long ago abandoned the idea of a stakeholder economy in favor of neoliberalism. The labor movement is in a unique position to regain the trust and loyalty of union members and join their struggle to that of other groups who are similarly exploited and marginalized. This is true for two reasons.

First, the labor movement has the authority to challenge Donald Trump for promising to bring back the blue-collar jobs that he and others like him have outsourced overseas. Corporate America will never agree to bring those jobs back, and even if they did, there is no guarantee that they would be good jobs. Indeed, those jobs were not "good," because they were mining or manufacturing jobs. Those of us from blue-collar families know that those jobs were back-breaking and mind-numbing. Workers made those jobs good jobs by sticking together in their unions and striking for a better life. The only real path to economic democracy is the path of collective struggle. Workers should not wait for one-percenters to bring back their old jobs: they should turn the bad service-sector jobs that are here—and can't easily be outsourced overseas—into the good jobs of the future. The labor movement can help workers organize their workplaces, negotiate contracts that improve their wages, and start them on the long road toward a more equal society.

Second, though the movement is down and out, the AFL-CIO remains the largest labor federation in the world in sheer numbers, and together with other unions like the Service Employees International Union they are even bigger. Organized labor still has the resources and time to channel its substantial resources toward mass mobilization: to unionize retail giants like Walmart and Amazon and to demand changes to the labor law, such as the repeal of right-to-work laws.

But the labor movement cannot succeed alone, and it must deal with the racial and gender inequalities in its own ranks. For economic democracy is by definition an inclusive idea. When women and people of color endure daily microaggressions on the job, we do not have economic democracy, because they are forced to choose between their jobs and their dignity. When someone or their partner is denied health benefits because they are queer or transgendered, we do not have economic democracy, because that person is effectively excluded from the workplace. Finally, when a supervisor hauls workers into his office and threatens to fire them if they join the union, we do not have economic democracy, because those workers must choose between feeding their families and having rights on the job. All of these struggles are connected, and unless the labor movement joins with other movements to improve the lives of all people, we can never truly have economic democracy.

* * *

People often ask me, "Can Donald Trump win in 2020?" My answer is, "Of course he can." He did it once; he can do it again. But the 2020 question assumes that only politicians can lead us to the promised land. The better question is whether we want something better than what either Mr. Trump or the establishment has to offer. There is an old adage that goes something like this: "*We* are the ones we have been waiting for." Every step toward a more perfect union has come because of movements of abolitionists and African Americans, of women and workers, of immigrants and queer folk. That is also the progressive path out of our present crisis, and anyone who says differently is trying to take the easy way out.

ACKNOWLEDGMENTS

As with all books, this one was a collective undertaking. I am particularly grateful for the assistance of Jessica Lacher-Feldman, Clark E. Center Jr., and Kevin Ray at the Hoole Special Collections Library at the University of Alabama in Tuscaloosa, and Ed Bridges at the Alabama Department of Archives and History in Montgomery. John Quist helped me navigate the Tuscaloosa archives. Mills Thornton was my guide through the hotly contested terrain of antebellum southern history.

I also want to thank those who read the original article manuscript, book proposal, and sample chapter. Those who deserve the most credit are the members of two writing groups. The first writing group consists of my dear friends, colleagues, and students Aisalkyn Botoeva, Diana Graizbord, and Michael Rodriguez-Muñiz. Aisa, Diana, and Michael were graduate students at Brown and are now off doing bigger and better things. I have cherished their honest feedback and company these last several years. My former colleague at Providence College, Trina Vithayathil, who was actually a member of that original crew, cofounded a second writing group that has been an invaluable source of support. Many, many thanks to Kara Cebulko, Orly Clergé, Silvia Dominguez, Zophia Edwards, and Trina. Kara, Zophia, and Trina deserve special thanks for keeping me sane at Providence College through our own mini-crisis; Orly was the one who asked, "Where is Donald Trump in all of this?"

I am grateful to my editor at Stanford University Press, Kate Wahl, for seeing what I saw in this book and for pushing me to be a better writer. Many thanks to Jeffrey Wyneken and Anne Fuzellier, also at Stanford, for their help in the home stretch. My friend and colleague Josh Pacewicz and the anonymous reviewers at the *Journal of Historical Sociology* helped me refine my contribution to this already well-traveled intellectual terrain at the journal article stage. As the project developed further, Barry Eidlin, Poulami Roychowdury, and Sarah Brauner-Otto at McGill University forced me to sharpen my analysis. My research assistant and former student at Providence College, Joanna Riccitelli, did a superlative job collecting and analyzing much of the data that appear in the second half of the book. Mercifully, she also completed the final wave of endnotes and citations. I am grateful to my former colleagues at Tufts University, especially Pawan Dhingra, for giving me the time and space to complete the book in the fall of 2017. My new colleagues at UMass Amherst have made me feel welcome during a complex transition. I owe special thanks to Amel Ahmed, Anna Branch, Dan Clawson, David Cort, Naomi Gerstel, Clare Hammonds, Moon-Kie Jung, Tom Juravich, Jasmine Kerrissey, Jennifer Lundquist, Joya Misra, Fareen Parvez, Ofer Sharone, Don Tomaskovic-Devey, Ana Villalobos, Eve Weinbaum, and Melissa Wooten for advising me and advocating on my behalf. The staff of the Labor Center, Katelyn Dreyer and Julie Rosier, make my work as director of the Labor Center possible.

Several people provided valuable feedback just before I submitted the final draft of the manuscript. I am grateful to the faculty, students, and staff at the Havens Center and Department of Sociology at the University of Wisconsin for inviting me to give a series of lectures based on the book, especially Patrick Barrett, Sara Trongone, Pete Ramand, Erik Olin Wright, Ivan Ermakoff, and Chaeyoon Lim. Fareen Parvez, Amy Schalet, and Ofer Sharone at UMass helped me prepare those lectures.

Last but certainly not least, for putting up with me through another book project, I want to express my love and gratitude to my family: my wife and fellow academic Emily Heaphy, our son Ellis, and our faithful companion Attie. You are my loves and my home.

NOTES

1. Widmer 2005, 145–46.
2. Widmer 2005, 146–47.
3. Greene 2007.
4. Penn 2007.
5. For a review of the research on realignments, see de Leon (2014). For an exception, see Carmines and Stimson (1990), who argue that after a long hiatus in which racial inequality was forced off the public policy radar, political elites like presidents John F. Kennedy and Lyndon B. Johnson, together with the civil rights movement, moved race to the center of party politics in the 1960s.
6. See Ayers (2005).
7. For a review of the research on populism and the Far Right, see Jansen (2011); and Veugelers (1999).
8. Slez and Martin 2007.
9. According to Jim Mahoney, a reactive sequence must have two features. First, in order to avoid the problem of infinite historical regress, the reactive sequence must begin with a contingent event, a breakpoint that could not have been anticipated or predicted. Second, the sequence must have inherent sequentiality. There are three dimensions to inherent sequentiality: events in the sequence are necessary or sufficient conditions for subsequent events; each intermediary event represents a causal mechanism that links an initial breakpoint with a final

outcome; and there is a clear temporal ordering among events in a sequence (Mahoney 2000, 527, 530–31).

10. Pew Research Center 2011.

11. Historian William L. Barney points out that by the end of the 1840s "the lower half of farming families owned 8% of the agricultural wealth," and by 1860 "their share fell to 6%" (Barney 1974, 3–6). Many historians reject the notion that secession and war were due exclusively to the economic interests of social groups and instead emphasize the importance of politicians. Classical accounts include Holt (1978); Randall (1940); and Thornton (1978). However, much of this work suggests that Civil War-era politicians were "irresponsible" or "blundering" agitators. In contrast, I argue that the dramatic triumphs and reversals of party politics that these studies point to foreshadow crises of hegemony.

12. Moore, 1966, 140–41. Similarly, Jonathan Wiener's controversial book, *Social Origins of the New South* (1978), was about how planters were able to stay in power in Alabama from 1850 through the Civil War and Reconstruction. Criticizing C. Vann Woodward's book *Origins of the New South* (1951), he wrote, "The planter elite, in whose interests the war was fought, is the proper starting point," for what occurred after the war "was not the 'downfall' or 'destruction' of the old planter class," as Woodward argued, "but rather its persistence" (Wiener 1978, 4–5). Around the same time, the sociologist Dwight Billings argued that "the civil war was the political expression of a conflict between aristocratic tendencies and planter interest on the one hand and the acquisitive middle class capitalism of the North on the other" (Billings 1979, 3).

13. Weingast 1998, 151–52.

14. Carpenter 2000, 660–62.

15. See McCurry (1995, 239–40).

16. Budros 2011.

17. de Leon 2015; Hacker 2011.

18. For a review of the literature, see Woods (2012). See also Huston (2006). My own position mirrors Elizabeth Varon's (2008) distinction between the overarching cause of the war (slavery) and the political twists and turns that precipitated the Civil War. A halfway point between interest-based approaches and my own is Meadwell and Anderson's (2008) emphasis on both "sequence and strategy in the secession of the American South." On their account, radical secessionists planned a "chain reaction" in which early seceders like South Carolina and Alabama would pressure laggards to secede later, once the Confederacy was established outside the Union.

Although I agree that we must think of the run-up to secession as a sequence, I see at least two gaps in their story. First, Meadwell and Anderson pay insufficient attention to the sequence of internal political maneuvers in states other than South Carolina. In particular they ignore the problem of defeating the Whig Party, which was the last remaining political obstacle to secession across the South. Even in South Carolina, which Meadwell and Anderson call the vanguard of the Southern Rights cause—the tip of the spear—former Whigs and Unionists roundly defeated the secessionists in an October 1851 election to choose delegates to a Southern Congress (Ford 1988, 205–6; Meadwell and Anderson 2008, 205–10).

Second, Meadwell and Anderson assume that the chain reaction occurred because Southern Rights advocates planned it that way. The problem is that resistance to secession was a plan, too, and until the mid-1850s quite a successful one at that. The question therefore remains why that resistance failed in 1861.

19.   Of course, there is significant debate on the trend lines of immigration, inequality, and other demographic shifts. Some researchers tell the opposite story of *mounting* economic inequality, for example, but because this too is a continuous trend, it remains difficult to discern where along the trend line the seeds of ethnic nationalism are supposed to have taken root and where they flowered.

20.   Ellis 2005, 176; Global Terrorism Database 2017; World Bank 2017.

21.   Judis 2016.

22.   Bivens et al. 2014.

23.   Similarly, Berezin (2009) traces right-wing populism to the European Union, which she argues compromised the economic security that ordinary Europeans used to feel in their individual nations; in doing so, the new economic order gave rise to a rhetoric of fear and insecurity. This is a plausible and indeed convincing account of the rise of the Far Right in Europe, but it is silent on two issues. First, and this is in part because the book was written a few years too early, it does not explain why the Far Right is now *winning* instead of *emerging* as important third parties. Second, Berezin's account is less focused on the political parties whose rhetoric and policies built and maintained popular support for the European Union and who now appear to be losing ground.

24.   Hochschild 2016.

25.   See, for example, Carmines and Stimson (1990); Paulson (2000); and Poole and Rosenthal (1997). The problem of timing also applies to those proclaiming a worldwide "culture shift." Ron Inglehart (1977; 1990), for example, argues that by shielding workers from the worst effects of capitalism (e.g., unemployment,

infant mortality), the welfare state gave rise to "postmaterialist" values, principles based less on class inequality and power, and more on personal well-being and environmental protection. This then generated a new division or "cleavage" between Far Right anti-postmaterialist parties on one side, and postmaterialist parties (e.g., the Greens) on the other. The first problem with this approach, as with other reflection theories, is once again timing. Assuming that Inglehart and his colleagues are correct, then the postmaterial "culture shift" has been underway for quite some time. Why has the Far Right just come to power? A second and related problem is the assumption that the culture shift has created a polarized political landscape pitting parties that represent old and new values. There is little acknowledgment that parties themselves play an active role in cultivating and politicizing values that divide the electorate (Veugelers 1999). For a similar approach, see Ignazi (1992).

26. See, for example, Ayers (2003); Holt (2004); Lankford (2007); Silbey (2007); and Varon (2008).

27. See Kitschelt (1995). For other approaches that are sensitive to institutional politics, see Veugelers (1999); and Schain, Zolberg, and Hossay (2002).

28. See especially de Leon, Desai, and Tuğal (2015).

29. de Leon 2017; Mahoney 2000; Pierson 2000.

30. Davis 1980; de Leon 2015; Montgomery 1979.

31. Glanton 2017.

CHAPTER 2

1. de Leon 2015.

2. Fraser and Gordon 1994.

3. Ashworth 1983; Blau 1954; de Leon 2015; Sellers 1991; Thornton 1978; Watson 1981; Watson 1990; Wilentz 2005; Wilson 1974.

4. Monroe 1959, 32–33.

5. Clay 1982 [1820], 766.

6. Adams 1951 [1820], 229.

7. Aldrich 1995, 112.

8. Crapol 2006, 177–78.

9. de Leon 2015, 38; Eyal 2007, 148; Jentz and Schneirov 2012, 2; Johnson 2013, 3; Lebergott 1961, 292; Nelson and Sheriff 2008, 12.

10. Morrison 1997, 17.

11. *Chicago Democrat*, February 21, 1844.

12. Breese 1844, 23.

13. Eyal 2007, 46–49, 117.

14. Widmer 2005, 149.

15. Van Buren 1844.

16. Merry 2009, 85; Niven 1983, 531; Widmer 2005, 149–50.

17. Widmer 2005, 150.

18. Van Buren 1973 [1920], 226–27.

19. Van Buren 1973 [1920], 226–27.

20. Varon 2008, 166–67.

21. Crapol 2006, 218; Niven 1983, 535.

22. Merry 2009, 1, 81–82, 84.

23. Niven 1983, 535.

24. Niven 1983, 535.

25. Merry 2009, 83.

26. Widmer 2005, 150.

27. Merry 2009, 84; Niven 1983, 536.

28. Merry 2009, 85–86.

29. Merry 2009, 86–87; Niven 1983, 537.

30. Merry 2009, 88; Niven 1983, 538.

31. Merry 2009, 89.

32. Merry 2009, 92–94; Niven 1983, 539–40.

33. Niven 1983, 540; Widmer 2005, 150.

34. Varon 2008, 169–72.

35. Widmer 2005, 151.

36. Morrison 1997, 29.

37. *Independent Monitor*, September 24, 1844.

38. *Independent Monitor*, June 18, 1845.

39. de Leon 2008; de Leon 2015; Holt 1999; Howe 1979; Quist 1996; Thornton 1978; Wilson 1974.

40. Quist 1996, 510.

41. Thornton 1978, 167–68.

42. de Leon 2015, 34; Holt 1999, 29; Quist 1996, 511.

43. *Independent Monitor*, September 4, 1844.

44. *Independent Monitor*, November 17, 1846.

45. Varon 2008, 171–72; Wilson 1974.

46. Owen 1921, 814.

47.   Henry Hilliard, "The War with Mexico: A Speech Delivered in the House of Representatives of the United States, January 5th, 1847," in Hilliard (1855), 105–6.

48.   Yancey 1845.

49.   *Independent Monitor*, September 4, 1844; Owen 1921, 411.

50.   Owen 1921, 1597.

51.   Jemison 1844, 902.

52.   County returns in this period were reported by rural "beat" or precinct, usually a general store, mill, or government building. The Whigs dominated the wealthier western half of the county, while the Democrats controlled the poorer, less populous east. The beats were further organized into quadrants. The planter strongholds were concentrated in the southwest quadrant, where the town of Tuscaloosa was located. Planters also owned the best farmland in the northwest portion of the county. The Democratic Party dominated the rest of the county, where the quality of the soil was middling to poor, where access to ground water was limited, and where fewer people, mostly small farmers and herdsmen, lived and worked.

53.   Alabama Department of Archives and History 1840; *Democratic Gazette*, November 14, 1844.

CHAPTER 3

1.   de Leon 2015; Eyal 2007, 123; Feller 2001, 67–68; Leonard 2002, 253–54; Merry 2009, 286–87; Morrison 1997, 39–41, 124; Varon 2008, 182; Yancey 1848.

2.   Morrison 1997, 37–38; Varon 2008, 175.

3.   Morrison 1997, 39; Varon 2008, 180–81.

4.   Morrison 1997, 68–69.

5.   Eyal 2007, 133.

6.   Varon 2008, 193.

7.   Morrison 1997, 45, 53.

8.   Morrison 1997, 98.

9.   Morrison 1997, 54.

10.   Morrison 1997, 54–57.

11.   Morrison 1997, 54.

12.   Morrison 1997, 59.

13.   Varon 2008, 191.

14.   Morrison 1997, 98.

15.   Morrison 1997, 60.

16. Morrison 1997, 86, 93.

17. Morrison 19967, 84; Varon 2008, 193.

18. Varon 2008, 194.

19. Morrison 1997, 84.

20. Morrison 1997, 99–100.

21. Varon 2008, 194–95.

22. Morrison 1997, 61, 99.

23. Holt 1999, 320–21, 323.

24. Holt 1999, 322–23.

25. Holt 1999, 324.

26. Holt 1999, 324–325.

27. Holt 1999, 325–26, 330.

28. Holt 1999, 326.

29. Morrison 1997, 95.

30. Morrison 1997, 100–106.

31. Morrison 1997, 108.

32. Varon 2008, 225.

33. Morrison 1997, 124.

34. de Leon 2015, 58–59; Fehrenbacher 1957, 117–18.

35. Varon 2008, 223–24.

36. Varon 2008, 224.

37. Varon 2008, 224.

38. Varon 2008, 227–28.

39. Ford 1988, 224–25.

40. Ford 1988, 204.

41. Ford 1988, 203–4.

42. Ford 1988, 198.

43. Ford 1988, 201.

44. Owen 1921, 854.

45. Hubbard 1850, 1, 6.

46. Hubbard 1850, 6.

47. Hilliard 1855, 224.

48. Thornton 1978, 180.

49. Dorman 1995 [1935], 49.

50. Hilliard 1855, 238.

51. Thornton 1978, 183, 186–87, 192–95.

52. Dorman 1995 [1935], 58–60, 64, 65, 67, 184; Thornton 1978, 183, 186–87, 192–95.

53. Yancey 1848.

54. Lewis 1848, 176–77.

55. Collier 1849.

56. Morrison 1997, 125.

57. Holt 1999, 324–25.

58. Yancey 1851.

CHAPTER 4

1. Morrison 1997, 140.

2. Morrison 1997, 142–43.

3. Gienapp 1987, 70–71.

4. Gienapp 1987, 71, 74.

5. Gienapp 1987, 77–78; Morrison 1997, 153–56.

6. de Leon 2015, 61–62; Morrison 1997, 205–6; Nichols 1948, 161, 171–75.

7. Morrison 1997, 197; Nichols 1948, 129–30, 218–20.

8. Nichols 1948, 217.

9. Gienapp 1987, 82.

10. Gienapp 1987, 83.

11. Gienapp 1987, 92–99.

12. Holt 1999, 907–8; Howe 1979, 248–49.

13. Howe 1979, 202.

14. Howe 1979, 203.

15. Howe 1979, 203.

16. Howe 1979, 278; de Leon 2015, 67. Later, in the run-up to the presidential election of 1860, Lincoln worked behind the scenes to write a proimmigrant plank into the Illinois Republican platform.

17. Holt 1999, 909–10.

18. Anbinder 1992, 44, 100.

19. Anbinder 1992, 106.

20. Anbinder 1992, 45.

21. Anbinder 1992, 66.

22. Holt 1999, 909–10.

23. Holt 1999, 908, 916.

24. Holt 1999, 925, 926, 928, 929.

25. Holt 1999, 929–31.

26. Holt 1999, 932.

27. Holt 1999, 932.

28. Holt 1999, 934, 939.

29. de Leon 2015; Holt 1999, 940–41, 943, 945, 947.

30. Holt 1999, 949.

31. Holt 1999, 965–66.

32. Holt 1999, 966.

33. Holt 1999, 976–77.

34. Holt 1999, 979; Morrison 1997, 185–87; Nichols 1948, 48.

35. Holt 1999, 981.

36. Holt 1999, 983.

37. The 1860 Republican National Convention in Chicago was itself a sectional third-party insurgency, so by definition there was no need to overcome the establishment.

38. Nichols 1948, 264–66.

39. Morrison 1997, 220, 224; Nichols 1948, 305, 308.

40. Morrison 1997, 226–27; Nichols 1948, 319.

41. Nichols 1948, 318.

42. Morrison 1997, 206.

43. Nichols 1948, 340.

44. Nichols 1948, 338, 347, 364.

45. Morrison 1997, 251; Nichols 1948, 370–71.

46. Nichols 1948, 387–91.

47. Nichols 1948, 402.

48. Nichols 1948, 409.

49. Nichols 1948, 410.

50. Nichols 1948, 429.

51. Nichols 1948, 431.

52. Nichols 1948, 431–32, 438.

53. Nichols 1948, 436.

54. Nichols 1948, 468–69.

55. Johannsen 1997 [1973], 820, 822, 825, 826.

56. Johannsen 1997 [1973], 826; Morris 2008, 213–14.

57. Nichols 1948, 456.

58. Nichols 1948, 505–6; Potter 1965 [1942], 371–75.

59. Potter 1965 [1942], 374.

60. Nichols 1948, 510. The remaining slaveholding states, Delaware, Maryland, Kentucky, and Missouri, voted to stay in the Union.

61. Dorman 1995 [1935], 176–92.

62. Democratic and Anti-Know-Nothing Party 1856.

63. Hilliard 1892, 276.

64. Dorman 1995 [1935], 141, 170, 173; Thornton 1978, 360–64.

65. Thornton 1978, 360–63.

66. Quist 1996, 496.

67. Quist 1998, 199–200.

68. Dorman 1995 [1935], 184–85.

69. *Independent Monitor*, November 9, 1860.

70. Nichols 1948, 252, 362.

71. Yancey 1860, 15.

72. Thornton 1978, 395–96.

73. Thornton 1978, 404, 409, 413–14.

74. Nichols 1948, 418; Thornton 1978, 426.

75. Smith 1861, 24–25.

76. Smith 1861, 26.

77. Smith 1861, 304.

78. Smith 1861, 97–98.

79. Barney 1974; Owen 1921, 902; Smith 1861, 97–98, 118–19.

CHAPTER 5

1. Bernstein 1970, 1; Gieske 1979, 131–32; Leuchtenberg 1963, 1, 19.

2. Leuchtenberg 1963, 19.

3. Leuchtenberg 1963, 19, 38–39.

4. Cohen 1990, 289; Leuchtenberg 1963, 2–3, 23, 52, 53.

5. Leuchtenberg 1963, 19–21.

6. Leuchtenberg 1963, 21–23.

7. Leuchtenberg 1963, 30.

8. Leuchtenberg 1963, 24, 51.

9. Leuchtenberg 1963, 24, 56.

10. Bubka 1970, 43–44.

11. Bubka 1970, 45–50.

12. Bubka 1979, 45–50, 52.

13. Bernstein 1979, 15.

14. Leuchtenberg 1963, 27.

15. Leuchtenberg 1963, 16–17.

16. Leuchtenberg 1963, 13.

17. Leuchtenberg 1963, 15.

18. Bernstein 1979, 3; Oestreicher 1988, 1273, 1281.

19. Eidlin 2016, 498; Leuchtenberg 1963, 5.

20. Eidlin 2016, 498; Leuchtenberg 1963, 6–7.

21. Leuchtenberg 1963, 9–11.

22. Eidlin 2016, 500; Kelley 1990; Oestreicher 1988, 1276.

23. See, for example, Finegold and Skocpol (1984).

24. Leuchtenberg 1963, 41.

25. Leuchtenberg 1963, 42–45.

26. Leuchtenberg 1963, 47.

27. Eidlin 2016, 500–501.

28. Cohen 1990; Leuchtenberg 1963, 53.

29. Leuchtenberg 1963, 52–53.

30. Leuchtenberg 1963, 57–58.

31. Bernstein 1970, 34; McFarland 1972, 402.

32. Bernstein 1970, 31–32, 34.

33. Bernstein 1970, 172–73.

34. Bernstein 1970, 217; Goldfield 1989, 172; Kolin 2017, 167–74.

35. Bernstein 1970, 308–9.

36. Bernstein 1970, 312–13; Kolin 2017, 174.

37. National Labor Relations Board 1985, 2789.

38. National Labor Relations Board 1985, 2342.

39. Montgomery 1979, 164.

40. Davis 1980, 52–53; Eidlin 2016, 501.

41. Davis 1980, 53; McFarland 1972, 402.

42. Davin 1996, 143–45.

43. Davis 1980, 53.

44. McFarland 1972, 407.

45. McFarland 1972, 411.

46. McFarland 1972, 402, 404, 412.

47. Davis 1980, 58, 60.

48. Lovin 1971, 25–26; Delton 2002, 17.

49. Eidlin 2016, 502–3; McCoy 1957, 89–90, 92.

50. Montgomery 1979, 163–66, 169–70.

51. Katznelson 2005.

52. Cohen 2003, 195; Jackson 1985, 203–18; de Leon 2011, 86–87.

53. Frymer 1999, 95–96.

54. de Leon 2011, 87–88; Frymer 1999, 94–95; Lassiter 2006, 229.

55. Scholars refer to the moderate racism of this period as "colorblind racism." See, for example, Bonilla-Silva (2003); and Lassiter (2006).

56. Agartan and de Leon 2016, 220–39.

57. See Arnold (2016), 34.

58. Congressional Budget Office 2011.

59. Wacquant 2009.

CHAPTER 6

1. Bureau of Labor Statistics 2012; Danziger, Chavez, and Cumberworth 2012, 1; Center on Budget and Policy Priorities 2017; Fronstin 2010, 6, 7, 9, 15; Mishel et al. 2012, 420; Pew Research Center 2011.

2. Borbely 2009, 4, 8, 9, 13; Danziger, Chavez, and Cumberworth 2012, 1; Lichtenstein and Weber 2015, 4, 6, 10; Mishel et al. 2012, 420.

3. *Guardian* 2009; McKinley 2009.

4. Brotman 2009.

5. Morgenson 2008.

6. *CBS News* 2008.

7. Farley and Holan 2008.

8. Dunbar and Donald 2009.

9. Frank 2016, 139–41.

10. Obama 2008a.

11. Obama 2008b.

12. Obama 2008c.

13. de Leon 2011.

14. White House Press Office 2009.

15. Krugman 2008.

16. Beinart 2008.

17. Grunwald 2012, 11.

18. Mahtesian 2008.

19. U.S. Census Bureau 2007; U.S. Census Bureau 2009.

20. *USA Today*, November 5, 2008.

21. Philpot, Shaw, and McGowen 2009, 998.

22. *Indianapolis Star*, April 21, 2008; July 25, 2008; July 26, 2008; November 9, 2008.

23. U.S. Census Bureau 2007; U.S. Census Bureau 2009.

24. Seelye 2008.

25. Philpot, Shaw, and McGowen 2009, 998.

26. de Leon 2011, 96–97.

27. According to U.S. Census data, the percentage of whites in all four counties either increased or remained constant between 2000 and 2009. If the in-migration of nonwhites played a role in North Carolina (which I do not deny), then they do not appear to have played a role in these four counties. It is possible that the in-migration of northern whites played a role, but substantial white migration to the Sunbelt has been ongoing since 1938. See, for example, Schulman 1991.

28. *Charlotte Observer*, November 6, 2008; U.S. Census Bureau 2009.

29. *News and Observer*, November 8, 2008; U.S. Census Bureau 2009.

30. Pew Research Center 2008.

31. Frymer 1999, 5.

32. Atler 2010, 19, 47, 52, 55, 57, 64.

33. Grunwald 2012, 77.

34. Grunwald 2012, 100–101.

35. Grunwald 2012, 111, 115.

36. Suskind 2011, 181.

37. Suskind 2011, 96.

38. Suskind 2011, 218–19.

39. Suskind 2011, 218–19.

40. Committee for a Responsible Federal Budget 2009; Lee Teslik 2009.

41. Obama 2010.

42. Atler 2010, 86; Frank 2016, 147–48; Suskind 2011, 220, 301.

43. Green 2011; Grunwald and Alarkon 2012.

44. Green 2011.

45. Green 2011.

46. Green 2011.

47. Kessler 2017.

48. Skocpol and Williamson 2012, 31.

49. Skocpol and Williamson 2012, 66, 69, 73–74.

50. Skocpol and Williamson 2012, 10, 103.

51. Skocpol and Williamson 2012, 10, 131–32, 135.

52. Heaney and Rojas 2015, 218–19; Skocpol and Williamson 2012, 9–10, 60, 62, 68–69, 170.

53. Jilani 2011.

54. *Democracy Now* 2011.

55. *Democracy Now* 2011.

56. *New York Times* 2012a.

57. Draper 2013; Stolberg and McIntire 2013.

58. Draper 2013.

59. Draper 2013.

60. Stolberg and McIntire 2013.

61. Pew Research Center 2015.

62. See Bonikowski (2017), S181–S213.

CHAPTER 7

1. Clinton 2017, 383.

2. Clinton 2017, 385.

3. Clinton 2017, 386.

4. Lightman 2016.

5. Kilgore 2017.

6. Skocpol and Williamson 2012, 169–70.

7. Skocpol and Williamson 2012, 107.

8. Skocpol and Williamson 2012, 173.

9. Green 2011.

10. Grunwald and Alarkon 2012.

11. Abramowitz 2012, 195–211; Lowndes 2012, 157.

12. Klinkner et al. 2013.

13. Klein 2011; Sharlet 2011.

14. Gitlin 2012.

15. Gitlin 2012, 50–51.

16. Figura and Ratner 2015.

17. Pew Research Center 2008.

18. Gitlin 2012, 27. Similarly, at an Occupy meeting at Providence College, where I was a sociology professor, a local leader of Occupy Wall Street revealed that he had campaigned for Mr. Obama in 2008 but soon realized that he was "a gutless wonder."

19. Gitlin 2012, 155.

20. Peterson-Smith 2015; Taylor 2016, 140.

21. de Leon 2011, 93; Obama 2008d.

22. Peterson-Smith 2015.

23. Price 2016, 35.

24. Taylor 2016, 135–36.

25. Rhodan 2016a.

26. Craven 2016.

27. American Presidency Project [n.d.].

28. American Presidency Project [n.d.].

29. American Presidency Project [n.d.].

30. American Presidency Project [n.d.].

31. American Presidency Project [n.d.].

32. American Presidency Project [n.d.].

33. Burns, Haberman, and Martin 2016.

34. Burns, Haberman, and Martin 2016.

35. Isenstadt 2016.

36. Burns, Haberman, and Martin 2016.

37. *New York Times* 2016a.

38. Burns and Martin 2016.

39. Burns and Martin 2016.

40. Burns, Haberman, and Martin 2016.

41. Funke 2016; Silver 2016; Tapper 2016.

42. Real Clear Politics 2017.

43. Kurrild-Klitgaard 2017.

44. American Presidency Project [n.d.].

45. American Presidency Project [n.d.].

46. American Presidency Project [n.d.].

47. American Presidency Project [n.d.].

48. American Presidency Project [n.d.].

49. American Presidency Project [n.d.].

50. American Presidency Project [n.d.].

51. American Presidency Project [n.d.].

52. *CNN* 2016.

53. Fletcher 2015.

54. *Democracy Now* 2016.

55. feelthebern.org [n.d.]; Gass 2016; Jamieson 2016; laborforbernie.org [n.d.];
McGill 2016; Moburg 2016.

56. Healy and Martin 2016.

57. Rhodan 2016b.

58. Nicholas and Lee 2016.

59. Gambino and Pankhania 2016.

60. *New York Times* 2016b.

61. Gambino and Pankhania 2016.

62. Blake 2016.

63. Rhodan 2016c.

64. *Daily Beast* 2016.

65. Lamont, Park, and Ayala-Hurtado 2017, S158, S160.

66. Clinton 2017, 400; Dutton, De Pinto, and Backus 2016; Mosendz 2016.

67. de Leon 2015; McQuarrie 2017, S139.

68. McQuarrie 2017, S122, S146.

69. McQuarrie 2017, S123–S124.

70. McQuarrie 2017, S126.

71. Krogstad and Lopez 2017.

72. McQuarrie 2017, S127.

73. Blendon, Casey, and Benson 2017, 5.

74. Clinton 2017, 412, 416–17; Klinkner 2017.

CHAPTER 8

1. Clinton 2017, xii.

2. Clinton 2017, viii.

3. Ermakoff 2008.

4. Desai and de Leon 2017.

5. Desai and de Leon 2017.

6. Douthat and Frum 2018.

7. Beinart 2016.

8. Hulse 2018.

9. Hulse 2018.

10. Werner and Lynch 2018.

11. Cassella, Kim, and Behsudi 2018.

12. Hulse 2018.

13. Brands 2018, 160–61.

14. Harris et al. 2017, 483.

15. Collins and Hoxie 2017.

REFERENCES

Abbott, Andrew. 1988. "Transcending General Linear Reality." *Sociological Theory* 6 (2): 169–86.

Abramowitz, Alan I. 2012. "Grand Old Tea Party: Partisan Polarization and the Rise of the Tea Party Movement." In *Steep: The Precipitous Rise of the Tea Party*, edited by Lawrence Rosenthal and Christine Trost, 195–211. Berkeley: University of California Press.

Abramson, Alana. 2016. "How Donald Trump Perpetuated the 'Birther' Movement for Years." *ABC News*, September 16. http://abcnews.go.com/Politics/donald-trump-perpetuated-birther-movement-years/story?id=42138176

Adams, John Quincy. 1951 [1820]. *The Memoirs of John Quincy Adams, Comprising Portions of His Diary from 1795–1848.* New York: Scribner's.

Agartan, Kaan, and Cedric de Leon. 2016. "Interns and Infidels: The Transformation of Work and Citizenship in Turkey and the United States under Neo-liberalism." *Global Labour* 7 (3): 220–39.

Alabama Department of Archives and History. 1840. "Returns of the vote for the Electors of the President & Vice President of the U.S. in Alabama 1840."Alabama Department of Archives and History, Montgomery.

Aldrich, John H. 1995. *Why Parties? The Origin and Transformation of Political Parties in America.* Chicago: University of Chicago Press.

American Presidency Project. [n.d.]. "Presidential Debates." Debate transcripts. Retrieved June 15, 2018. www.presidency.ucsb.edu/debates.php

Anbinder, Tyler G. 1992. *Nativism and Slavery: The Northern Know Nothings and the Politics of the 1850s*. Oxford: Oxford University Press.

Arnold, Colin P. 2016. "Talking Trade: The Discursive Evolution and Divisive Articulation of Trade in American Politics." Unpublished manuscript. University of Virginia.

Ashworth, John. 1983. *"Agrarians" and "Aristocrats": Party Political Ideology in the United States, 1837–1846*. London: Royal Historical Society; Atlantic Highlands, NJ: Humanities Press.

Atler, Jonathan. 2010. *The Promise: President Obama, Year One*. New York: Simon & Schuster.

Ayers, Edward L. 2003. *In the Presence of Mine Enemies: War in the Heart of America, 1859–1863*. New York: Norton.

———. 2005. *What Caused the Civil War? Reflections on the South and Southern History*. New York: Norton.

Barney, William L. 1974. *The Secessionist Impulse, Alabama and Mississippi in 1860*. Princeton: Princeton University Press.

Beard, Charles A., and Mary R. Beard. 1927. *The Rise of American Civilization*. New York: Macmillan.

Beinart, Peter. 2008. "The New Liberal Order." *Time*, November 24. search.ebscohost.com/login.aspx?direct=true&db=aph&AN=35289855&site=ehost-live

———. 2016. "Why Are Some Conservative Thinkers Falling for Trump?" *The Atlantic*, September. www.theatlantic.com/magazine/archive/2016/09/trumps-intellectuals/492752/

Berezin, Mabel. 2009. *Illiberal Politics in Neoliberal Times: Culture, Security, and Populism in the New Europe*. Cambridge: Cambridge University Press.

Bernstein, Irving. 1970. *Turbulent Years: A History of the American Worker, 1933–1941*. Boston: Houghton Mifflin.

Billings, Dwight B., Jr. 1979. *Planters and the Making of a "New South": Class, Politics, and Development in North Carolina, 1865–1900*. Chapel Hill: University of North Carolina Press.

Bivens, Josh, Elise Gould, Lawrence Mishel, and Heidi Shierholz. 2014. "Raising America's Pay: Why It's Our Central Economic Policy Challenge." Washington, DC: Economic Policy Institute. www.epi.org/publication/raising-americas-pay/

Blake, Aaron. 2016. "The First Trump-Clinton Presidential Debate Transcript, Annotated," *Washington Post*, September 26. www.washingtonpost.com/news/the-fix/wp/2016/09/26/the-first-trump-clinton-presidential-debate-transcript-annotated/?utm_term=.4a8cbcc2d7eb

Blau, Joseph L. 1954. *Social Theories of Jacksonian Democracy: Representative Writings of the Period, 1825–1850*. New York: Liberal Arts Press.

Blendon, Robert J., Logan S. Casey, and John M. Benson. 2017. "Public Opinion and Trump's Jobs and Trade Policies." *Challenge* 60 (4): 1–17.

Bonikowski, Bart. 2017. "Ethno-nationalist Populism and the Mobilization of Collective Resentment." *British Journal of Sociology* 68 (S1): S181–S213.

Bonilla-Silva, Eduardo. 2003. *Racism without Racists: Color-Blind Racism and the Persistence of Racial Inequality in the United States*. Lanham, MD: Rowman & Littlefield.

Borbely, James Marschall. 2009. "U.S. Labor Market in 2008: Economy in Recession." Bureau of Labor Statistics. www.bls.gov/opub/mlr/2009/03/art1full.pdf

Borneman, Walter R. 2008. *Polk: The Man Who Transformed the Presidency and America*. New York: Random House.

Brands, Hal. 2018. *American Grand Strategy in the Age of Trump*. Washington, DC: Brookings Institution Press.

Breese, Sidney. 1844. "Speech of Mr. Breese, of Illinois, on the Oregon Territory: delivered in the United States Senate, February 27, 1844. Washington: Printed at the Globe Office." Library collection of the Chicago History Museum.

Brotman, Barbara. 2009. "Surviving the Recession: One Family's Story." *Chicago Tribune*, May 15. www.chicagotribune.com/business/yourmoney/chi-051909 -recession-lead-story.html

Bubka, Tony. 1970. "The Harlan County Coal Strike of 1931." *Labor History* 11 (1): 41–57.

Budros, Art. 2011. "Explaining the First Emancipation: Social Movements and Abolition in the US North, 1776–1804." *Mobilization* 16 (4): 439–54.

Bump, Philip. 2016. "Donald Trump Got Reagan-Like Support from Union Households." *Washington Post*, November 10. www.washingtonpost.com/news /the-fix/wp/2016/11/10/donald-trump-got-reagan-like-support-from-union-households/?utm_term=.a11057b032a1

Bureau of Labor Statistics. 2012. "The Recession of 2007–2009." www.bls.gov/spotlight /2012/recession/pdf/recession_bls_spotlight.pdf

Burns, Alexander, Maggie Haberman, and Jonathan Martin. 2016. "Inside the Republican Party's Desperate Mission to Stop Donald Trump." *New York Times*, February 27. www.nytimes.com/2016/02/28/us/politics/donald-trump-republican-party.html

———, and Jonathan Martin. 2016. "Facing Long Odds, G.O.P. Leaders Map Strategy to Derail Trump." *New York Times*, March 20. Academic OneFile. www.nytimes .com/2016/02/28/us/politics/donald-trump-republican-party.html

Carmines, Edward G., and James A. Stimson. 1990. *Issue Evolution: Race and the Transformation of American Politics*. Princeton: Princeton University Press.

Carpenter, Daniel P. 2000. "Commentary: What Is the Marginal Value of Analytic Narratives?" *Social Science History* 24 (4): 653–67.

Carson, E. Ann. 2014. "Prisoners in 2013." *Bureau of Justice Statistics Bulletin*, September. www.bjs.gov/content/pub/pdf/p13.pdf

Cassella, Megan, Seung Min Kim, and Adam Behsudi. 2018. "GOP Senators Push Trump on Trade." *Politico*, February 7. www.politico.com/story/2018/02/07/trump-trade-republican-senators-330024

CBS News. 2008. "McCain Blames Recession on Wall St." *60 Minutes*, September 21. www.cbsnews.com/news/mccain-blames-recession-on-wall-st/

Center on Budget and Policy Priorities. 2017. "Chart Book: The Legacy of the Great Recession." www.cbpp.org/research/economy/chart-book-the-legacy-of-the-great-recession

Clay, Henry. 1982 [1820]. "To Adam Beatty, Washington, January 22, 1820." In *The Papers of Henry Clay*, vol. 2, *The Rising Statesman, 1815–1820*, edited by James F. Hopkins, 766. Lexington: University of Kentucky Press.

Clinton, Hillary Rodham. 2017. *What Happened*. New York: Simon & Schuster.

Clinton, Matthew W. 1958. *Tuscaloosa, Alabama: Its Early Days, 1816–1865*. Tuscaloosa: Zonta Club.

CNN. 2016. "Election 2016: Primaries and Caucuses." edition.cnn.com/election/primaries

Cohen, Lizabeth. 1990. *Making a New Deal*. Cambridge: Cambridge University Press.

———. 2003. *A Consumers' Republic: The Politics of Mass Consumption in Postwar America*. New York: Knopf.

Collier, Henry W. 1849. "To the Hon. Jere. Clemens, H. W. Hilliard, David Hubbard, S. W. Inge, Sampson W. Harris, Wm. J. Alston, and F. W. Bowdon," December 22. H. W. Collier Papers. 1849 Administrative Files, SG014793, Folder 1. Alabama Department of Archives and History, Montgomery.

Collins, Chuck, and Josh Hoxie. 2017. "Billionaire Bonanza: The Forbes 400 and the Rest of Us." Institute for Policy Studies. https://inequality.org/wp-content/uploads/2017/11/BILLIONAIRE-BONANZA-2017-Embargoed.pdf

Committee for a Responsible Federal Budget. 2009. "Analysis of the American Recovery and Reinvestment Act." www.crfb.org/sites/default/files/documents/StimulusAnalysis.pdf

Congressional Budget Office. 2011. "Trends in the Distribution of Household Income between 1979 and 2007." www.cbo.gov/publication/42729

Converse, Philip E. 2006. "Researching Electoral Politics." *American Political Science Review* 100 (4): 605–12.

Crapol, Edward P. 2006. *John Tyler: The Accidental President*. Chapel Hill: University of North Carolina Press.

Craven, Julia. 2016. "People Aren't Too Happy about President Obama's Town Hall on Race." *Huffington Post*, July 15. www.huffingtonpost.com/entry/obama-race-town-hall_us_578844e0e4b08608d333f057

Daily Beast. 2016. "Trump: Hillary Clinton's a 'Nasty Woman.'" October 19. www.thedailybeast.com/trump-hillary-clintons-a-nasty-woman

Danziger, Sheldon, Koji Chavez, and Erin Cumberworth. 2012. *Poverty and the Great Recession*. Stanford: Stanford Center on Poverty and Inequality.

Davin, Eric Leif. 1996. "The Very Last Hurrah? The Defeat of the Labor Party Idea, 1934–36." In *"We Are All Leaders": The Alternative Unionism of the Early 1930s*, edited by Staughton Lynd, 117–71. Urbana: University of Illinois Press.

Davis, Mike. 1980. "The Barren Marriage of American Labour and the Democratic Party." *New Left Review* 124 (November–December): 43–84.

de Leon, Cedric. 2008. "'No Bourgeois Mass Party, No Democracy': The Missing Link in Barrington Moore's American Civil War." *Political Power and Social Theory* 19: 39–82.

———. 2011. "The More Things Change: A Gramscian Genealogy of Barack Obama's 'Post-Racial' Politics, 1932–2008." *Political Power and Social Theory* 22: 75–104.

———. 2014. *Party and Society: Reconstructing a Sociology of Democratic Party Politics*. Cambridge: Polity.

———. 2015. *The Origins of Right to Work: Antilabor Democracy in Nineteenth-Century Chicago*. Ithaca: Cornell University Press.

———. 2017. "The Crisis Sequence: The Case of Secessionism in Tuscaloosa County, Alabama." *Journal of Historical Sociology* 30 (3): 518–44.

———, Manali Desai, and Cihan Tuğal (eds.). 2015. *Building Blocs: How Parties Organize Society*. Stanford: Stanford University Press.

Delton, Jennifer A. 2002. *Making Minnesota Liberal: Civil Rights and the Transformation of the Democratic Party*. Minneapolis: University of Minnesota Press.

Democracy Now. 2011. "Cornel West and Tavis Smiley on Obama: 'Many of Us Are Exploring Other Possibilities in Coming Election.'" *Democracy Now*, August 9. www.democracynow.org/2011/8/9/cornel_west_tavis_smiley_on_obama

————. 2016. "We Endorse No One: Black Lives Matter and the 2016 Presidential Race." *Democracy Now*, February 9. democracynow.org/2016/2/9/we_endorse_no_one_black_lives

Democratic and Anti-Know-Nothing Party. 1856. "Official Proceedings of the Democratic and Anti-Know-Nothing State Convention of Alabama, held in the city of Montgomery, January 8th and 9th, 1856." William Lowndes Yancey Papers, 1834–1941, Alabama Department of Archives and History, Montgomery.

Desai, Manali, and Cedric de Leon. 2017. "A Sequential Analysis of Right, Left, and Failed Ethnic Nationalisms." Paper presented at "The Lineages of the People: Embedded and Transregional Histories of Contemporary Populism," Social Science Research Council and the University of Göttingen, August 18, Göttingen, Germany.

Dorman, Lewy. 1995 [1935]. *Party Politics in Alabama from 1850 through 1860*. Tuscaloosa: University of Alabama Press.

Douthat, Ross, and David Frum. 2018. "Has the U.S. Become a 'Trumpocracy'?" *New York Times*, January 23. www.nytimes.com/2018/01/23/opinion/david-frum-trumpocracy.html

Draper, Robert. 2013. "The War Within." *Politico*, November. www.politico.com/magazine/story/2013/11/war-within-shutdown-tea-party-robert-draper-099378

Dunbar, John, and David Donald. 2009. "The Roots of the Financial Crisis: Who Is to Blame?" Center for Public Integrity, May 6. www.publicintegrity.org/2009/05/06/5449/roots-financial-crisis-who-blame

Dutton, Sarah, Jennifer De Pinto, and Fred Backus. 2016. "Who's Voting in the Democratic Primaries?" *CBS News*, May 17. www.cbsnews.com/news/democratic-primary-electorate-key-findings-from-the-exit-polls/

Eidlin, Barry. 2016. "Why Is There No Labor Party in the United States? Political Articulation and the Canadian Comparison, 1932–1948." *American Sociological Review* 81 (3): 488–516.

Ellis, Faron. 2005. *The Limits of Participation: Members and Leaders in Canada's Reform Party*. Calgary: University of Calgary Press.

Ermakoff, Ivan. 2008. *Ruling Oneself Out: A Theory of Collective Abdications*. Durham: Duke University Press.

Eyal, Yonatan. 2007. *The Young America Movement and the Transformation of the Democratic Party, 1828–1861*. New York: Cambridge University Press.

Farley, Robert, and Angie Drobnic Holan. 2008. "What Caused Crisis? No One Thing." *Politifact*, November 30. www.politifact.com/truth-o-meter/article/2008/nov/30/what-caused-crisis-no-one-thing/

Federal Election Commission. 2008. "2008 Presidential Popular Vote Summary for All Candidates Listed on at Least One State Ballot." https://transition.fec.gov /pubrec/fe2008/tables2008.pdf

feelthebern.org. [n.d.]. "Endorsements for Bernie Sanders." Retrieved December 6, 2017. http://feelthebern.org/endorsements-for-bernie-sanders/

Fehrenbacher, Don E. 1957. *Chicago Giant: A Biography of "Long John" Wentworth.* Madison: American History Research Center.

Feller, Daniel. 2001. "A Brother in Arms: Benjamin Tappan and the Antislavery Democracy." *Journal of American History* 88 (1): 48–74.

Figura, Andrew, and David Ratner. 2015. "The Labor Share of Income and Equilibrium Employment." *FEDS Notes*, June 8. Board of Governors of the Federal Reserve System. www.federalreserve.gov/econresdata/notes/feds-notes/2015 /labor-share-of-income-and-equilibrium-unemployment-20150608.html

Finegold, Kenneth, and Theda Skocpol. 1984. "State, Party, and Industry: From Business Recovery to the Wagner Act in America's New Deal." In *State Making and Social Movements: Essays in History and Theory*, edited by Charles Bright and Susan Harding, 159–92. Ann Arbor: University of Michigan Press.

Fletcher, Bill, Jr. 2015. "From Hashtag to Strategy: The Growing Pains of Black Lives Matter." *In These Times*, September 23. http://inthesetimes.com/article/18394 /from-hashtag-to-strategy-the-growing-pains-of-blacklives-matter

Foner, Eric. 1970. *Free Soil, Free Labor, Free Men: The Ideology of the Republican Party before the Civil War.* Oxford: Oxford University Press.

Ford, Lacy K. 1988. *Origins of Southern Radicalism: The South Carolina Upcountry, 1800–1860.* New York: Oxford University Press.

Frank, Thomas. 2016. *Listen, Liberal: Or, What Ever Happened to the Party of the People?* New York: Metropolitan Books.

Fraser, Nancy, and Linda Gordon. 1994. "A Genealogy of Dependency: Tracing a Keyword of the U.S. Welfare State." *Signs* 19 (2): 33–58.

Freehling, William W. 2001. *The South vs. The South: How Anti-Confederate Southerners Shaped the Course of the Civil War.* Oxford: Oxford University Press.

Fronstin, Paul. 2010. "The Impact of the Recession on Employee-Based Health Coverage." Employee Benefit Research Institute. www.ebri.org/pdf/briefspdf /EBRI_IB_05-2010_No342_Recssn-HlthBns.pdf

Frymer, Paul. 1999. *Uneasy Alliances: Race and Party Competition in America.* Princeton: Princeton University Press.

Funke, Jonathan. 2016. "Why Marco Rubio Should Join Forces with John Kasich as a

VP Candidate." *Fortune*, March 3. http://fortune.com/2016/03/03/marco-rubio-vp-john-kasich-trump/

Gambino, Lauren, and Madhvi Pankhania. 2016. "How We Got Here: A Complete Timeline of 2016's Historic US Election." *Guardian*, November 8. www.the guardian.com/us-news/2016/nov/07/us-election-2016-complete-timeline -clinton-trump-president

Gass, Nick. 2016. "Sanders Snags Another Union Endorsement." *Politico*, April 24. www.politico.com/blogs/2016-dem-primary-live-updates-and-results/2016/04 /sanders-snags-another-union-endorsement-222357

Gienapp, William E. 1987. *The Origins of the Republican Party, 1852–1856*. Oxford: Oxford University Press.

Gieske, Millard L. 1979. *Minnesota Farmer-Laborism: The Third-Party Alternative*. Minneapolis: University of Minnesota Press.

Gitlin, Todd. 2012. *Occupy Nation: The Roots, the Spirit, and the Promise of Occupy Wall Street*. New York: HarperCollins.

Glanton, Dahleen. 2017. "Thanks, Mr. Trump, for Reminding Us of Lessons from the Civil War." *Chicago Tribune*, May 2. www.chicagotribune.com/news/columnists /glanton/ct-trump-civil-war-glanton-20170501-column.html

Global Terrorism Database. 2017. "Search the Database." University of Maryland. www.start.umd.edu/gtd/

Goldfield, Michael. 1989. "Worker Insurgency, Radical Organization, and New Deal Labor Legislation." *American Political Science Review* 83 (4): 1257–82.

Goodwin, Joe. 1974. *The Place-Names of Tuscaloosa County, Alabama*. Center for Southern Regional Folklife Studies, University of Alabama, Tuscaloosa.

Gramsci, Antonio. 1971. *Selections from the Prison Notebooks of Antonio Gramsci*. New York: International.

Green, Joshua. 2011. "Strict Obstructionist." *The Atlantic*, January/February. www .theatlantic.com/magazine/archive/2011/01/strictobstructionist/308344/

Greene, Richard Allen. 2007. "Hillary the Inevitable." *Politico*, July 9. www.politico. com/blogs/ben-smith/2007/07/hillary-the-inevitable-002123

Grunwald, Michael. 2012. *The New New Deal: The Hidden Story of Change in the Obama Era*. New York: Simon & Schuster.

———, and Walter Alarkon. 2012. "The Party of No." *Time*, September 3. search.ebsco host.com/login.aspx?direct=true&db=aph&AN=79387874&site=ehost-live

Guardian. 2009. "US Tent Cities Highlight New Realities as Recession Wears On." March 26. www.theguardian.com/world/2009/mar/26/tent-city-california -recession-economy

Hacker, J. David. 2011. "A Census-Based Count of the Civil War Dead." *Civil War History* 57 (4): 307–48.

Harris, Jerry, Carl Davidson, Bill Fletcher, and Paul Harris. 2017. "Trump and American Fascism," *International Critical Thought* 7 (4): 476–92.

Healy, Patrick, and Jonathan Martin. 2016. "His Tone Dark, Donald Trump Takes G.O.P. Mantle," *New York Times*, July 21. www.nytimes.com/2016/07/22/us/politics/donald-trump-rnc-speech.html?login=email&auth=login-email

Heaney, Michael T., and Fabio Rojas. 2015. *Party in the Street: The Antiwar Movement and the Democratic Party after 9/11.* New York: Cambridge University Press.

Hilliard, Henry. 1855. *Speeches and Addresses by Henry W. Hilliard.* New York: Harper and Brothers.

———. 1892. *Politics and Pen Pictures at Home and Abroad.* New York: G. P. Putnam's Sons.

Hochschild, Arlie. 2016. *Strangers in Their Own Land: Anger and Mourning on the American Right.* New York: New Press.

Holt, Michael F. 1978. *The Political Crisis of the 1850s.* New York: Wiley.

———. 1999. *The Rise and Fall of the American Whig Party: Jacksonian Politics and the Onset of the Civil War.* Oxford: Oxford University Press.

———. 2004. *The Fate of Their Country: Politicians, Slavery Extension, and the Coming of the Civil War.* New York: Hill and Wang.

Howe, Daniel W. 1979. *The Political Culture of the American Whigs.* Chicago: University of Chicago Press.

Hubbard, David. 1850. "The Territorial Question: Speech of Hon. David Hubbard of Alabama, in the House of Representatives, Thursday, June 6, 1850." Washington, DC: Congressional Globe Office.

Hulse, Carl. 2018. "Facing a Democratic Wave, Republicans Refuse to Throw Trump Overboard." *New York Times*, March 15. www.nytimes.com/2018/03/15/us/politics/trump-congressional-republicans-midterms.html

Huston, James. 2006. "Review: Interpreting the Causation Sequence: The Meaning of the Events Leading to the Civil War." *Reviews in American History* 34 (3): 324–31.

Ignazi, Piero. 1992. "The Silent Counter-Revolution: Hypotheses on the Emergence of Extreme Right-Wing Parties in Europe." *European Journal of Political Research* 22 (1): 3–34.

Inglehart, Ronald. 1977. *The Silent Revolution: Changing Values and Political Styles among Western Publics.* Princeton: Princeton University Press.

———. 1990. *Culture Shift in Advanced Industrial Society.* Princeton: Princeton University Press.

Isenstadt, Alex. 2016. "Marco Rubio Rejected 'Unity Ticket' with Ted Cruz." *Politico*, March 21. www.politico.com/story/2016/03/exclusive-marco-rubio-rejected -unity-ticket-with-ted-cruz-221066

Jackson, Kenneth T. 1985. *Crabgrass Frontier: The Suburbanization of the United States*. New York: Oxford University Press.

Jamieson, Dave. 2016. "Another Major Union Just Endorsed Bernie Sanders." *Huffington Post*, March 14. www.huffingtonpost.com/entry/bernie-sanders -amalgamated-transit-union_us_56c6151ee4b0c3c550541c2a

Jansen, Robert S. 2011. "Populist Mobilization: A New Theoretical Approach." *Sociological Theory* 29 (2): 75–96.

Jemison, Robert, Jr. 1844. "To Mr. Clay." Robert Jemison Jr. Papers, 1797–1973. Hoole Special Collections Library, Tuscaloosa, Alabama.

Jentz, John B., and Richard Schneirov. 2012. *Chicago in the Age of Capital: Class, Politics, and Democracy during the Civil War and Reconstruction*. Urbana: University of Illinois Press.

Jilani, Zaid. 2011. "Bernie Sanders Says It Would Be a 'Good Idea' to Primary President Obama." Washington, DC: Think Progress. https://thinkprogress.org /bernie-sanders-says-it-would-be-a-good-idea-to-primary-presidentobama -313b4f05f3c1/

Johannsen, Robert W. 1997 [1973]. *Stephen A. Douglas*. Urbana: University of Illinois Press.

Johnson, Walter. 2013. *River of Dark Dreams: Slavery and Empire in the Cotton Kingdom*. Cambridge: Belknap Press of Harvard University Press.

Judis, John B. 2016. *The Populist Explosion: How the Great Recession Transformed American and European Politics*. New York: Columbia Global Reports.

Katznelson, Ira. 2005. *When Affirmative Actions Was White: An Untold History of Racial Inequality in Twentieth-Century America*. New York: Norton.

Kelley, Robin. 1990. *Hammer and Hoe: Alabama Communists during the Great Depression*. Chapel Hill: University of North Carolina Press.

Kessler, Glenn. 2017. "When Did Mitch McConnell Say He Wanted to Make Obama a One-Term President?" *Washington Post*, January 11. www.washingtonpost. com/news/fact-checker/wp/2017/01/11/when-did-mitch-mcconnellsay-he-wanted-to-make-obama-a-one-term-president/?utm_term=.54f274723df3

Kilgore, Ed. 2017. "GOP Senator Explains Party's Disarray: Nobody Expected Trump to Win." *New York Magazine*, July 6. http://nymag.com/daily/intelligencer/2017/07 /senator-explains-gop-disarray-nobody-expected-trump-to-win.html

Kitschelt, Herbert. 1995. *The Radical Right in Western Europe: A Comparative Analysis*. Ann Arbor: University of Michigan Press.

Klein, Rick. 2011. "Democrats Seek to Own 'Occupy Wall Street' Movement." *ABC News*, October 10. http://abcnews.go.com/Politics/democratsseek-occupy-wall-street-movement/story?id=14701337

Klinkner, Philip. 2017. "Anti-immigrant Views Helped Trump Win: Will They Also Cause His Undoing?" *Chicago Tribune*, April 18. www.chicagotribune.com/news/opinion/commentary/ct-trump-supporters-anti-immigrant-20170418-story.html

———, Nicholas Anastasi, Jack Cartwright, Matthew Creeden, Will Rusche, Jesse Stinebring, and Hashem Zikry. 2013. *The 2012 Election and the Sources of Partisan Polarization: A Survey of American Political Attitudes*. Clinton, NY: Arthur Levitt Public Affairs Center at Hamilton College. www.hamilton.edu/documents/HamiltonSurvey.pdf

Kolin, Andrew. 2017. *Political Economy of Labor Repression in the United States*. Lanham, MD: Lexington.

Krogstad, Jens Manuel, and Mark Hugo Lopez. 2017. "Black Voter Turnout Fell in 2016, Even as a Record Number of Americans Cast Ballots." Pew Research Center, May 12. www.pewresearch.org/fact-tank/2017/05/12/black-voter-turnout-fell-in-2016-even-as-a-record-number-of-americans-cast-ballots/

Krugman, Paul. 2008. "Franklin Delano Obama?" *New York Times*, November 10. www.nytimes.com/2008/11/10/opinion/10krugman.html

Kurrild-Klitgaard, Peter. 2017. "Trump, Condorcet and Borda: Voting Paradoxes in the 2016 Republican Presidential Primaries." *European Journal of Political Economy* 50 (December). https://doi.org/10.1016/j.ejpoleco.2017.10.003

laborforbernie.org. [n.d.]. "What Trade Unionists Are Saying." Retrieved December 6, 2017. www.laborforbernie.org/#unionists

Lamont, Michele, Bo Yun Park, and Elena Ayala-Hurtado. 2017. "Trump's Electoral Speeches and His Appeal to the American White Working Class." *British Journal of Sociology* 68 (S1): S153–S180.

Lankford, Nelson D. 2007. *Cry Havoc! The Crooked Road to Civil War, 1861*. New York: Penguin.

Lassiter, Matthew D. 2006. *The Silent Majority: Suburban Politics in the Sunbelt South*. Princeton: Princeton University Press.

Lebergott, Stanley. 1961. "The Pattern of Employment since 1800." In *American Economic History*, edited Seymour E. Harris, 281–310. New York: McGraw-Hill.

Leonard, Gerald. 2002. *The Invention of Party Politics: Federalism, Popular Sovereignty, and Constitutional Development in Jacksonian Illinois*. Chapel Hill: University of North Carolina Press.

Leuchtenberg, William E. 1963. *Franklin D. Roosevelt and the New Deal*. New York: Harper and Row.

Lewis, Dixon H. 1848. "My Dear Yancey." William Lowndes Yancey Papers—LPR 87. Box 1, Folder 2: Correspondence—Political, 1844–1860. Alabama Department of Archives and History, Montgomery.

Lichtenstein, Bronwen, and Joe Weber. 2015. "Women Foreclosed: A Gender Analysis of Housing Loss in the US Deep South." *Sociology and Cultural Geography* 16 (1): 1–21.

Lightman, David. 2016. "McConnell: 'I Didn't Think President Trump Had a Chance of Winning.'" *McClatchy DC*, December 20. www.mcclatchydc.com/news/politics-government/article121970954.html

Lovin, Hugh T. 1971. "The Fall of the Farmer-Labor Parties, 1936–38." *Pacific Northwest Quarterly* 62 (1): 16–26.

Lowndes, Joseph. 2012. "The Past and Future of Race in the Tea Party Movement." In *Steep: The Precipitous Rise of the Tea Party*, edited by Lawrence Rosenthal and Christine Trost, 152–70. Berkeley: University of California Press.

Lynch, Denis Tilden. 1929. *An Epoch and a Man: Martin Van Buren and His Times*. New York: Horace Liveright.

Mahoney, James. 2000. "Path Dependence in Historical Sociology." *Theory and Society* 29 (4): 507–48.

Mahtesian, Charles. 2008. "Obama Gains in Fastest Growing Counties." *Politico*, November 9. www.politico.com/story/2008/11/obama-gains-in-fast-growing-counties-015456

McCoy, Donald R. 1957. "The National Progressives of America, 1938." *Mississippi Valley Historical Review* 44 (1): 75–93.

McCurry, Stephanie. 1995. *Master of Small Worlds: Yeoman Households, Gender Relations, and the Political Culture of the Antebellum South Carolina Low Country*. New York: Oxford University Press.

McFarland, C. K. 1972. "Coalition of Convenience: Lewis and Roosevelt, 1933–1940." *Labor History* 13 (3): 400–414.

McGill, Andrew. 2016. "Bernie Sanders, Union-Buster." *The Atlantic*, April 17. www.theatlantic.com/politics/archive/2016/04/bernie-sanders-union-local-endorsement-labor/478527/

McKinley, Jesse. 2009. "Cities Deal with a Surge in Shantytowns." *New York Times*, March 25. www.nytimes.com/2009/03/26/us/26tents.html

McQuarrie, Michael. 2017. "The Revolt of the Rustbelt: Place and Politics in the Age of Anger." *British Journal of Sociology* 68 (S1): S120–S152.

Meadwell, Hudson, and Lawrence M. Anderson. 2008. "Sequence and Strategy in the Secession of the American South." *Theory and Society* 37 (3): 199–227.

Merry, Robert W. 2009. *A Country of Vast Designs: James K. Polk, the Mexican War, and the Conquest of the American Continent*. New York: Simon & Schuster.

Mishel, Lawrence, Josh Bivens, Elise Gould, and Heidi Shierholz. 2012. "Poverty: The Great Recession Adds Injury to Insult." In *The State of Working America*, 419–54. Ithaca: Cornell University Press. www.jstor.org.ezproxy.library.tufts .edu/stable/10.7591/j.cttq42t8.10

Moburg, David. 2016. "Bernie Sanders and Unions' Relationship Status: It's Complicated." *In These Times*, January 19. http://inthesetimes.com/working/entry/18786/unions-bernie-sanders-hillary-clinton-labor

Monroe, James. 1959. *The Autobiography of James Monroe*, edited by Stuart Gerry Brown. Syracuse: Syracuse University Press.

Montgomery, David. 1979. *Workers' Control in America: Studies in the History of Work, Technology, and Labor Struggles*. Cambridge: Cambridge University Press.

Moore, Barrington. 1966. *Social Origins of Dictatorship and Democracy: Lord and Peasant in the Making of the Modern World*. Boston: Beacon Press.

Morgenson, Gretchen. 2008. "Your Money at Work, Fixing Others' Mistakes." *New York Times*, September 20. www.nytimes.com/2008/09/21/business/21gret .html?8dpc

Morris, Roy, Jr. 2008. *The Long Pursuit: Abraham Lincoln's Thirty-Year Struggle with Stephen Douglas for the Heart and Soul of America*. New York: HarperCollins.

Morrison, Michael A. 1997. *Slavery and the American West: The Eclipse of Manifest Destiny and the Coming of the Civil War*. Chapel Hill: University of North Carolina Press.

Mosendz, Polly. 2016. "What This Election Taught Us about Millennial Voters." *Bloomberg News*, November 9. www.bloomberg.com/news/articles/2016-11-09 /what-this-election-taught-us-about-millennial-voters

National Labor Relations Board. 1985. *Legislative History of the National Labor Relations Act, 1935*. 2 vols. Washington, DC: Government Printing Office.

Nelson, Scott Reynolds, and Carol Sheriff. 2008. *A People at War: Civilians and Soldiers in America's Civil War, 1854–1877*. New York: Oxford University Press.

New York Times. 2012a. "President Exit Polls." www.nytimes.com/elections/2012
/results/president/exit-polls.html

———. 2012b. "Election 2012: President Map." www.nytimes.com/elections/2012
/results/president.html

———. 2016a. "Transcript of Mitt Romney's Speech on Donald Trump." March 3.
www.nytimes.com/2016/03/04/us/politics/mitt-romney-speech.html

———. 2016b. "Transcript: Donald Trump's Taped Comments about Women." October 8. www.nytimes.com/2016/10/08/us/donald-trump-tape-transcript.html

———. 2016c. "Presidential Election Results: Donald J. Trump Wins." www.nytimes
.com/elections/results/president

Nicholas, Peter, and Carol E. Lee. 2016. "Bernie Sanders Wins Policy Concessions
as Democrats Seek Unity." *Wall Street Journal*, July 10. www.wsj.com/articles
/bernie-sanders-wins-policy-concessions-as-democrats-seek-unity-1468197358

Nichols, Roy Franklin. 1948. *The Disruption of American Democracy*. New York:
Macmillan.

Niven, John. 1983. *Martin Van Buren: The Romantic Age of American Politics*. New
York: Oxford University Press.

Obama, Barack. 2008a. "Remarks of Senator Barack Obama: Reclaiming the
American Dream." January 29, El Dorado, Kansas. www.barackobama.com
/speeches/

———. 2008b. "Remarks of Senator Barack Obama." April 10, Gary. www.barack
obama.com/speeches/

———. 2008c. "Remarks of Senator Barack Obama: An Agenda for Middle-Class
Success." July 7, St. Louis. www.barackobama.com/speeches/

———. 2008d. "Remarks of Senator Barack Obama: 99th Annual Convention of
the NAACP." July 14, Cincinnati. www.barackobama.com/speeches/

———. 2010. "State of the Union: President Obama's Speech." *ABC News*, January
27. http://abcnews.go.com/Politics/State_of_the_Union/state-of-the-union
-2010-president-obama-speech-transcript/story?id=9678572

Oestreicher, Richard. 1988. "Urban Working-Class Political Behavior and Theories
of American Electoral Politics, 1870–1940." *Journal of American History* 74 (4):
1257–86.

Owen, Thomas M. 1921. *History of Alabama and Dictionary of Alabama Biography*.
Chicago: S. J. Clarke Publishing Company.

Paulson, Arthur C. 2000. *Realignment and Party Revival: Understanding American
Electoral Politics at the Turn of the Twenty-First Century*. Westport: Praeger.

Penn, Mark. 2007. "Campaign Memo: After 6 Months." *Politico*, July 9. www.politico
.com/pdf/PPM43_070709_hillarymessage.pdf

Peterson-Smith, Khury. 2015. "Black Lives Matter." *International Socialist Review*
(Spring). https://isreview.org/issue/96/black-lives-matter

Pew Research Center. 2008. "Inside Obama's Sweeping Victory." www.pewresearch.
org/2008/11/05/inside-obamas-sweeping-victory/

———. 2011. "Wealth Gaps Rise to Record Highs between Whites, Blacks and
Hispanics." www.pewsocialtrends.org/2011/07/26/wealth-gaps-rise-to-record
-highs-between-whites-blacks-hispanics/

———. 2015. "Public Trust in Government: 1958–2015." www.people-press.org/2015/11
/23/1-trust-in-government-1958-2015/trust-1/

Philpot, Tasha S., Daron R. Shaw, and Ernest B. McGowen. 2009. "Winning the
Race: Black Voter Turnout in the 2008 Presidential Election." *Public Opinion
Quarterly* 73: 995–1022.

Pierson, Paul. 2000. "Not Just What, but *When*: Timing and Sequence in Political
Processes." *Studies in American Political Development* 14 (1): 72–92.

———. 2004. *Politics in Time: History, Institutions, and Social Analysis*. Princeton:
Princeton University Press.

Poole, Keith T., and Howard Rosenthal. 1997. *Congress: A Political-Economic History
of Roll Call Voting*. Oxford: Oxford University Press.

Potter, David M. 1965 [1942]. *Lincoln and His Party in the Secession Crisis*. New Haven: Yale University Press.

Price, Melanye T. 2016. *The Race Whisperer: Barack Obama and the Political Uses of
Race*. New York: New York University Press.

Quist, John W. 1996. "Slaveholding Operatives of the Benevolent Empire: Bible,
Tract, and Sunday School Societies in Antebellum Tuscaloosa County, Alabama." *Journal of Southern History* 62 (3): 481–526.

———. 1998. *Restless Visionaries: The Social Roots of Antebellum Reform in Alabama
and Michigan*. Baton Rouge: Louisiana State University Press.

Randall, James G. 1940. "The Blundering Generation." *Mississippi Valley Historical
Review* 27 (1): 3–28.

Real Clear Politics. 2017. "2016 Republican Popular Vote." www.realclearpolitics
.com/epolls/2016/president/republican_vote_count.html

Remington, W. Craig, and Thomas J. Kallsen. 1999. *Historical Atlas of Alabama*, vol. 1,
Historical Locations by County, 2nd ed. Department of Geography, College of
Arts and Sciences, University of Alabama, Tuscaloosa.

Rhodan, Maya. 2016a. "Black Lives Matter Activist Snubs White House Invite." *Time*, February 18. http://time.com/4229329/black-livesmatter-activist-snubs-white -house-invite/

———. 2016b. "Bernie Sanders Supporters Storm Out of Convention in Protest," *Time*, July 26. http://time.com/4425475/dnc-bernie-sanders-protest-walkout -convention/

———. 2016c. "Donald Trump Raises Eyebrows with 'Bad Hombres' Line," *Time*, October 20. *http://time.com/4537847/donald-trump-bad-hombres/*

Schain, Martin, Aristide Zolberg, and Patrick Hossay (eds.). 2002. *Shadows over Europe: The Development and Impact of the Extreme Right in Western Europe*. New York: Macmillan.

Schulman, Bruce J. 1991. *From Cotton Belt to Sunbelt: Federal Policy, Economic Development, and the Transformation of the South, 1938–1980*. New York: Oxford University Press.

Seelye, Katharine Q. 2008. "Obama Wins North Carolina." *New York Times*, November 6. https://thecaucus.blogs.nytimes.com/2008/11/06/obama-wins-north-carolina/

Sellers, Charles. 1991. *The Market Revolution: Jacksonian America, 1815–1846*. New York: Oxford University Press.

Sewell, Richard H. 1976. *Ballots for Freedom: Antislavery Politics in the United States, 1837–1860*. New York: Norton.

Sharlet, Jeff. 2011. "Inside Occupy Wall Street." *Rolling Stone*, November 10. www .rollingstone.com/politics/news/occupy-wallstreet-welcome-to-the-occupa- tion-20111110

Silbey, Joel H. 2007. *Storm over Texas: The Annexation Controversy and the Road to Civil War*. Oxford: Oxford University Press.

Silver, Nate. 2016. "Ted Cruz Might Still Be Able to Stop Donald Trump." *FiveThirtyEight*, March 10. https://fivethirtyeight.com/features/ted-cruz-might-still-be -able-to-stop-donald-trump/

Skocpol, Theda, and Vanessa Williamson. 2012. *The Tea Party and the Remaking of Republican Conservatism*. New York: Oxford University Press.

Slez, Adam, and John Levi Martin. 2007. "Political Action and Party Formation in the United States Constitutional Convention." *American Sociological Review* 72 (1): 42–67.

Smith, Ben, and Carrie Budoff Brown. 2008. "The Clinton Band Is Back Together." *Politico*, November 14. www.politico.com/story/2008/11/the-clinton-band-is -backtogether-015617

————, and Byron Tau. 2011. "Birtherism: Where It All Began." *Politico*, April 22. www.politico.com/story/2011/04/birtherismwhere-it-all-began-053563?o=1

Smith, William R. 1861. "The history and debates of the Convention of the people of Alabama: begun and held in the city of Montgomery, on the seventh day of January 1861: in which is preserved the speeches of the secret sessions, and many valuable state papers." Montgomery; Tuscaloosa; Atlanta: White Pfister & Co.; D. Woodruff; Wood, Hanleiter, Rice & Co.

Stolberg, Sheryl Gay, and Mike McIntire. 2013. "A Federal Budget Crisis Months in the Planning." *New York Times*, October 5. www.nytimes.com/2013/10/06/us/a -federal-budget-crisis-months-in-the-planning.html

Suskind, Ron. 2011. *Confidence Men: Wall Street, Washington, and the Education of a President*. New York: HarperCollins.

Tapper, Jake. 2016. "Cruz Campaign: We Could Have Stopped Trump If Rubio Became Running Mate." *CNN*, May 9. www.cnn.com/2016/05/08/politics/republican -officials-donald-trump-marco-rubio-ted-cruz/

Taylor, Keeanga-Yamahtta. 2016. *From #BlackLivesMatter to Black Liberation*. Chicago: Haymarket Books.

Teslik, Lee Hudson. 2009. "Backgrounder: The U.S. Economic Stimulus Plan." *New York Times*, January 27. www.nytimes.com/cfr/world/slot3_20090126 .html?pagewanted=all

Thornton, J. Mills, III. 1978. *Politics and Power in a Slave Society: Alabama, 1800–1860*. Baton Rouge: Louisiana State University Press.

Tuğal, Cihan. 2017. "An Unmoving Wall or a Shifting One? The American Right's Deep Emotional Politics and Its Emaciated Counterpart." *British Journal of Sociology* 68 (1): 137–42.

U.S. Bureau of Soils. 1911. "Soil Map, Alabama, Tuscaloosa County Sheet." Map Collections, Hoole Special Collections Library, Tuscaloosa, Alabama.

U.S. Census Bureau. 2007. "Housing Unit Estimates for the 100 Fastest Growing Counties with 5,000 or More Housing Units in 2007." April 1, 2000, and July 1, 2007 (HU-EST2007-05). www.census.gov/popest/housing/HU-EST2007-top100 .html

————. 2009. "State and County Quickfacts." http://quickfacts.census.gov/qfd /index.html

U.S. Census Office. 1985 [1850]. "1850 Federal Census of Tuskaloosa County Alabama/ Extracted from National Archives Microfilm copy 432, population schedule, 7th census of the U.S., Alabama Free Schedule, 1850, Roll 16. Enumerated by E.A. Powell, assistant Marshall, 4 October 1850–11 February 1851." Alabama Collection, Hoole Special Collections Library, Tuscaloosa, Alabama.

Van Buren, Martin. 1844. "To W[illiam] H[enry] Hammet[t], 20 April 1844." Van Buren Papers. http://vanburenpapers.org/content/martin-van-buren-william -henry-hammett-20-april-1844

———. 1973 [1920]. *The Autobiography of Martin Van Buren*. New York: Da Capo Press.

Varon, Elizabeth R. 2008. *Disunion! The Coming of the American Civil War, 1789–1859*. Chapel Hill: University of North Carolina Press.

Veugelers, John W. P. 1999. "A Challenge for Political Sociology: The Rise of Far-Right Parties in Contemporary Western Europe." *Current Sociology* 47 (4): 78–100.

Wacquant, Loïc. 2002. "From Slavery to Mass Incarceration: Rethinking the Race Question in the U.S." *New Left Review* 13 (January–February).

———. 2009. *Punishing the Poor: The Neoliberal Government of Social Insecurity*. Durham: Duke University Press.

Watson, Harry L. 1981. *Jacksonian Politics and Community Conflict: The Emergence of the Second American Party System in Cumberland County North Carolina*. Baton Rouge: Louisiana State University Press.

———. 1990. *Liberty and Power: The Politics of Jacksonian America*. New York: Hill and Wang.

Weingast, Barry R. 1998. "Political Stability and Civil War: Institutions, Commitment, and American Democracy." In *Analytical Narratives*, edited by Robert H. Bates, Avner Greif, Margaret Levi, and Jean-Laurent Rosenthal, 149–93. Princeton: Princeton University Press.

Werner, Erica, and David J. Lynch. 2018. "GOP Senators Urge Trump to Stay in NAFTA," *Washington Post*, January 30. www.washingtonpost.com/business /economy/gop-senators-urge-trump-to-stay-in-nafta/2018/01/30/298a5320-060 c-11e8-b48c-b07fea957bd5_story.html?utm_term=.fa4b182b31be

White House Press Office. 2009. "President Barack Obama's Inaugural Address." https://obamawhitehouse.archives.gov/blog/2009/01/21/president-barack -obamas-inaugural-address>

Widmer, Ted. 2005. *Martin Van Buren*. New York: Times Books.

Wiener, Jonathan M. 1978. *Social Origins of the New South: Alabama, 1860–1885*. Baton Rouge: Louisiana State University Press.

Wilentz, Sean. 2005. *The Rise of American Democracy: Jefferson to Lincoln*. New York: Norton.

Wilson, Major L. 1974. *Space, Time and Freedom: the Quest for Nationality and the Irrepressible Conflict, 1815–1861*. Westport: Greenwood Press.

Woods, Michael E. 2012. "What Twenty-First-Century Historians Have Said about the Causes of Disunion: A Civil War Sesquicentennial Review of the Recent Literature." *Journal of American History* 99 (2): 415–39.

Woodward, C. Vann. 1951. *Origins of the New South, 1877–1913*. Baton Rouge: Louisiana State University Press.

World Bank. 2017. "World Bank Open Data." https://data.worldbank.org/

Yancey, William L. 1845. "Annexation of Texas." In *The Congressional Globe containing Sketches of the Debates and Proceedings of the Second Session of the Twenty-Eighth Congress*, vol. 14, edited by Francis P. Blair and John C. Rives, 85–90. Washington, DC: Congressional Globe Office.

———. 1848. "An Address to the People of Alabama, by W. L. Yancey, Late a Delegate, at Large, for the State of Alabama, to the National Democratic Convention, Held at Baltimore, on 22d May, A. D. 1848." William Lowndes Yancey Papers, 1834–1941, Alabama Department of Archives and History, Montgomery.

———. 1851. "Letter to Messrs. Joel E. Matthews, G. C. Pegues, J. H. Campbell, C. H. Cleveland, G. W. Gayle, Committee, &C. Montgomery, May 10, 1851." William Lowndes Yancey Papers—LPR 87. Box 1, Folder 2: Correspondence—Political, 1844–1860. Alabama Department of Archives and History, Montgomery.

———. 1860. "Speech of the Hon. William L. Yancey, of Alabama, delivered in the National Democratic Convention, Charleston, April 28th, 1860, with the Protest of the Alabama Delegation," William Lowndes Yancey Papers, 1834–1941, Alabama Department of Archives and History, Montgomery.

INDEX